MW01154627

What's Hecuba to Him?

Literature & Philosophy

A. J. Cascardi, General Editor

This series publishes books in a wide range of subjects in philosophy and literature, including studies of the social and historical issues that relate these two fields. Drawing on the resources of the Anglo-American and Continental traditions, the series is open to philosophically informed scholarship covering the entire range of contemporary critical thought.

Already published:

J. M. Bernstein, *The Fate of Art: Aesthetic Alienation from Kant to Derrida and Adorno*

Peter Bürger, *The Decline of Modernism*

Mary E. Finn, *Writing the Incommensurable: Kierkegaard, Rossetti, and Hopkins*

Reed Way Dasenbrock, ed., *Literary Theory After Davidson*

David Haney, *William Wordsworth and the Hermeneutics of Incarnation*

David Jacobson, *Emerson's Pragmatic Vision: The Dance of the Eye*

Gray Kochhar-Lindgren, *Narcissus Transformed: The Textual Subject in Psycho-analysis and Literature*

Robert Steiner, *Toward a Grammar of Abstraction: Modernity, Wittgenstein, and the Paintings of Jackson Pollock*

Sylvia Walsh, *Living Poetically: Kierkegaard's Existential Aesthetics*

Michel Meyer, *Rhetoric, Language, and Reason*

Christie McDonald and Gary Wihl, eds., *Transformations in Personhood and Culture After Theory*

Charles Altieri, *Painterly Abstraction in Modernist American Poetry: The Contemporaneity of Modernism*

John C. O'Neal, *The Authority of Experience: Sensationist Theory in the French Enlightenment*

John O'Neill, ed., *Freud and the Passions*

Sheridan Hough, *Nietzsche's Noontide Friend*

What's Hecuba to Him?

Fictional Events
and
Actual Emotions

E. M. Dadlez

The Pennsylvania State University Press
University Park, Pennsylvania

An early version of Chapter 1, now revised, appeared under the title "Fiction, Emotion, and Rationality" in the *British Journal of Aesthetics* 36 (July 1996): 292–306. Used by permission of Oxford University Press.

Library of Congress Cataloging-in-Publication Data

Dadlez, E. M. (Eva M.), 1956–
    What's Hecuba to him? : fictional events and actual emotions / by
E.M. Dadlez.

        p.   cm.
    Includes bibliographical references and index.
    ISBN 0-271-01650-7 (alk. paper)
    ISBN 0-271-01651-5 (pbk. : alk. paper)
    1. Psychology and literature.   2. Literature — Psychology.
3. Literature — Philosophy.   4. Emotions in literature.   5. Emotions
and cognition.   I. Title.
PN49.D23   1997
801'.92 — dc20   96-42211
                                                                               CIP

Copyright © 1997 The Pennsylvania State University
All rights reserved
Printed in the United States of America
Published by The Pennsylvania State University Press,
University Park, PA 16802-1003

It is the policy of The Pennsylvania State University Press to use acid-free paper for the first printing of all clothbound books. Publications on uncoated stock satisfy the minimum requirements of American National Standard for Information Sciences — Permanence of Paper for Printed Library Materials, ANSI Z39.48-1992.

for
Catherine Lord
and
Jamie Mock

Contents

Introduction

Is it not monstrous that this player here,
But in a fiction, in a dream of passion,
Could force his soul so to his own conceit
That from her working all the visage wann'd,
Tears in his eyes, distraction in his aspect,
A broken voice, an' his whole function suiting
With forms to his conceit? And all for nothing,
For Hecuba!
What's Hecuba to him, or he to Hecuba,
That he should weep for her?

Hamlet II.ii

Hamlet's question can be re-
garded as the first step in a philosophical inquiry. We respond to fiction
with a range of feeling and emotion otherwise reserved for actual events.
Like the player, we can weep over the plight of merely fictional entities.
Like Hamlet, we may ask how it is that what we know to be a fiction can
nonetheless provide a motive and a cue for passion. Over the past twenty
years, this question has attracted a widening philosophical audience and
prompted a variety of philosophical answers. My book is another such
response to Hamlet's question, and also a response to the answers and
explanations the question has recently provoked.

To ask how we can be moved by fiction can be to pose a paradox that
brings the apparatus of philosophical inquiry into play. If the player's tears
are all for nothing, if he responds to no one's plight and is aware that there
is nothing in the world to move him at that moment, then his reaction
seems at odds with what he knows is true. His sadness and his grief are
inconsistent and irrational, according to Colin Radford. Emotions like pity
and distress seem incoherent when it is not believed that someone suffers.
Radford's claim has given rise to a virtual industry in commentary and
attempted refutation. Indeed, it is possible to trace the progression of

argument and counterargument to the present day, as Radford's series of replies to critics and commentators can itself attest.[1]

However, Radford's analysis is not by any means the only one available. Consider that it is a *player* whose reactions and condition Hamlet thinks to question. A player's role is one dictating that he should respond to Hecuba as if both she and her experiences were genuine. His part invites him to participate in games of make-believe. His purpose is to make believe the fictional is real. Kendall Walton suggests that imaginative engagement with fiction makes one a player in such games. The experience of making-believe can lead to certain characteristic sensations and physical symptoms. It can make the visage wan and cause the voice to break. It can cause tears. However, it is only in the game that it is true the player grieves, for he only makes believe that there is someone whose experience warrants any such response. Only make-believe emotions can be felt toward what is made believe. The player thus cannot be said to feel a genuine emotion, since he does not believe in Hecuba or in her pain, and since he cannot be at all inclined to act in her defense. The affective response that follows from participation in this game can constitute what Walton calls a "quasi emotion." Published shortly after Radford's paper, Walton's account of our reactions to fiction is equally influential and, for some philosophers, equally controversial.[2]

---

1. Colin Radford's initial paper, "How Can We Be Moved by the Fate of Anna Karenina? (I)," appeared under the same title with a reply from Michael Weston (II) in *Proceedings of the Aristotelian Society* 49, suppl. 6 (1975): 67–93. This was followed by Radford's response to Weston in "Tears and Fiction," *Philosophy* 52 (1977): 208–18. Barrie Paskins's "On Being Moved by Anna Karenina and *Anna Karenina*," *Philosophy* 52 (1977): 344–47, prompted Radford's "The Essential Anna," *Philosophy* 54 (1979): 390–94. H. O. Mounce's "Art and Real Life," *Philosophy* 55 (1980): 183–92, led to Radford's "Stuffed Tigers: A Reply to H. O. Mounce," *Philosophy* 57 (1982): 529–32. Radford's "Philosophers and Their Monstrous Thoughts," *British Journal of Aesthetics* 22 (1982): 261–63, is a response to Kendall Walton's "Fearing Fictions," *Journal of Philosophy* 75 (1978): 5–27, and Peter Lamarque's "How Can We Fear and Pity Fictions?," *British Journal of Aesthetics* 21 (1981): 291–304. Next, Radford responds to William Charlton's "Feeling for the Fictitious," *British Journal of Aesthetics* 24 (1984): 206–16, in his own "Charlton's Feelings About the Fictitious: A Reply," *British Journal of Aesthetics* 25 (1985): 380–83. Radford's "Replies to Three Critics," *Philosophy* 64 (1989): 93–97, addresses the work of Don Mannison in his "On Being Moved by Fiction," *Philosophy* 60 (1985): 71–87, as well as the work of two other philosophers. Most recently, Radford has given us "The Incoherence and Irrationality of Philosophers," *Philosophy* (1990): 349–54.

2. Kendall Walton's landmark article is entitled "Fearing Fictions," *Journal of Philosophy* 75 (1978): 5–27. An extended treatment of the topic is offered in his book *Mimesis as Make-Believe: On the Foundations of the Representational Arts* (Cambridge: Harvard University Press, 1990).

Is Hecuba the source of a pseudogrief that is merely make-believedly or imaginarily genuine? Is she instead a source of inconsistent or irrational grief? Any attempt to answer Hamlet's question must first address these two analyses, not only because they are central in many philosophical discussions of the topic, but because they make fundamental and fundamentally incompatible assumptions about the nature of emotion and its relation to belief. To discover what Hecuba can be to the player, we must first consider the relation between them. Accordingly, the first two chapters of this book will constitute an inquiry into the conditions necessary for emotion and investigate several cognitive characterizations of emotional response. It is the identification of the emotional with the cognitive that provides a basis for allegations of inconsistency in emotional response and that explains why it may be held that there is an intimate connection between what we believe and what we feel.

It should be emphasized that neither Radford nor Walton means to diminish the significance of the player's experience. Our irrationality or quasi emotionality in responding as we do to fiction is regarded as a happy fact about our faculties and predilections. We are, it is stressed, much better off for having this capacity. Experiences like the player's can prove rewarding. Yet I cannot help but find myself adopting Gertrude's point of vantage on the player queen when I consider protestations such as these. However enriching the player's experience may be, to call it irrational, while this is not to call it monstrous, is still to impugn his reason and to promote an alliance between the rational and the unimaginative. However beneficial the experience, the claim that it cannot be a genuine emotion makes of it an illusion on account of which the player may himself be quite deceived.

As I will attempt to establish, there are reasons for thinking that what the player feels for Hecuba and what we may feel for Hamlet are neither irrational nor pseudo-emotional. I will argue that the adoption of a cognitive characterization of emotion cannot provide grounds for an ascription of irrationality or inconsistency to our response to fiction without thereby classifying a number of seemingly unproblematic responses as equally irrational. I will also maintain that irrationality in our reactions to the fictional cannot be established on the basis of an argument from analogy, for obvious cases of irrationality differ from our responses to fiction in significant respects. The contention that such responses are not genuine emotions will also be disputed. It does not follow from the assumption that emotions are cognitive that only one particular candidate can assume the role of their constituent cognition. Maintaining that emotions must be

accompanied or constituted by cognitions does not commit us to the
further characterization of these cognitions as existentially committed
beliefs. (Neither does it appear that a genuine pity must involve some
inclination to offer aid, if feelings about historical figures and incidents can
be considered genuine despite the absence of such inclinations.) Thus, an
investigation of the cognitive character of emotion not only clarifies the
grounds for the claims in contention but may make evident the grounds for
possible counterarguments.

Asking what Hecuba is to the player prompts questions about what
Hecuba is in herself. Is she merely a conceit, a stand-in for more ontologically correct emotional objects? In asking what it is that moves the player,
one asks about the objects one's emotional response can take when one
contemplates a fiction. As several philosophers have claimed, such objects
can be real. The player may, in fact, pity those whose suffering is like the
pain that he imagines. The thoughts he entertains may make him recollect
and resurrect some previous personal reaction to a circumstance resembling that of Hecuba. The player may be moved by the human capacity for
cruelty brought to mind by what he contemplates. It is true that our
experience of fiction may lead us to consider and react to objects such as
these. However, it is important to understand that the objects of emotion
mentioned here cannot entirely replace the character. Pity or fear for
Hecuba cannot be analyzed away and so reduced to pity for less problematic objects.

And Hecuba does present us with a puzzle, for she, her circumstances,
and her fate are only entertained in imagination. She occupies the player's
thoughts when they are of a certain kind of woman in distress. At most, it
seems that Hecuba can be identified with the content of the player's
thoughts and with his mental representations.[3] This need not make of
Hecuba a chimera or insubstantial dream whose serious contemplation
seems ridiculous. When the player entertains the thought of Hecuba's
misery in imagination, he entertains it sadly. His grief is not what he
imagines, as a number of philosophers would claim. Rather, he imagines
Hecuba *with* sadness or distress. His emotion can be tied to the way he
entertains a thought about the kind of experience he believes to be both
miserable and tragic. Hecuba exists in the player's thoughts. She can be to

---

3. Peter Lamarque has suggested this in his "How Can We Fear and Pity Fictions?," *British
Journal of Aesthetics* 21 (1981): 291–304, and, more recently, in Peter Lamarque and Stein
Haugom Olsen, *Truth, Fiction, and Literature: A Philosophical Perspective* (Oxford:
Clarendon Press, 1994).

him what he imagines sadly or sorrowfully, for imagining something with grief or regret can be seen as a *manner* of imagining.[4]

For all that characters are only people in imagination, it is the contemplation of their world that Hamlet hopes will catch the conscience of his enemy. But how can what is merely fictional have the moral impact Hamlet's wish implies? If it can be demonstrated that emotion is related to one's repertoire of normative beliefs, then an emotional response to fiction may take on a distinctly ethical significance. Emotional reactions frequently involve evaluations. For instance, anger may be associated with the belief that some action or policy is unjust. We can assume that the player, in thinking about what's been done to Hecuba and Priam, believes that the *kind* of act he contemplates is cruel, that to kill a woman's husband before her eyes is heinous, that no one deserves to feel the kind of pain afflicting Hecuba. These are beliefs about universals, which can lead him to focus his attention on particular thoughts and to entertain them with distress. If the player's grief for Hecuba and his anger at the agents of her misery has at its base some set of personal convictions about what kinds of acts are just or fair, or other thoughts concerning what can constitute a just desert, then the bare fact of our emotional response to fiction can attest to the possibility of its moral significance. I will maintain that fiction can rehearse our moral judgments and that it can make us aware of them as newly challenged or substantiated.

Martha Nussbaum and others have been eloquent in their claims that literature can have such significance for us, that it can demonstrate ways in which a life ought or ought not be lived.[5] Yet the play performed at Hamlet's own behest is not a masterpiece but melodrama. What can be said of fictions that cannot aspire to the learned or the literary? I propose to redistribute some of the arsenal of arguments defending the moral importance of literature to the folks in the trenches: the rollicking as well as the profound. What fictions can make salient about our lives and how they could be lived is a function of what can capture our attention and our conscience, and thus a function of what can move us. That some works are more likely to do so than others does not preclude responses both to the trashy and to the sublime.

If the player's response to the fiction that he contemplates involves beliefs about the universal rather than beliefs about particulars, then he

4. Richard Moran suggests this in "The Expression of Feeling in Imagination," *Philosophical Review* 103 (1994): 75–106.

5. Martha C. Nussbaum, *Love's Knowledge: Essays on Philosophy and Literature* (New York: Oxford University Press, 1990).

imagines the instantiation of the kinds of actions and events that those beliefs concern. In that he weeps for Hecuba, we may assume that he believes the kind of torment to which she has been exposed is both unfair and cruel. This assessment can apply to real actions and actual torments. The player's own evaluation spans the actual and the fictional. In doing so, it may constrain or limit what he can imagine. Are there indeed such limits on imagination? Surely Puck and Prospero would join the player in rejecting any such hypothesis. To imagine is in most ways to be *un*constrained by what's believed. Yet David Hume has spoken of our occasional reluctance or incapacity to enter into moral sentiments that a work of fiction may endorse.[6] This can suggest a limit on the kind of imaginative engagement that involves one in an emotional response to fiction.

I do not think the player could in some way will himself to think or to imagine as right or good the injuries done to Hecuba, for to imagine the rightness of an act is to entertain the thought of it with approval or at least with equanimity. It is to imagine the instantiation of a set of characteristics one believes sufficient for an action's being right. The limitation that belief imposes can be found in how it is we entertain thoughts in imagination. The beliefs tied to emotion are evaluative, and it is by imagining the instantiation of the kind of act we will evaluate in certain ways that we can entertain the thought of it in certain ways. To entertain the thought of an action disapprovingly is to construe that kind of action as unkind or wrong. To entertain the thought of an action contemptuously is to construe that kind of action as contemptible. The limits on imagination involve no prohibitions on the fantastic or bizarre. The player cannot be restrained by his beliefs from entertaining thoughts of Ariel and Prospero. What he believes determines *how* he will evaluate, not what it is that the evaluation will concern. It can be true, of course, that what the player thinks about proves an exception to some general rule to which he has subscribed or demonstrates an inconsistency among those judgments he already holds. In such a case, I think the player's repertoire of beliefs may change, if only to allow occasional exceptions.

The player imagines a world populated by certain people, Hecuba and Priam among them. Yet what's imagined may exceed what any fiction indicates. Our engagement with the fictional can and often does involve our own imaginative construction of worlds. In contemplating fictional states of affairs, we infer and we extrapolate. Thus, we imagine states of

---

6. David Hume, "Of the Standard of Taste," in *Of the Standard of Taste and Other Essays* (New York: Bobbs-Merrill, 1965), 21–22.

affairs that are not included in the worlds of fictional works. The same work can be associated with a variety of different imaginary worlds. For instance, beliefs about what would occur if some event depicted in the work were to occur could differ radically across readers or viewers. For this reason, I have tentatively allied imaginary worlds with interpretations. This need not render the comparison and evaluation of different interpretations impossible, since the inferences and beliefs upon which an imaginary world is based can be critically assessed. Moreover, these assumptions demonstrate that the events with which a fiction presents us signify the initial stage of an imaginative process whose culmination can make us collaborators in and architects of the worlds we have imagined.

Imagining, considered as a mental *activity*, need not be relegated to some ontologically suspect domain inhabited exclusively by fictions, fantasies, and pipe dreams. We constantly imagine. We speculate about possible motivations or the possible causes of events. We consider ways our own experience or another's could be or could have been. Indeed, the world that Claudius imagines when he contemplates the play that Hamlet has commissioned leads him to entertain the thought of what his own experience was. He could, for that brief moment, entertain the thought of what the fictional murderer had done from that fictitious entity's point of vantage.

To empathize is to imagine having the thoughts and beliefs, the desires and impulses, of another. No stretch for Claudius, in this particular circumstance. Any inferences he makes concerning mental states experienced by those whose conduct duplicates that of the fictional killer are likely to be accurate. Such inferences can constitute the initial condition for an empathetic reaction. Empathy also provides us with another criterion for differentiation among emotional reactions. One can feel for someone, as the player feels for Hecuba, or one can feel *with* someone, as Claudius may vicariously fear discovery.

Imagination is involved in empathetic emotion both when one empathizes with fictional entities and when one empathizes with actual persons. To empathize is to adopt a different point of vantage on the actual or the fictional world. It is to regard that world from the perspective of certain beliefs and thoughts and predilections, just the beliefs and thoughts a character is imagined to have or a person is believed to possess. Further, it is to imagine having those thoughts and beliefs, to imagine believing what and as another does. To imaginatively inhabit the worlds of others — whether our apprehension of such worlds is constrained by what we believe others believe or by what we imagine characters believe — has ethical significance not only in that it permits us to imagine that a life could be lived in a certain way but in that it enables us to contemplate how it might be to live just such a life.

The player's fondness for the tragic and melodramatic has yet to be considered. If he takes satisfaction in performances that cause distress and delights in fictions that induce him to feel fear and pity, then yet another paradox may confront us. How can someone enjoy what is grieved over? How can one regard with satisfaction the very source of one's distress? I will contend that the enjoyment of tragic or terrifying fictions poses no difficulty when what terrifies is quite distinct from that which is enjoyed. The player may take satisfaction in the insights that a tragic fiction can afford, or may himself enjoy the freedom and excitement of emotional release. We may take pleasure in the satisfaction of a curiosity concerning what we fear. We may delight in Shakespeare's eloquence while feeling nothing but distress about events a work of his describes. In every case, the thought one entertains with pity or fear is wholly different from that entertained with satisfaction or delight.

This book is an attempt to answer a question asked by the denizen of one story about the inhabitant of yet another. In what follows, I embark on an exploration of stories, sometimes by telling them and sometimes by examining the ways in which they can and do affect us. The pursuit and review of answers to Hamlet's question both leads to the gradual emergence of a set of necessary conditions for an emotional response to the fictional and ushers in an adverbial approach in the characterization of that response. That the player weeps for Hecuba reflects both on our capacity to envision and to understand a seemingly limitless variety of human situations and on the capacity of fiction to facilitate such understanding and such imaginative engagement.

1

Fiction, Emotion, and Irrationality

People sometimes respond emotionally to fictions. How does it come about that fictions can so engage the imagination as to arouse fear, pity, or anger toward something in whose existence we do not believe? What might this suggest about the role of fiction in our lives? Are such reactions even rational? Is it the case that they cannot be characterized as full-fledged emotions?

Such questions have been repeatedly posed in the philosophical literature with varying degrees of urgency. Implicit in many of these investigations are certain assumptions about what emotions are and how they can be characterized. That such assumptions are seldom made explicit has, I think, obscured some of the most important aspects of this dialogue behind a series of exchanges based on incompatible premises about the nature of emotion. It is crucial to begin any investigation of responses to fiction by discovering what they have in common with and what distinguishes them from other instances of emotional response by considering them against a backdrop of patterns of response to other, less ontologically problematic, phenomena. That this is no simple procedure is a foregone conclusion. Theories of emotion are numerous, diverse, and frequently incompatible. Agreement on what constitutes an emotion is by no means readily discernable.

In this chapter, my intention is to sketch in broad strokes an account of emotional response that will provide some idea of conditions considered necessary for emotion and that will make sense of ascriptions of rationality or irrationality to emotional response. What follows is a rough and ready foray into some of the literature on emotion, organized not by individual theory but by features identified or associated with emotion. While any theories cited are necessarily oversimplified, this piecemeal approach has the dual advantage of brevity and directness, allowing an immediate investigation of conditions necessary for emotion. Cognitivist analyses will prove the most amenable to a discussion of irrationality in emotional response. Several different criteria for the ascription of irrationality to such responses will be considered. Finally, an analysis of Colin Radford's claim that our emotional responses to fiction are irrational will be attempted on the basis of these criteria.[1]

EMOTIONS

Any number of conditions, states, and qualities have been and are associated with emotion. Nearly all of these have at one time or another been put forward as necessary or sufficient for an emotion's identification. It should be made clear at the outset that there is considerable disagreement about whether emotions happen to us or whether they are something we do, about whether they are attributes or states or perceptions, about whether they are cognitive or noncognitive. Nevertheless, there exist candidates that have been repeatedly cast as constituents or concomitants of emotions, and a survey of these seems appropriate to the organization of this analysis. Physiological perturbations, sensations/feelings, behaviors and behavioral dispositions, desires and motivations, intentionality or object-directedness, evaluative beliefs or normative judgments, appraisals, construals, and other cognitions have all been said, at one time or another, to be integral to emotion.

Theories that focus on physiological disturbances and sensations, like that of William James, identify emotion with an awareness (either acute or obscure) of a change in physiological condition brought about by the experience of (and perhaps instinctive reaction to) certain kinds of events.[2] For example, fear may be characterized as the way a quickened pulse and shallow breathing feel to an agent. The difficulty with the Jamesian view is that neither overt physiological changes nor the way they feel accounts for our ability to discriminate among emotions, as the work

---

1. For instance, in "How Can We Be Moved by the Fate of Anna Karenina? (I)," *Proceedings of the Aristotelian Society* 49, suppl. 6 (1975): 67–80.

2. William James, "What Is an Emotion?," *Mind* (1884).

of Stanley Schachter and Jerome Singer suggests. Schachter and Singer conclude:

> Given a state of physiological arousal for which an individual has no immediate explanation, he will label this state and describe his feelings in terms of the cognitions available to him. To the extent that cognitive factors are potent determiners of emotional states, it should be anticipated that precisely the same state of physiological arousal can be labeled "joy" or "fury" or "jealousy" or any of a great diversity of emotional labels depending on the cognitive aspects of the situation.[3]

That is, it is held that cognitions are integral to emotion in a way for which James's treatment cannot fully account. James does speak of our "awareness" of events, describing it as the stimulus of physiological changes the perception of which is said to constitute emotion. However, he never affiliates such awareness with the kinds of brain processes that are identified with thought or belief, as opposed to sensory perception.

Physical changes involving heightened pulse and shallow breathing can be associated variously with fear, excitement, or rage. In fact, they can be associated with illness rather than emotion, as Walter B. Cannon has pointed out.[4] There even seem to be emotions with which no overt physiological changes of the sort that James describes are associated. What physical condition corresponds to envy or pity? This is not to deny that sensations and physiological changes are concomitants of emotion. My only claim is that, as the case stands, there is no specific and readily identifiable condition of the body that can be indisputably and exclusively identified with some particular emotion in every instance in which the emotion is held to occur.

Perhaps the difficulty here simply involves the lack of precision inherent in an account based on century-old notions of physiology. Biochemical and neurological criteria could be brought into play. That is, proponents of a physiologically based analysis of emotion could regroup and proceed to argue from the bastion of materialism. Such a step would change the arena

---

3. Stanley Schachter and Jerome Singer, "Cognitive, Social, and Physiological Determinants of Emotional State," excerpted in Cheshire Calhoun and Robert C. Solomon, eds., *What Is an Emotion? Classic Readings in Philosophical Psychology* (New York: Oxford University Press, 1984), 183.

4. Walter B. Cannon, *Bodily Changes in Pain, Hunger, Fear and Rage*, excerpted in *What Is an Emotion?*, 147.

of the debate, however. The thoroughgoing materialist would identify *any* mental event with physiological and neurological phenomena. Naturally, thoughts and beliefs would not be excluded. Rather than resolving the debate about emotion, such a step would simply require a whole new level of verification for its resolution. In other words, nothing particularly new is added to the debate by the contention that emotions are changes in physiological condition, if beliefs, desires, thoughts, and imaginings are characterized in precisely the same way. The debate would still be open with respect to claims that emotions were cognitive, normative, and so on, since these hypotheses would also be taken to refer ultimately to neurological events.

Accounts like that of James have typically been contrasted with others, especially with cognitivist and constructionist theories, because Jamesian accounts put emotions pretty much out of the subject's control. The implication is that emotions are fundamentally *non*rational events for which we are seldom, if ever, responsible. However, if processes like thinking and reasoning and being disposed to behave in certain ways are also characterized as neurological and physiological phenomena, the force of a Jamesian account is entirely lost. We no longer have a competing theory; we simply have a new way of characterizing other analyses.[5]

My conclusion about this criterion, then, is that a commitment to emotions as physiological or neurological phenomena commits us neither to the view that emotions are noncognitive nor to the view that they are *inevitably* beyond our control. Even if it is impermissible to hold that our beliefs are wholly voluntary, it is still possible to maintain that voluntary actions and behaviors can lead to the development of one belief-forming process, habit, or disposition rather than another. While many of our beliefs could be said to be involuntarily or automatically (rather than deliberately) formed, we could still be held responsible for them insofar as their maintenance in the face of counterevidence or the absence of corroboration was concerned. Thus, some distinction would remain between cognitivist and noncognitivist approaches.

The view that emotions are cognitive is to some extent borne out by recent studies focusing on the manner in which emotions are processed in the brain. Some researchers believe emotions are the brain's interpreta-

---

5. I hesitate to say that this provides us with a method of verification. Until it is possible to determine precise neurological criteria for the identification of certain kinds of cognitive events (e.g., thoughts with a certain content, such as a normative assessment of another's action as unjust or unfair), most hypotheses about cognitive constituents of emotion cannot be verified.

tion of our visceral reaction to the world at large.[6] Certain neural pathways are said to be responsible for our emotional responses, which are founded on "a perception of both body changes and cognitive changes induced by the evaluation of a particular stimulus in terms of earlier experience."[7] A cognitive aspect of emotion is here recognized and acknowledged, for the process of evaluating a stimulus in terms of previous experience cannot be other than cognitive.

However, "feelings" may not have been done justice in the above discussion. Perhaps a feeling is not an awareness of one's *physiological* state but a kind of unanalyzable awareness of one's *psychological* state or changes therein. Those who espouse such an analysis might reject all other candidates on the list I have offered, characterizing them as causes or effects of the emotion proper rather than constituents of the emotion.[8] Yet what is this psychological state? If the state itself is what resists analysis, then perhaps we should characterize the state as the emotion. Such a step raises further questions, however. How could a feeling or awareness not be logically distinct from what it was a feeling or an awareness *of*? Aside from the need for some explanation of this confusion, it seems unsatisfying to maintain emotion as an enigma, a black box whose contents we will never be in a position to peruse.

There is also some question of whether our inner states are so readily and precisely identifiable. Can we distinguish between indignation and annoyance by their *feel*?[9] There may even be a difference between the claim that someone *is* resentful or *is* insecure and the claim that she or he *feels* so. Resentment, especially, lends itself to hypotheses about repression. Certainly, if one can *have* an emotion without being aware of it, feelings cannot be necessary conditions for emotion. Robert C. Solomon even suggests that emotions can be characterized in the same way as dispositional beliefs. Consider a person who holds a grudge, resenting something or someone for years. This would not mean, probably could not mean, that the person had continuously experienced a certain feeling for that length of time.[10] An unfelt feeling seems a contradiction in terms, whereas an unfelt emotion need not be.

---

6. Sandra Blakeslee, "Tracing the Brain's Pathways for Linking Emotion and Reason," *New York Times*, 6 December 1994, Medical Science suppl., B5, B11.

7. Ibid., B11.

8. For instance, G. F. Stout, *A Manual of Psychology* (London: University Tutorial Press, 1938), 371–75.

9. Errol Bedford asks this in "Emotions and Statements About Them," in Rom Harre, ed., *The Social Construction of Emotions* (New York: Basil Blackwell, 1988), 16.

10. Robert C. Solomon, "Emotions and Choice," in *What Is an Emotion?*, 309.

A purely behavioral account of emotion poses several difficulties similar to those already discussed, for emotions can be experienced in the absence of any behavioral manifestations we think are characteristic of them, and a subject can exhibit behavior thought typical of some particular emotion without experiencing that emotion. Not all such accounts focus exclusively on behavior, however. John Dewey, for instance, held that behavior was only one component of an emotion, but a central one.[11] Still, the fact that one can experience an emotion without exhibiting *any* of the behavior typically associated with it seems to militate against considering behavior a necessary condition.

A different behavioral approach is taken by Gilbert Ryle, who suggests that emotions can be understood as primarily behavioral dispositions, motivations, and propensities (he refers in particular to the sense of "emotion" that classifies it as the motive for behavior).[12] Dispositional adjectives provide us with lawlike propositions. Solubility indicates a tendency to dissolve when immersed in liquid, brittleness a tendency to shatter when struck. Similarly, fear might be characterized as a disposition to remove oneself from danger or to attempt to avert it. To say that someone did something from the motive of fear is to say that was the kind of thing he or she was disposed to do. Emotion words identify dispositions to behave in characteristic ways given certain stimuli.

However, some of the problems posed for simpler behaviorist accounts remain to plague the dispositional approach, since to accept that some type of behavior is characteristic of an emotion does not imply that it invariably accompanies that emotion. As Errol Bedford points out, we can accept behavioral evidence of a certain characteristic sort as true (Sam bellowed and pounded on the table), while denying the experience of the emotion (anger) that the behavior is usually identified with (That Sam! Can he ever party!).[13]

It is also clear that there is a wide variation across individuals, both in the behavior and the behavioral dispositions associated with their experience of a given emotion. Take anger, for instance. Some persons are utterly averse to violent behavior or recrimination, while others are disposed to swing at the drop of an ill-considered remark. What would warrant our claim that both are angry, if their behavioral dispositions are so distinct? It

---

11. John Dewey, "The Theory of Emotion" (1894), reprinted in *What Is an Emotion?*, 154–72.

12. Gilbert Ryle, *The Concept of Mind* (New York: Barnes and Noble, 1949), excerpted in *What Is an Emotion?*, 252–63.

13. Errol Bedford, "Emotions," in *What Is an Emotion?*, 269–70.

is all very well to say that Snopes responded to the stimulus by compressing his lips while Filbert responded with assault because both were inclined to respond in those different ways, but why should a habit or disposition of compressing one's lips be identified with a radically different habit of hitting people? What warrants calling them by the same name? Neither the behaviors nor the inclinations of the subjects give us a clue. That both Snopes and Filbert may admit to anger if asked, that both may be disposed to answer a question about how they feel in a certain way, does not resolve the difficulty. First, Ryle is suspicious of a person's own assessment of his motives and habits, placing greater trust in impartial observers, and clearly does not have in mind any disposition to identify one's own mental states in a particular way. Second, such an account of behavioral dispositions may not allow for the existence of any form of repression or denial (being angry or jealous without admitting to oneself or to others that one is). Behavioral evidence of anger may vary with the individual involved and with the social context in which the individual finds himself. The latter point is emphasized by Bedford when he considers that the same behavior can constitute evidence for different emotions in different contexts.[14] Sam's pounding and bellowing could be a sign of enthusiasm and acceptance at a friendly, drunken party and a sign of anger in a different social context.

Moreover, a dispositional story of this sort does not acknowledge a cognitive element that seems embedded in the account itself. Behavioral dispositions can be rendered as sets of stimulus-response conditionals: if one is stimulated in a certain way (for example, being placed in a certain situation or confronted with a certain event), one will respond with certain characteristic behavior. It is the antecedent of the conditional that is neglected, for the apprehension of that event or situation is thought sufficient for the response. In fact, the apprehension that one has been unjustly or rudely treated seems to be what the mildly disposed Snopes and the wildly disposed Filbert have in common. If what a behavioral disposition is in itself makes reference to the apprehension or awareness of particular kinds of situations, then such an account exhibits a kind of closet cognitivism.

Errol Bedford also points out that emotion words are deprived of any explanatory force by the adoption of the dispositional approach,[15] something that Ryle was perfectly happy to acknowledge in the body of his own

---

14. Ibid., 271.
15. Ibid., 277–78.

work. Nevertheless, it does seem that when we request an explanation of the window's shattering, we would rather hear about Filbert's rock-throwing than the brittleness of glass. Similarly, if we use anger to explain Smith's abruptness with Jones, we generally mean more than the simple fact that Smith just tends to be abrupt in certain situations. If we attempt to fill in more of the story by claiming that Smith tends to treat people abruptly when he takes it that they have insulted him, we no longer have a vitiated explanatory function for emotion words, but we have incorporated a cognitive element in the explanation.

Yet another candidate is frequently identified as a constituent or concomitant of emotion. Many philosophers, particularly Aristotle, associate desire with emotional response. Few hold that it is a sufficient condition, though some accounts suggest that it may be necessary, while others refer to it as a frequent concomitant of emotion. Thus, a fear for oneself might be associated with a desire to avoid or avert some threat or danger, anger might involve a desire for redress or vengeance, and pity could be associated with a desire that suffering be relieved. It is beyond dispute that desires can accompany emotions, but the claim that they necessarily do so is problematic. First, it is not clear that, for example, pity inevitably involves the desire to relieve suffering. I can feel sorry for a student who failed my course without desiring to change the grade that he deserved. I might have a counterfactual desire of some sort, of course: I might wish that he had bothered to study, because that would have prevented his failure. A counterfactual analysis would obviously apply to many of our reactions to events in the past or to historical persons whose lives and situations are now unalterable. We might desire that things had happened otherwise, that certain events or experiences had not occurred. I do not think that we could accept desire as necessary for emotion without adopting an extended application of this sort, though some might believe that it plays havoc with what we ordinarily take desires to be.

Finally, emotions are very frequently held to be intentional states or attitudes with propositional objects. That is, emotions are thought to be *about* something. Naturally, intentionality cannot be sufficient for emotion, but many identify it as a necessary condition. Standard counter-examples to the claim that emotions are object-directed present us with conditions such as depression, free-floating anxiety, euphoria, and apathy. Here we have cases of what Irving Thalberg would call emotions that cannot take objects.[16] There are at least two ways in which it might be maintained that intentionality is a necessary feature of emotions, even in

---

16. Irving Thalberg, "Emotion and Thought," in *What Is an Emotion?*, 293.

the face of counterexamples such as these. First, it could be maintained that we can be depressed or apathetic or euphoric about particular things or situations. Someone could be apathetic about the health care controversy or depressed about his finances. One could append to this a further claim that conditions like free-floating anxiety and general depression only *appear* to lack objects because they are so all-encompassing. In the case of a full-fledged depression, every situation in one's experience could be apprehended as infelicitous or bleak. Free-floating anxiety might be characterized as taking every circumstance in one's life to involve the possibility of negative consequences. In other words, it could be held that there are indeed intentional objects in such cases but that the emotions are generally rather than specifically focused. For instance, Robert C. Solomon suggests that such emotions may be " 'about' the world."[17] Alternatively, depression, anxiety, and euphoria could be classified as moods rather than emotions.

Some commitment to the intentionality of emotion, some acknowledgment that emotion can be characterized as object-directed, is often taken to imply that cognitions are necessary constituents of emotion. If emotions take objects, then the experience of them must involve some awareness of those objects. For example, if fear is of or about something (or for someone), then it must involve an apprehension of that thing or situation as dangerous or threatening (or an apprehension of another's situation as risky). An enormous number of current theories make claims of this sort. While it is impossible to enumerate all of them here, it is significant that their heritage goes back to the work of Aristotle, whose views might be taken to ally emotions with ways of conceiving objects and situations.

In the *Rhetoric*, certain emotions are said to take certain objects. Contempt, for instance, takes an object one considers or believes unimportant.[18] In *De Anima*, Aristotle stresses that emotions are neither purely cognitive nor purely physiological.[19] The criteria that distinguish justifiable from unjustifiable emotions are described Aristotle's *Nicomachean Ethics*. Excessive or inappropriate anger is said sometimes to involve the mistaken or unjustified apprehension of an offense.[20] In each case, there is a focus on the subject's *apprehension* of an object or situation, a focus that

17. Solomon, "Emotions and Choice," in *What Is an Emotion?*, 306.

18. Aristotle, *Rhetoric* 1378a20–1380a4, trans. W. Rhys Roberts, in *Aristotle: II* of *Great Books of the Western World*, vol. 9 (Chicago: Encyclopedia Britannica, 1952), 622–25.

19. Aristotle, *De Anima* 403a2–403b19, trans. J. A. Smith, in *Aristotle: I* of *Great Books of the Western World*, vol. 8 (Chicago: Encyclopedia Britannica, 1952), 632–33.

20. Aristotle, *Nicomachean Ethics* 1126a, trans. Terence Irwin (Indiana: Hackett, 1985), 105–6.

has emerged repeatedly in the work of other philosophers. Max Scheler goes so far as to characterize feeling as a form of cognition, a perception or disclosure of objective values.[21] Franz Brentano compares certain emotions to directly evident judgments, the truth of which is clear from the concepts involved. He indicates that judging and thinking can be necessary conditions for feeling.[22] More recently, Anthony Kenny has held that a given emotion is necessarily tied to a certain restricted range of epistemic objects. It is not possible, states Kenny, to feel remorse for or about something in which one did not believe one had played a part, or to envy the possession of some object one already believed oneself to possess.[23] As Irving Thalberg states, each sort of emotion requires a particular cognitive cohort. Emotions with objects are logically tied to some form of thought about the object.[24] Robert Solomon identifies this thought with normative judgment.[25]

In some of the most interesting contemporary accounts, emotions are said to involve "construals," or evaluations of objects or situations.[26] This approach makes considerable sense of our tendency to refer to certain emotional responses as irrational or unjustified, since we often ascribe unreasonableness to the evaluations or evaluative judgments of others. Indeed, the very fact that we frequently speak of emotions in this way is often adduced as evidence for the claim that they are, at least in part, cognitive.[27] How could we call someone's anger *irrational* if it were

---

21. Max Scheler, *Formalism in Ethics and Non-formal Ethics of Values*, excerpted in *What Is an Emotion?*, 219–28.

22. Franz Brentano, *On the Origin of Our Knowledge of Right and Wrong* (1889), excerpted in *What Is an Emotion?*, 205–14.

23. Anthony Kenny, *Action, Emotion, and Will*, excerpted in *What Is an Emotion?*, 284.

24. Thalberg, "Emotion and Thought," in *What Is an Emotion?*, 292, 304.

25. Solomon, "Emotions and Choice," in *What Is an Emotion?*, 305–26.

26. For example, in Rom Harre's "An Outline of the Social Constructionist Viewpoint" (8–9), and Claire Armon-Jones's "The Thesis of Constructionism" (41–50) and "Social Functions of the Emotions" (70–71), all of which appear in Rom Harre, ed., *The Social Construction of Emotions*. Robert C. Roberts offers the most detailed account of such construals in "What an Emotion Is: A Sketch," *Philosophical Review* 87 (1988): 183–209. Ronald de Sousa associates emotions with the projection of paradigm scenarios and speaks of construing or interpreting situations in terms of such scenarios in *The Rationality of Emotion* (Cambridge: MIT Press, 1990), 181–88.

27. For instance, Errol Bedford discusses a sense in which emotions may be thought justified in "Emotions and Statements About Them" (24–25), Claire Armon-Jones mentions two types of unwarrantedness in emotion in "Social Functions of Emotion" (71), and J. Coulter speaks of emotions as reasonable and unreasonable in "Affect and Social Context" (123–24), all of which appear in *The Social Construction of Emotions*.

merely a biochemical reaction over which that individual had not the slightest control? How could we consider an overprotective parent's dire foreboding about an offspring's plight unreasonable, if there were nothing *in* or *about* the emotion itself to which reason could appeal?

Thus, emotions can be characterized as both intentional and cognitive and are frequently described as or associated with attentive construals or evaluations of objects and situations. It is held that there is a logical connection between the emotion and the concept in terms of which its object is construed or evaluated. To fear someone would be to construe or evaluate that person as dangerous or threatening to oneself in some way. To pity someone would be to construe that person's experience as painful or disadvantaged. According to many accounts, one could not feel fear in the absence of any thought or belief about danger, nor could one be proud of something with which one did not think oneself affiliated or for which one did not hold oneself responsible.

It is seldom that cognitive characterizations are intended to provide sufficient as well as necessary conditions for the identification of emotion. Such characterizations are usually offered to establish construals, thoughts, or evaluative beliefs as necessary constituents or concomitants of emotion. These accounts neither deny nor preclude physiological theories of emotion but could be held to co-opt many of the claims such theories make. It could be suggested, for instance, that neurological models of brain processing and interactions establish the fundamental interpretive or evaluative — and thus cognitive — features of emotion.[28] It could also be held that cognitions constituted an essential feature of behavioral dispositions, insofar as an apprehension or awareness of some particular stimulus seems built into the disposition itself.

More important for the purposes of the present enterprise, cognitive accounts of emotion can be brought to bear on an investigation of Colin Radford's claim that our emotional responses to fiction are irrational and (in the next chapter) on Kendall Walton's claim that most of our affective responses to fiction are merely pseudo-emotions (given the lack of an appropriate existentially committed belief and behavioral inclination on the part of an individual who is moved by fiction). Such claims can only make sense against a backdrop of assumptions that permit us to hold there is some cognitive element of emotion that can be consistent or inconsistent with reason (or, in Walton's case, that existentially committed belief or the motivational force associated with it are necessary for emotion). In

---

28. Blakeslee, "Tracing the Brain's Pathways for Linking Emotion and Reason," B5, B11.

particular, it is the cognitivist approach to analysis that most easily permits us to speak of the rationality or irrationality of emotion without forcing us to abandon aspects of the physiological, dispositional, and desiderative accounts.

From this point forward, discussion will focus exclusively on those accounts of emotion that facilitate the ascription of rationality or irrationality to an emotional response. Theories maintaining that emotions have cognitive constituents or concomitants are the most suitable candidates, as Alex Neill has recently pointed out.[29] Several versions of such theories will ground an analysis and investigation of Colin Radford's characterization of our responses to fiction as irrational. Once a set of candidate criteria for irrationality in emotion is established, an investigation of the claim that our emotional responses to fiction are irrational will be attempted. It will be my contention that such a claim cannot be supported either on the basis of analogies drawn to comparison cases or on the basis of more general allegations of inconsistency.

IRRATIONALITY IN EMOTION

Let us begin by once more considering evaluations or construals as the cognitive constituents of emotion. The characterization of emotion in terms of construal or evaluation is particularly interesting, since current neurological research suggests that emotions necessarily involve bodily and cognitive changes "induced by the *evaluation* of a particular stimulus in terms of earlier experience."[30] This reinforces the claims of Ronald de Sousa, who indicates that

> we are made familiar with the vocabulary of emotion by association with paradigm scenarios. These are drawn first from our daily life as small children and later reinforced by the stories, art, and culture to which we are exposed. . . . Paradigm scenarios involve two aspects: first, a situation type providing the characteristic *objects* of the specific emotion type . . . and second, a set of characteristic

---

29. Alex Neill, "Fiction and the Emotions," *American Philosophical Quarterly* 30 (1993): 1–13.

30. Blakeslee, "Tracing the Brain's Pathways for Linking Emotion and Reason," B11. Emphasis mine.

or "normal" *responses* to the situation, where normality is first a biological matter and then very quickly becomes a cultural one.[31]

Paradigm scenarios are at one point described as interpretations of situations,[32] and might even be understood as ways of apprehending situations (i.e., in terms of characteristic scenarios). This is in some ways compatible with the different account of emotion put forward by Robert C. Roberts, in which he speaks of emotions as ways of "concernfully" construing one thing in terms of another, as mental states in which one thing is grasped in terms of something else. For instance, fear of an interviewer can involve seeing the interviewer as threatening to oneself. This "can be analyzed into my construing her as having great power over my life and having contempt for my answers on the one hand, and my having a big concern to get a job and esteem myself as a capable person, on the other."[33]

On such an account of emotion, taking umbrage or offense at someone's behavior might be described in terms of construing that behavior as rude and disrespectful. Let us say that Smith takes umbrage at the familiarity of his younger colleague Jones, who addresses Smith by his first name during the course of a philosophical dispute. Smith construes Jones's familiarity as disrespectful. Such treatment, Smith feels, is incommensurate with his stature in the philosophical community. Were I to call Smith's emotional response irrational (in the context of accounts that identify emotions with construals), I would be taking issue with Smith's construal of Jones's behavior as a manifestation of disrespect, or taking issue with Smith's notion about what kinds of behavior constitute rudeness, or perhaps taking issue with Smith's assessment of the *degree* of disrespect involved. Usually, I would be questioning either Smith's appraisal or the grounds for it.

A number of philosophers would identify Smith's construal with a belief about Jones's behavior. For instance, Solomon might say that Smith made a hasty and dogmatic normative judgment about Jones and her behavior, since it is his contention that judgments are, or are embedded in, emotional responses.[34] The assessment of rationality might, in this case, involve an attempt to discover whether such a belief is justified.[35] If char-

31. Ronald de Sousa, *The Rationality of Emotion*, 182.
32. Ibid., 201.
33. Roberts, "What an Emotion Is: A Sketch," 192.
34. Solomon, "Emotions and Choice," in *What Is an Emotion?*, 317.
35. This may not always prove to be a straightforward matter, given the relativism inherent in certain constructionist theories.

acterized as constituents of emotion or identified outright with emotions, unjustified beliefs could, on some accounts, invite the ascription of irrationality to the emotion itself.

What of an affective response to which no existentially committed belief could be said to correspond? If existential commitment is necessary for emotion, the response could not be characterized as emotional. Alex Neill has focused on this as a central difficulty in explicating our response to fiction,[36] and such criteria have been considered by several philosophers who discuss these responses, Kendall Walton among them.[37] Acceptance of such a view dissolves Radford's charge of irrationality. There would no longer be an emotion against which the charge could be leveled. If Smith's state lacked a cognitive constituent, how could we speak of its *ir*rationality, as distinct from its *non*rationality? It is not clear that it is permissible to impugn the rationality or coherence of a set of physiological symptoms, for instance. What could there be *in* the state or condition that could be held inconsistent with some proposition the subject believed? However, while Radford's allegation of irrationality suggests the adoption of a cognitive view of emotion, accounts that identify the cognitive constituent of emotion with existentially committed belief are not the only alternative. Radford himself appears to reject these and to hold only that existentially committed belief is necessary for *rationality* in emotion. Given this, and given that the present discussion is concerned with the question of rationality in emotion rather than necessary conditions for emotion in general, the aforementioned cognitive account of emotion will be reserved for future chapters. It is, in fact, possible to maintain that emotions are cognitive without mandating existentially committed beliefs as the constituent cognitions.

For instance, it has been convincingly argued that we cannot rule out the possibility of emotions that are unaccompanied by corresponding existentially committed beliefs.[38] Sometimes our beliefs seem to be in outright conflict with our emotions. If such possibilities are not denied outright, we could propose that emotions be associated with construals or evaluations involving the ascription of a property in imagination. Smith may *imagine* of Jones that she is disrespectful without *believing* this of Jones.

---

36. Neill, "Fiction and the Emotions," 1–2.

37. Kendall Walton, *Mimesis as Make-Believe: On the Foundations of the Representational Arts* (Cambridge: Harvard University Press, 1990).

38. Roberts, "What an Emotion Is: A Sketch," 196–201. Cheshire Calhoun, "Cognitive Emotions?," in *What Is an Emotion?*, 327–42.

David Hume, I think, described it best when he contrasted inferences drawn on the basis of general rules with those drawn on the basis of habitual associations. The former are ascribed to the judgment and the latter to the imagination in an example of an inconsistent emotional response.[39] The occupant of an iron cage suspended from a tower cannot forbear trembling when he surveys the precipice below, though he knows himself safe and has had every assurance of security. Despite such knowledge and assurance, "his imagination runs away with its object, and excites a passion proportion'd to it."[40] He construes his situation as dangerous (he imagines of the situation that it is dangerous) but does not believe it is.

Certainly, those who take evaluative beliefs to be necessary constituents of emotions will try to argue that Hume's subject cannot *know* himself safe if he is afraid. The subject might be thought to focus his beliefs on remote possibilities, since a fall is not absolutely out of the question. He might be thought to have all the evidence a reasonable man could ask for that he is safe without drawing the prescribed conclusion. Such critics might point out that their disinclination to take literally Hume's claim that the subject *knows* himself safe has some support from Hume. Elsewhere in *A Treatise of Human Nature,* Hume speaks of ill-founded emotions in a somewhat different way and suggests that "passions can be contrary to reason only so far as they are accompany'd with some judgment or opinion."[41]

Yet Robert C. Roberts, Cheshire Calhoun, and others offer convincing examples in support of the view that construals linked to emotional response need not be accompanied by corresponding existentially committed judgments.[42] These cases roughly resemble that of Hume's caged man, illustrating an imaginative misconstruction independent of belief. Calhoun and Roberts, although some of their terminology differs, make similar points and even employ some of the same metaphors. Both speak of construal in terms of "seeing as," of bringing some concept or image to bear on an object or situation (e.g., if I have contempt for a politician, I may

---

39. David Hume, *A Treatise of Human Nature* 1.3.13, ed. L. A. Selby-Bigge (Oxford: Clarendon Press, 1967), 147–49.

40. Ibid., 148.

41. Hume, *A Treatise of Human Nature* 2.3.3, 416. In one respect, Hume treats emotions as unanalyzable sensations. However, his claims about indirect emotions suggest that they are, in a sense, intentional and that they are thought to have cognitive concomitants.

42. Roberts, "What an Emotion Is: A Sketch," 196–201. Calhoun, "Cognitive Emotions?," in *What Is an Emotion?*, 335–42. In Calhoun's case, a belief that is held intellectually may not be held evidentially. A given emotional response may thus prove at odds with a belief that is only held intellectually.

see that individual as greedy and dishonest).[43] Both also compare misconstruals occurring in the absence of some corresponding belief to optical
illusions.[44]

Let us consider the further adventures of Smith, who so recently took
umbrage at the familiarity of Jones. Smith, the purchaser of a new personal
computer whose workings remain largely a mystery to him, has just finished typing the first draft of his magnum opus. It is due at the publisher's
the very next day. Smith carefully positions his mouse and clicks on the
print command. Nothing happens. He clicks again. Nothing. A frenzied
perusal of several manuals follows, to no avail. The cursor blinks in malign
satisfaction, impervious to Smith's salvage attempts. Smith grows enraged.
He smashes his fist down on the keyboard. "Stupid machine!" he yells (just
as he yells at his car when it stalls).

Let us absolve Smith of any unjustified beliefs about sentient computers.
He does not believe that inanimate objects can be guilty of either malicious
obstructionism or willful incompetence. He does, however, respond as if
he did believe this. Roberts might suggest that Smith *construes* the computer as culpable or malicious, even though he would disavow any such
judgment. The computer seems so to him, despite his firm belief that
inanimate objects cannot possess such properties. Calhoun might indicate
that Smith believed intellectually that the computer could not be morally
culpable but that he could not bring himself to hold the belief evidentially.
His experience of the computer as culpable could be attributed to a
cognitive set of associations and patterns of attention that constituted an
interpretive framework different from that of belief, insofar as it was
prereflective rather than consciously articulated.[45]

It seems that Smith entertains some type of thought about or attitude
toward the computer, one which might even be specified propositionally.
As Noel Carroll and others suggest, he may entertain a proposition unasserted.[46] My own inclination is to suggest that Smith entertains the
thought in imagination. It might be held that Smith imagines of the com-

---

43. Roberts, "What an Emotion Is: A Sketch," 187. Calhoun, "Cognitive Emotions?," in
What Is an Emotion?, 339–42.

44. Roberts, "What an Emotion Is: A Sketch," 196. Calhoun, "Cognitive Emotions?," in
What Is an Emotion?, 338. Again, in Calhoun's case, what is missing is a belief that is held
evidentially.

45. Calhoun, "Cognitive Emotions?," in *What Is an Emotion?*, 340.

46. Noel Carroll, "Critical Study: *Mimesis as Make-Believe*," *Philosophical Quarterly* 45
(1995): 93. Distinctions between the mere entertainment of a proposition and imaginative
involvement will be made in later chapters. At present, it should be sufficient to point out
that imagining can involve more than entertaining propositions.

puter that it is culpably obstructive. Thus, construal becomes an act of interpretation or property ascription to which one's degree of commitment may vary. To construe may be to believe, or it may be merely to imagine. The construal need not be considered wholly involuntary, though it is clear that construals like Smith's cannot involve extensive deliberation.

There are, of course, many other ways of analyzing Smith's reaction. Instead of claiming Smith is angry with his computer, we could point out Smith's frustration with his situation, or with the writers of his manual, or with his own lack of technical expertise. I will concentrate on my initial analysis mainly because it provides a readily accessible comparison to cases that will be discussed later, and because none of the competing analyses can explain Smith's words and actions without bringing to bear complicated psychological concepts of displacement.

Let us take a brief hiatus from Smith and consider further examples of misconstrual. I will clarify a bit further by providing a parallel from my own experience. Take the case of my dog, who rouses me at three in the morning with desperate entreaties to be taken out of doors. I stagger bleary-eyed into subzero temperatures only to discover that the sole purpose of this expedition is the retrieval of a cherished marrow bone. I experience a strong feeling of ill usage. She lied to me, I fume, about why she wanted to go out. Now, I am not inclined to believe that my dog deceived me with malice aforethought about the motives for her request, nor am I inclined to believe that she took unfair advantage of my concern for the state of the carpet. However, I respond as if I did believe this — with anger and irritation. I have, in imagination, construed the dog as an entity that deliberately deceived and inconvenienced me for base and self-interested reasons, even though I deny any corresponding assumptions about the cognitive capacities of canines.

Similar claims could be made about phobic reactions.[47] Spike fears spiders. He has taken several entomology courses at the university and is well aware that the type of spider infesting his home is utterly harmless. Nevertheless, he shrieks when he sees one, begs others to kill it, and carries a spray can of insecticide in a manner usually exhibited only by insecure gunslingers in spaghetti westerns. Some might hold that Spike has conflicting beliefs. On the other hand, Calhoun and Roberts might suggest that Spike does not believe that these kinds of spiders are danger-

---

47. Cheshire Calhoun makes such a claim in her "Cognitive Emotions?," in *What Is an Emotion?*, 331, 340.

ous but interprets or construes them that way. These interpretations or construals are something I have linked to an individual's imagination. As Calhoun does, I think they involve associations and patterns of attention, and I agree that the cognitions associated with a given emotion may not be fully articulated. I suggest, however, that they are articulable, and I see no inconsistency in forging the same alliance Hume did between such attention patterns or associations and the workings of the imagination.

Here is another possible ground, then, for ascribing irrationality to an emotional response. Holding a belief that denies the substance of the construal linked to the emotion, that contradicts or denies the property ascription the construal makes, suggests irrationality in an emotion. To rehearse the grounds for irrationality in emotion, I return briefly to the case of Smith. It is irrational for Smith to feel rage toward his computer when he misconstrues it as a morally culpable agent. If such a construal were to take the form of a belief, Smith's belief (and his anger, for those claiming belief is a constituent of emotion or those identifying belief with emotion) could clearly be labeled irrational. If, as in Hume's example, Smith's construal is at odds with his belief (Smith doesn't *believe* the computer is a morally responsible agent but nevertheless imaginatively construes it that way), we might consider adducing irrationality on the ground of inconsistency, since what Smith believes of his computer is inconsistent with what he imagines of it.

One other possibility remains, for those who wish to deny that we can ever characterize beliefs as constituents of emotion. Here, it might be held that emotions are only rational to the extent that they are *consistent* with beliefs.[48] Thus, a fear of Martian invasion could be held rational if a subject (unreasonably, let us hope) believed such an invasion were imminent. On such an account, the belief could be held irrational while the subject's fear was not. This, of course, yields different results from those obtained by considering the belief a constituent of emotion. In this latter case, the fear could be deemed irrational on account of considering its constituent cognition — the belief — irrational. The former approach also differs from any treatment that permits us to characterize the emotion as a construal that *can* be existentially committed. The approach appears to multiply cognitions unnecessarily. If the construal identified with an emotional response *cannot* be a belief (though it must retain the capacity to be at odds with belief), we would have to associate a duality of cognitions with

---

48. This is an analysis to which I believe Colin Radford may subscribe, as will become evident in the next section.

every emotional response. Each emotion, rational or irrational, would involve two evaluations or construals of its object: one of these a belief; the other, a thought of some sort (since we could not speak of sensations or biochemical reactions as items whose consistency with a belief we were in any position to assess).

The preceding survey has provided us with several criteria for the identification of irrationality in emotion. Depending on the specific cognitive account of emotion adopted, we may consider an emotion irrational when what is held to be a constituent belief is irrational or when the construal associated with the emotion is at odds with what is believed of the intentional object.

FICTIONAL EVENTS AND IRRATIONAL EMOTIONS

Alarms blare, steam pipes explode, and lights flash as the spaceship officer, sweaty and battered, shoulders a flamethrower and staggers through a doorway. The emergency destruct system has been activated, and Ripley must reach the shuttle before the ship detonates. I lean forward in my theater seat, engrossed in the film, terrified that the titular and wholly unprepossessing alien lurks around the next bend of the corridor. This is more exciting than *Star Wars*. The hero is more emotionally riveting than Luke Skywalker. And the protagonist is even cast against type. She is a woman.

Undoubtedly, I am responding emotionally to the film. I fear for Ripley. I am distressed by her plight: trapped aboard a spaceship with only a hostile alien and understandably irritable cat for company. I admire Ripley's courage and resourcefulness. I exhibit many of the physiological symptoms of fear and some of the behavior associated with it. My pulse rate is up. I yell when the alien makes an unannounced entrance. This is, in fact, not an unusual response to *Alien*, a film that was calculated to terrorize, and succeeded admirably in the endeavor.

The fact that such experiences are usual can raise several interesting philosophical questions in itself, the most pertinent of which has been repeatedly asked by Colin Radford.[49] How can I be moved by this improbable space opera? How can I fear for Ripley when I do not believe that she

---

49. Radford has written extensively on this topic. For a complete list of these writings and of responses to them, see footnote 1 in my introduction.

exists? My emotional engagement is irrational (albeit benignly), according to Radford. To pity or to fear for an entity that one is certain does not exist involves one in inconsistency and incoherence.

Different grounds for the ascription of irrationality to an emotion have been canvased. Can irrationality in emotional response to fiction be established on their basis? In the above example, my beliefs do not appear to pose a problem. I believe that, fictionally, there is a woman named Ripley who is in danger.[50] I do not believe that I am contemplating actual events, nor do I believe that a heroic fighter of aliens named Ripley exists. I have not mistakenly ascribed Ripley's experiences to the actress who portrays her. In short, I am aware that I am dealing with a fiction. I even, for those who wish to identify emotions outright with evaluative judgments, have justified evaluative beliefs that might be thought to ground or constitute a part of my emotional response: I believe that to be trapped with a hostile and cunning adversary of superior powers is dangerous, for instance.[51] None of the beliefs related to my experience of the fiction appears to be unreasonable. Those who assess rationality in emotion solely by assessing the evaluative and other beliefs thought to compose or to accompany emotion would probably exonerate our responses to fictions from charges of inconsistency on this basis. But the kinds of emotional responses such criteria rule irrational are not involved in the cases to which Radford has drawn attention. Many of Radford's writings suggest that it is when an emotional response is at odds with what is believed to be the case that the difficulty arises.[52]

Being moved by fictions seems far more comparable to situations of the

---

50. Beliefs about what is fictionally the case are taken as central to emotional response to fiction by Eva Schaper in "Fiction and the Suspension of Disbelief," *British Journal of Aesthetics* 18 (1978), and, most recently, by Alex Neill in "Fiction and the Emotions." The accounts are attractive if one requires only that *some* belief accompany any emotion. However, such approaches pose certain problems when one attempts to account for the intentional object of an emotional response, as will be discussed in Chapter 6. Beliefs about what is fictionally the case do not seem to be evaluative in the same way that beliefs associated with emotion are. Pity, for instance, could be thought to involve our construing someone's experience as undeservedly painful. A belief that, fictionally, someone suffers seems to leave us pitying authorial fabrications, which cannot suffer.

51. This kind of an approach is suggested by Bijoy H. Boruah in *Fiction and Emotion: A Study in Aesthetics and the Philosophy of Mind* (Oxford: Clarendon Press, 1988), 108–17.

52. Radford holds that an emotion is rational to the extent that it is consistent with what is believed. Were I to believe *Alien* a documentary, my fear for Ripley would be considered rational, even though my belief that I observed actual events was not in itself rational. See Radford's "Philosophers and Their Monstrous Thoughts," *British Journal of Aesthetics* 22 (1982): 262.

kind described by Hume, Roberts, and Calhoun, which I have maintained display an opposition between what is imagined and what is believed. Radford's own comparisons appear to suggest this. In one paper, he compares our being moved by fictions to a child's fear of a stuffed tiger in a museum. The child *knows* that the tiger is stuffed but fears it nonetheless.[53] The parallels to cases of irrationality discussed in the preceding section are obvious. Radford might claim, for instance, that when we are moved by fictions we have (without believing them real) construed fictional situations as real ones. Just as Smith construed his computer as culpable without believing it, I might be thought to construe, for example, a fictional instance of danger as a real one, despite having no mistaken beliefs about the ontological status of fictional situations. In both cases there appears to be a kind of error, for the computer is not believed capable of deliberate malice and the fictional danger is not believed to be actual.

The parallels are not as clear as they appear at first glance, however. The examples given by those who propose such an account of irrational emotion always involve the imaginative construal of *actual* objects or events in terms of attributes they are believed not to possess or scenarios they are believed not to resemble. Roberts, for instance, mentions a case in which someone *looks* guilty to the agent (is imaginatively endowed with guilt by the agent) even though she is not believed to be guilty.[54] Here, the charge of irrationality is leveled precisely because there is an imaginative misascription of a quality (guilt, culpability) or scenario (that of a guilty party) to an object or situation whose properties are incompatible with the projection. Ronald de Sousa makes a similar point and does not condemn our emotional responses to fictions as irrational. Literature, he states, educates us in how to picture and understand human situations.[55] De Sousa even considers whether there is something wrong with wanting to

---

53. Radford, "Stuffed Tigers: A Reply to H. O. Mounce," *Philosophy* 57 (1982): 529–32. Those espousing a cognitivist account of emotion that identifies it with belief might deny that one could know oneself safe while fearing for one's safety. They would probably suggest that the child was not quite certain of safety, despite possessing good reasons for believing it. Cheshire Calhoun, in her previously cited work, makes a distinction between holding beliefs intellectually and evidentially. She might propose that the child only intellectually believed himself safe, but that he did not believe this evidentially. Despite possible controversy about the beliefs of the subject in this example, I will for the moment (and for the purpose of furthering the investigation at hand) take Radford's word for the child's knowledge of safety.

54. Roberts, "What an Emotion Is: A Sketch," 201.

55. de Sousa, *The Rationality of Emotion*, 184.

experience an emotion without paying the price of its natural context, with evoking "paradigm scenarios without needing to live through their natural causes." He does not think there is, because "emotions aroused by art need not pose as applying to reality."[56] It is in other contexts that the problem of irrationality can arise, for an emotion that is suspended from its natural context can pretend to be otherwise and prove viciously projective. True irrationality of emotion involves the perception of an actual situation in terms of a scenario it does not resemble.[57] Similarly, the child's fear of the stuffed tiger could be thought irrational because dangerousness is misascribed to an entity we are told is *known* to be incapable of possessing any such quality. Note that the charge of irrationality is never leveled because actuality or existence in the real world is imaginatively misascribed to the purely imaginary.

The properties whose misascription seems central to the identification of an irrational emotion are those with some variety of analytic connection to the emotion. Fear is linked with the construal of a situation as dangerous, taking umbrage with the construal of behavior as insulting. In other words, the properties ascribed (e.g., danger) are essential to the emotion (e.g., fear). Perhaps it may be held that existence is a necessary condition for the rational ascription of properties (even a purely imaginative ascription)—that is, that *any* construal must involve existential commitment to its object in order to be rational.[58]

Yet this makes the contemplation of possible or hypothetical events highly suspect. Consider that we frequently entertain hypothetical events in imagination without being existentially committed to any aspect of them. To say that I contemplate a hypothetical event or scene does not necessitate my being a player in it, nor does it require feature roles for anyone with whom I am acquainted or even of whose existence I am aware. I might be an environmentalist who worries about the plight of merely *possible* future generations (the depletion of the ozone layer might have more fatal effects than is currently suspected) and construes their environmentally hazardous hypothetical situation as distressing. Consider further that construals are usually taken as necessary but insufficient for an

---

56. Ibid., 320-21.

57. Ibid., 188.

58. For example, this may be suggested by Rom Harre in his discussion of Schachter's work. Harre states that "some belief in the existence of a suitable intentional object is necessary" for the correct use of emotion words. The preceding quotation is from Harre's "An Outline of the Social Constructionist Viewpoint," 8.

emotional response. On this account, any vivid imaginative construal could suggest irrationality, whether or not it amounted to emotion.

Such a claim seems unacceptable. I can imagine the way a government might be (in no particular country or time) and construe it as effective, if improbable. In ethics, hypothetical cases are frequently entertained in thought experiments aimed at considering what would follow from various assumptions. Indeed, our response to imagined cases (though it is seldom a full-blown emotion) is often taken as revelatory of an assumed principle's success or failure.[59] Are such imaginings *irrational*? Surely the alliance of rationality with a dearth of imagination is a less than happy one.

One might respond that only those construals that are constituents of emotions can be correctly judged irrational on the basis of a lack of existential commitment. Yet what could warrant the attribution of inconsistency only to these isolated cases? It is difficult to find grounds for such a distinction. It seems that emotional responses directed toward fictional events and characters cannot be considered irrational on account of their lack of existential commitment without thereby jettisoning the rationality of undeniably respectable construals.

Granted, when I construe Ripley's situation vis-à-vis the alien as dangerous, I know it is not the case that there *is* a woman named Ripley who is in danger, even though that is what I imagine. However, the property ascription is not what is central to my denial. The stuffed animal phobic does not believe that there is a stuffed tiger that is dangerous, but he does believe that there is a stuffed tiger. There is a disparity between construals of fictional events and the comparison cases of irrational response that were ventured earlier (Smith's computer, the stuffed tiger, my dog, Spike's spider). These comparison cases involve existential commitment to one term of the construal, whereas responses to fiction do not.

Consider that there is a difference between imagining *of* some existing thing that it has a certain property and imagining *that* there is something with a certain property. If it were possible to demonstrate such a distinction in logical form,[60] the contrast might be illustrated by the following:

Case 1
There is a stuffed tiger of which S imagines that it is dangerous and
of which he believes that it is not the case that it is dangerous.
$(\exists x)[Tx \ \& \ Im(S,Dx) \ \& \ Bel(S,-Dx)]$

---

59. The last example is suggested by the work of Richard Moran: "The Expression of Feeling in Imagination," *Philosophical Review* 103 (1994): 94.

60. Thanks to my colleague Joseph Bessie for his suggestions.

Case 2
S imagines that there is a space alien that is dangerous and S believes
that it is not the case that there is an alien that is dangerous.
$$Im[S, (\exists x)(Ax \& Dx)] \& Bel[S, -(\exists x)(Ax \& Dx)]$$

Case 2 involves no projection of the imaginary onto the real since the
existential quantifier is within the scope of "imagines that" and thus avoids
contradicting the belief. In Case 1, what is imagined about a real thing is
denied in the corresponding belief about the same real thing. Case 1 recalls
the kind of situation that Hume described: a case in which one's response
to an actual situation is governed by what one imagines of it, despite one's
belief to the contrary.

It is debatable, however, whether Case 1 represents a condition sufficient for the ascription of irrationality to any construal, whether emotional
or not. Imaginative construals of actual objects in terms of properties those
objects do not possess can seem blameless. I can imagine what it would be
like if I were the greatest fencer in the world (the fame, the product
endorsements, the complementary equipment from Santelli) or what it
would be like to win the lottery without thereby rendering myself liable to
charges of irrationality.

Case 1 may instead provide a necessary condition for the ascription of
irrationality to imaginative construals. In particular situations, the imaginative projection of a property onto an object not believed to possess it
does seem irrational. In the case of Smith and his computer, for instance,
Smith's imaginative projection alters his attitude and behavior toward the
object of his construal. He bellows abuse at the computer. He strikes it. Yet
he does not believe it is a responsible or responsive agent, even though his
behavior and attitude toward an object in the real world have been altered
by what he imagines. In other words, Smith's response appears irrational
not only because his construal is at odds with his belief but because his
behavior and behavioral inclinations are under the influence of his imaginative construal *rather than* under the influence of what he believes.
Hume's caged man at least appears inclined to escape his cage. The child
who fears the stuffed tiger is described as behaving in such a way as to
prompt reassurance from adults. Thus, paradigm cases of irrationality that
take the form of Case 1 are not just associated with emotion but with an
inclination to act on the basis of what is imagined rather than what is
believed.

I am disinclined to state categorically that every *emotional* construal
that takes the form of Case 1 is irrational. First, nonemotional construals
can be considered irrational when they take the form of unjustified beliefs.

Even if we consider only imaginative property ascriptions, these need not be the cognitive constituents of emotions in order to invite allegations of irrationality. Certain kinds of compulsive behavior can be as easily associated with imagination as belief. Consider a fairly typical scenario. One may believe that one has closed the garage door or turned out the garage lights upon departing for work. Nevertheless, before one reaches the end of the block, one begins to imagine that one has forgotten to perform these tasks. That is, one can imagine of oneself that one has neglected tasks one believes one has performed or imagine of actions one believes have been performed that they have not been performed.[61] If one goes back to check, perhaps more than once, one's actions and one's inclinations to act are clearly under the influence of what is imagined rather than what is believed. One behaves (or is strongly inclined to behave) as if one believed something that one does not. In such cases, the only real emotion felt might be a frustration with *oneself* for feeling compelled to go back to check on the door or the lights. One can behave in such a way without believing that any real dangers attach to an open or lit garage. Thus, I do not think that irrationality need attach only to *emotional* construals that take the form of Case 1.

Second, some emotional construals that are associated with imaginative property ascriptions and that could be held to take the form of Case 1 do not seem to be irrational. Empathetic emotion, the subject to which Chapter 6 is devoted, involves imagining the possession of thoughts and beliefs one does not believe oneself to possess. To feel empathetic fear, for instance, can be to imagine believing oneself endangered. That is, in empathizing with a frightened friend, one considers the beliefs and thoughts one believes that friend to possess and imagines *having* those thoughts and beliefs. It is through the imaginative adoption of such a point of vantage that an empathetic response becomes possible. I do not think that empathetic fear is irrational, however. It differs from the paradigm cases of irrationality already discussed. The empathizer does not project onto an actual situation some property she does not believe it to possess but imaginatively projects herself into an alternate perspective on a situation. Like an imaginative response to fiction, which begins with beliefs about what is fictional, empathy begins with beliefs about what is believed or thought by another (the person with whom one empathizes).

---

61. Since such actions are virtually automatic, it may be the case that one simply does not recollect having performed them. In that case, however, the individual will probably believe it is *possible* that he has not closed the garage door or turned out the lights. We are at present considering a case in which the subject does believe he has done so.

The empathizer's imaginative adoption of certain beliefs could, I suppose, be characterized as an ascribing to oneself of properties that are incompatible with those one believes one possesses. That is, just like the child who fears the stuffed tiger, the empathizer could be described as projecting a property onto a real object: herself. The case of the stuffed tiger could be reworded, and the child could be taken to imagine believing himself endangered, just as the empathizer does. However, a distinction lies in the fact that the child imagines an object he knows to be benign as threatening, whereas the empathizer will in most cases imagine as threatening an object she believes would pose a threat to certain people in certain circumstances. I am willing to concede that if the empathizer imagines having unjustified beliefs about what threatens (whether she regards them as irrational or not), there are grounds for considering her empathetic fear irrational, since the fear with which she empathizes is irrational.[62] If her own beliefs about the beliefs of another are unjustified, then her response may well be irrational and is certainly not genuinely empathetic. My contention is merely that many cases of empathy differ from scenarios like that of the stuffed tiger in several respects.

Consider my empathy with someone undergoing an experience quite likely to induce terror: review by a tenure committee. I fear the tenure committee on behalf of my friend. I believe that my friend believes herself at risk from the committee. In empathizing, I imagine believing I am at risk. While I believe that the tenure committee would be a threat to certain people in certain circumstances, I do not believe that it threatens me even though I imagine believing that I stand in that relation to it. But the self whose danger I imagine is imaginatively endowed with all the properties that *would* make the tenure committee a threat. I imagine believing I am up for tenure at a certain university; I imagine thinking that I have not published enough; I imagine recollecting the acrimonious argument about counterfactuals I just had with the committee chair; I imagine suspecting that I am doomed. Someone who had such thoughts and beliefs could justifiably believe herself at risk. This is unlike the case of the stuffed tiger, for the child does not believe the stuffed tiger could pose a threat to anyone in any circumstances.

The empathetic imagination is both hypothetical and, in Richard Mo-

---

62. The contemplation of beliefs one believes irrational or ludicrous would appear to make empathetic emotion unlikely. Considering such a world view could certainly lead to pity for an individual, or even to contempt. Yet imagining that one has such beliefs oneself seems a tall order. It would be far easier (and not, I think, irrational) to imagine having false but justified beliefs.

ran's words, dramatic.[63] It involves imagining what a situation or an experience *would* be like if one had certain thoughts, beliefs, desires, and impulses. To imagine having these thoughts and beliefs is not to imagine changes in oneself or one's doxastic repertoire but to imagine how life is for somebody else, to imagine how it could be to be such a person in such a situation. The imaginative construal tied specifically to the empathizer's fear is not a simple evaluation of the tenure committee as threatening to herself. The empathizer imaginatively occupies a certain point of vantage and considers the tenure committee from the perspective of the thoughts and beliefs she imagines having. If the property ascribed is to be regarded as self-referential ("dangerous-to-me" rather than "dangerous"), then its imaginative ascription to the tenure committee is contingent on certain imaginative assumptions. The empathizer believes that the tenure committee would be a threat to anyone placed as she imagines being placed. This belief is not contradicted by what she imagines. She does not imagine that she *personally* (i.e., *she*: the individual who works at a different university) is threatened by the committee any more than she believes it. The empathizer imagines the threateningness the committee would have for her were she to have certain thoughts and beliefs, just because she imagines believing and thinking certain things.

Of course, she imagines having beliefs and experiences she does not believe she has, and this does take the form of Case 1. However, it is interesting to note that this imaginative property ascription of beliefs and experiences to oneself would not be the cognitive constituent of one's empathic fear, which would involve the imaginative ascription of dangerousness to a different object. Imagining having certain beliefs has no necessary connection to an explicitly emotional construal and in itself does not seem dissimilar to the cases of hypothesizing mentioned earlier. Neither does the empathizer act or feel inclined to act under the influence of her construal rather than her belief. For these reasons, I do not think that most empathetic emotions (excepting problem cases already mentioned) can be considered irrational. Empathy will be discussed at far greater length in Chapter 6.

I therefore conclude that Case 1 provides us with a necessary rather than a sufficient condition for classifying an imaginative property ascription as irrational. A sketch of conditions that might prove sufficient would have to take the considerations raised in preceding examples into account. The

---

63. Moran, "The Expression of Feeling in Imagination."

emotional construal *itself* (rather than any accompanying property ascription) would have to take the form of Case 1. Perhaps an imaginative property ascription taking that form would have to be shown to influence deliberate behaviors or behavioral inclinations despite and in opposition to the subject's beliefs. When what one imagines influences one's attitude toward one's own life and one's own surroundings and experiences *despite* what one believes of them, then there appear to be grounds for the ascription of irrationality.

The above is merely intended as a sketch of the direction investigations of necessary and sufficient conditions for the ascription of irrationality to imaginative construals might take. The purpose of the present project has already been accomplished by establishing the distinction between Cases 1 and 2, for our emotional responses to fiction do not even meet conditions necessary for the assignment of irrationality to imaginative property ascriptions. At the very least, the clear differences between construals taking the form of Case 1 and those taking the form of Case 2 demonstrate that an argument from analogy based on similarities between such cases could not be sustained. The grounds for allegations of inconsistency that pertain to cases taking the first form are not applicable to cases that take the second.

Certain difficulties might still be raised in the case of fictions, however. To say that I fear for Ripley is to say that I construe her situation as dangerous. Yet I know there *is* no Ripley. My emotion and the construal identified with it appear to have no intentional object, and I am fully aware of this. How can one construe nothing, fear for no one? Am I not contemplating screen images of events I do not believe have occurred, events I know are fakes, and construing *them* as dangerous? Is there not some fundamental inconsistency in this? I think that the above does not accurately reflect what occurs when we are moved by fictions, and I further believe that my distinction between Cases 1 and 2 bears this out.

First, what is generally ascertainable about my particular situation vis-à-vis the fiction is my apprehension of a fictional world within whose boundaries certain propositions are true — namely, that a woman named Ripley is trapped aboard a spacecraft with a hostile alien that has quite efficiently eradicated every other human being in its vicinity. It is perfectly apparent to all undistracted film viewers that this proposition is fictionally true, that such a state of affairs obtains within the world of the work. Naturally, some viewers will be more imaginatively engaged than others. For those who do not attend to the belief that they are contemplating a fiction (though they certainly would not deny it), there is, as per the hypotheses of David Novitz, a world they imagine.[64] Such a world may be one in which certain propositions are true that are neither true nor false in the world of the work, or are never specifically indicated in the world of the work.[65]

For instance, I imagine Ripley's mental states on the basis of behavioral and situational cues given by states of affairs that obtain in the world of the work. I could, of course, watch a film of an actual event and make assumptions of the same sort about the mental states of its subject. The difference is this. I can be mistaken in my assumptions about the mental states of the actual person, even if my construals are consistent with behavioral and situational evidence. That my assumption may be a perfectly justifiable or reasonable one does not alter the possibility of its falsity. In the case of my assumptions about Ripley, however, provided that they are consistent with what is indicated in the world of the work (and perhaps provided that they *would* be less improbable than a variety of alternatives, were these events actually to occur),[66] I cannot be mistaken in just this way. Consider the following example.

Both the imaginative assumption that Ripley's antipathy toward the alien is slightly greater than her fear and the assumption that her fear is slightly greater than her antipathy seem equally consistent with evidence available in the world of the work. Of course, imaginative construals can be inconsistent with such evidence. For example, the assumption that Ripley feels deep affection for the alien is inconsistent with all behavioral cues. The point is that some assumptions consistent with the work's world, say assumptions about Ripley's fear very slightly exceeding her antipathy, cannot be verified, since they are neither true nor false in the world of *Alien*.

My reason for making the above distinction involves demonstrating the kind of irreducibility inherent in purely imaginative construals. To imagine the situation depicted in the final moments of the film *Alien* is to imagine an imperiled and frightened woman. My sympathetic fear for Ripley can be identified with the way such a thought or imagining is entertained. The thought we take seriously and attend to at a specific

---

64. David Novitz, *Knowledge, Fiction and Imagination* (Philadelphia: Temple University Press, 1987), 75–85.

65. See, for instance, the assumptions of Nicholas Wolterstorff in his *Works and Worlds of Art* (Oxford: Clarendon Press, 1980).

66. I have in mind here Nicholas Wolterstorff's assumptions about extrapolation on the basis of fictional states of affairs in *Works and Worlds of Art* and David Lewis's treatment of the same subject in "Truth in Fiction," *American Philosophical Quarterly* 15 (1978): 37–46. These accounts will be discussed further in later chapters.

moment—the thought of a woman's being in perilous circumstances—involves an imagined instantiation of the kind of event that is believed dangerous. The thought can thus be entertained fearfully. Construals involving fictions can be subject to criticism, of course, when they are inconsistent with the world of the work or based on flawed inferences from propositions that are true in that world. But when such difficulties do not arise, there is no further ground for allegations of inconsistency.

My imagining a woman whose experience is unpleasant and perilous involves an existential quantification *within* the context of "imagining that," not a quantification *into* it. I do not imagine of Sigourney Weaver, or of a screen image, or of a theoretical entity of literary criticism (having the same ontological status or lack thereof as would plots or themes)[67] that she or it is imperiled. I imagine an imperiled woman. As Peter Lamarque has suggested, talk of object-directedness in such cases seems to lead not to talk of one's thoughts (which are entertained in imagination) but to talk of their content.[68] This is a content that, in the case of fictions, encompasses both the object and the property ascribed to it. Most of our emotional reactions to fiction, therefore, cannot be held inconsistent on the ground that they involve the projection of a real property onto a merely imaginary entity that can possess no such property, for it is imagined that the property in question is instantiated.

Furthermore, if imagining a woman in Ripley's situation prior to the advent of any danger (and thus prior to any emotion on my part, though I may construe Ripley as competent and intelligent, i.e., imagine a competent and intelligent woman) does not impugn my rationality, what further illegitimate maneuver is my imagination thought to conduct once the story progresses and I begin to fear for Ripley (i.e., imagine an imperiled woman)? To imagine Ripley's peril and thus construe her situation as dangerous (i.e., entertain the thought of it fearfully) surely involves the same kind of cognitive gymnastic as imagining Ripley secure and construing her situation as safe (i.e., imagining it complacently or calmly). Whence the sudden onset of irrationality?

---

67. Peter van Inwagen suggests this as one way of understanding characters in his "Creatures of Fiction," *American Philosophical Quarterly* 14 (1977): 299–308.

68. Peter Lamarque, "How Can We Fear and Pity Fictions?," *British Journal of Aesthetics* 21 (1981): 291–304. Lamarque's hypothesis that thought contents or mental representations can be the objects of our emotions will be discussed at length in Chapter 3.

CONCLUSION

To say that we take fiction as real in imagination, despite our belief that it is not, seems most significantly a commentary on our ability to grasp and contemplate hypothetical human situations. That such a construal can often comprise part of an emotional response adds nothing new to the picture. If the act of imagining a hypothetical human situation, and construing it in a particular way in doing so, is not irrational in itself, what further ground is left on the basis of which to call emotional responses to fictions irrational?

I suggest that our emotional responses to fiction need not invite an inevitable ascription of irrationality. First, for those who hold that some (justified) evaluative belief is necessary either for emotions as such or for rational emotions (whether the belief in question is characterized as a necessary concomitant or a necessary constituent of emotion), it seems that appropriate candidates are available. My fear for Ripley does in fact involve the justified belief that to be stranded with a hostile adversary of superior powers is dangerous and unpleasant.

Second, I have attempted to demonstrate that the kinds of misconstruals with which emotional responses to fictions are typically compared (e.g., the stuffed tiger case) differ significantly from construals involved in response to fiction, for the former involve existential commitment to the object of the construal while the latter do not. It therefore seems that no argument from analogy made on the basis of such comparisons could be sustained. It further appears that no general principle tying rationality to existential commitment could be established without relegating much of our purely hypothetical thinking to the outer darkness of irrationality.

There is hope, I think, for maintaining that we can on occasion feel a coherent and unparadoxical fear for Ripley and that Radford's pity for Anna Karenina is consistent with many of his more general normative judgments and evaluations. The paradox may lie not in our fearing and pitying fictions but in the unquestioning acceptance of an alliance between the rational and the unimaginative.

2

Nearing Fictions: Feeling as Believing

To say, as I have done, that we can take a fiction as real in imagination, whatever this indicates about our ability to grasp and contemplate human situations, may ground some claim to the effect that the construal taken to constitute or accompany an emotion is imaginary rather than imaginative — that we only imagine making it and thus only imagine experiencing a particular emotion. Indeed, several philosophers appear to support such a claim, and many, on this basis or on other grounds, refer to affective responses to fictional entities and situations as quasi emotions or make-believe emotions. This chapter will address the question of whether our reactions to the fictional can be characterized as genuine emotions.

THE EMOTIONAL AND THE QUASI EMOTIONAL

The term "quasi emotion" originates with Kendall Walton. It appeared first in his well-known paper "Fearing Fictions"[1] and has since been adopted by other philosophers.[2] What we are confronted with is the claim that re-

---

1. Kendall Walton, "Fearing Fictions," *Journal of Philosophy* 75 (1978): 5–27. His hypotheses are elaborated in his book, *Mimesis as Make-Believe: On the Foundations of the Representational Arts* (Cambridge: Harvard University Press, 1990).
2. For instance, Gregory Currie utilizes the concept of quasi emotions in *The Nature of*

sponses made specifically to fictional events and entities are not genuine emotions, and this claim seems at least in part to rest on our lack of existential commitment to the objects of those emotions.[3] Since we do not have existentially committed beliefs about the situations of fictional entities and since what we feel toward and about them is said to have no motivational force, Walton maintains that our reactions to the fictitious are quasi emotional.[4]

Quasi emotions can apparently exhibit every feature of a genuine emotion *except* existential commitment to the intentional object and the desires and motivational connections said usually to accompany it. To acknowledge as Walton does that one can genuinely fear that a suspenseful film will give one a heart attack (202), or that historical fictions can lead us to feel (genuine) emotions about actual historical persons (252), is not to acknowledge that we feel genuine emotions toward *fictional* entities and situations to which we are existentially uncommitted and concerning which we have no inclination to act. Neither does it alter Walton's contention that "grief, as well as pity or admiration, would seem to require at the very least awareness of the existence of their objects. It is arguable that for this reason alone, appreciators cannot be said actually to pity Willy [Loman] or grieve for Anna [Karenina] or admire Superman" (204).

While acknowledging that "fear may not *require* a belief that one is in danger" (245), Walton maintains that an emotion like fear must nevertheless be "similar to such a belief (combined with a desire not to be harmed) in its motivational force" (202). Ultimately, he thinks it preferable to assimilate fear to a belief-desire complex, though he allows that there may be cases of, for instance, phobic reactions in which fear is felt in the absence of a belief about danger (like that of Spike in Chapter 1). Such cases, however, will involve the exhibition of deliberate behaviors or involve behavioral inclinations and desires (conceived here as motivations). These are features our responses to fiction are said to lack.

As Walton concedes, there is no reason to take the claim that an existentially committed belief is a necessary condition for emotion as, a priori, unchallengeable. Given the cases of emotional irrationality discussed in

---

Fiction (Cambridge: Cambridge University Press, 1990), although there are distinctions between Walton's and Currie's accounts of the fictional.

3. Colin Radford explicitly rejects this kind of interpretation in "How Can We Be Moved by the Fate of Anna Karenina?," *Proceedings of the Aristotelian Society*, 49, suppl. 6 (1975): 75–76. For him, lack of existential commitment is allied with irrationality in *genuine* emotion.

4. Walton, *Mimesis as Make-Believe*, 202.

the preceding chapter, given the claims of philosophers like Robert C. Roberts about the possibility of emotional construal in the absence of doxastic commitment, and given the contention of Cheshire Calhoun that intellectually held beliefs can conflict with emotions, such a characterization of emotion seems challengeable indeed.

So the absence of an existentially committed belief about the intentional object of one's affective response need not be taken to classify that response as nonemotional. Irving Thalberg and others indicate that an emotion must be, or be accompanied by, some form of thought.[5] Thus, fear is said to be accompanied by a thought of or about danger, the construal of a situation as dangerous. Pity is accompanied by a thought about suffering, the construal of a situation or experience as painful or unpleasant. This thought, however, need not be a belief. We can always claim that such a thought is entertained unasserted in imagination. I could, for instance, claim that my fear for the heroine of *Alien* was accompanied by (or partly constituted of) the thought of a woman in the power of a hostile and alien adversary, a thought I entertained fearfully. The thought is simply entertained in imagination rather than believed.[6]

Furthermore, I hold several evaluative beliefs that are relevant to my emotional response. I believe that to be pursued by a hostile, cunning, and powerful adversary is both potentially threatening to one's health and wholly unpleasant. I believe that to be trapped with an individual of this kind is both dangerous and distressing. Beliefs of this sort are not like beliefs about specific situations, of course. They are about kinds of events and situations rather than particular ones. In holding such a belief, one is, I think, committed to the possibility of events of that *kind* (i.e., broadly construed) but not to the actual occurrence of some specific event. These are beliefs about universals, about what further property ascriptions are warranted when certain characteristics are instantiated. Should a belief's lack of specificity make it impossible to experience a genuine emotion? That beliefs of the type just described have application both to the actual and to the fictional seems rather to support a claim of *similarity* between

---

5. Irving Thalberg, "Emotion and Thought," in Cheshire Calhoun and Robert C. Solomon, eds., *What Is an Emotion? Classic Readings in Philosophical Psychology* (New York: Oxford University Press, 1984).

6. Walton briefly addresses such an approach (*Mimesis*, 203) but rejects it because he takes it to suggest that thoughts are to become the intentional objects of our affective response. Of course, it is not one's thought that one (fictionally or actually) fears when one is said to fear a character. However, I do not think that the adoption of an account like Peter Lamarque's has any such consequences, as I will contend in Chapter 3.

responses to different objects, especially if beliefs are thought constituents
of emotions.

However, Walton holds that our responses to fiction fail to meet other
criteria. That is, even if a phobic reaction is not accompanied by an
appropriate existentially committed belief, it satisfies other conditions
that our reactions to the fictional do not. Thus, our affective responses to
fiction still fail to meet conditions Walton thinks are necessary for emotion.
What might such conditions be? O. K. Bouwsma has offered some suggestions similar to several offered by Walton. Walton identifies our affective
reactions to fictional events with involuntary physiological responses (and
attendant sensations) to beliefs about what is fictionally the case. This
claim, coupled with the contention about quasi emotions, is in several
respects reminiscent of Bouwsma's approach in "The Expression Theory
of Art."[7]

Bouwsma's central example revolves around the experiences of Cassie,
a young woman with a taste for both tragic literature and popcorn. She
ensconces herself in her room with the latest in a series of tragic novels, an
enormous bowl of popcorn, and her cat. As she reads and stuffs herself
with popcorn, tears stream down her face. She sobs. The tears and sobs are
involuntary, certainly not phony. When she has finished the story, Cassie
puts the book down and engages in a perfectly cheerful game with her cat.
If we were to ask Cassie what she felt when she was reading the book, she
would say she was sad. (She would say the book was sad too, but that
would lead us into an entirely different discussion.) Yet how could she
have been genuinely sad while munching popcorn and reveling in her
experience? How could anyone recover so swiftly from a *genuine* sadness?

Bouwsma says that we can come to describe Cassie as sad (and perhaps
Cassie comes to describe herself as sad) because of her involuntary physiological response. According to Bouwsma, Cassie's tears are real, but her
sadness is not. The statement "Cassie is sad," when used in these circumstances, is used to refer only to Cassie's tears.[8] The emotion is expressed,
but Cassie does not have the emotion, just as we "might say there was the
thought of an elephant, but no elephant."[9] We tend to call Cassie's state

---

7. O. K. Bouwsma, "The Expression Theory of Art," in *Philosophical Essays* (Lincoln:
University of Nebraska Press, 1965), 21–50.

8. Bouwsma, "The Expression Theory of Art," 31, 33–35.

9. Ibid., 37. Note the similarity to Walton's claim about physiological responses in the
absence of existential commitment. Bouwsma actually vacillates in answering the question
about whether there is genuine sadness in this case or not. At one point, he suggests that if

one of sadness, because tears are frequently a symptom, an expression, of sadness. It is not, Bouwsma stresses, that Cassie's sadness is imaginary, for no one (including Cassie) imagines her sadness.[10] It is, rather, that some of the outward physiological manifestations of sadness are present. Just as Walton does, Bouwsma contends that Cassie's state has only *some* of the characteristics of genuine emotion: involuntary physiological responses. Not all such responses are necessary concomitants of sadness. One can be sad without crying or expressing one's sadness in any way at all.

What, then, could make an affective state count as genuine sadness? Bouwsma does not supply explicit criteria, but in the course of his discussion he points to certain features that Cassie's experience lacks and genuine emotional responses presumably would not lack. Cassie's tears are not accompanied by the kind of prolonged state of distress or anxiety that may be thought to accompany genuine emotion. She is said to revel in her experience in a way that she would not, were she to be moved by something that had actually occurred. The following list combines the contentions of Walton and Bouwsma about what may be missing in a response like Cassie's:

1. existential commitment to objects of one's construal (a condition I have associated with both accounts, and one that has already been discussed);
2. the endurance of the affective reaction beyond the moment during which one contemplates its object, which is thought less typical of responses to fiction (a condition espoused by Bouwsma; Walton does not concur, suggesting that responses to fiction may be prolonged);
3. the unalleviated discomfort typically associated with negative emotional responses, as opposed to the pleasure or satisfaction we can take in fictional tragedy or horror (once again, a condition put forward by Bouwsma; Walton disagrees, indicating that one may want to experience negative emotions in real-life contexts);[11]
4. the kinds of behaviors, inclinations, motivations, and desires typically associated with emotional response to actual events.

The first point has already been dealt with. Adopting a cognitivist account of emotion does not require the adoption of the view that emotions must

---

there *were* genuine emotion, it would be weak and watered down. I will focus here, however, on the claim that Cassie is not really sad.

10. Ibid., 31. Kendall Walton would dispute this point.

11. Walton, *Mimesis as Make-Believe*, 257.

be accompanied by existentially committed beliefs about their objects. Moreover, Cassie probably does believe that to have certain experiences (the kind that the characters in her novel undergo) is painful and wretched. Indeed, in Chapter 4 I will claim that such a belief is necessary for pity or distress, as is the belief that such wretchedness is possible. Thus, Cassie could possess evaluative beliefs that have the right kind of explanatory connection to a state of sadness. Assuming that Cassie does have beliefs that explain her affective response, and given that cognitive theories of emotion do not inevitably require existentially committed beliefs as the only possible cognitive constituents of emotion, I do not think we must conclude that Cassie cannot be sad on the basis of her lack of existential commitment to the object of her response.

Neither the second nor the third condition appears necessary for emotion, unless a lot of our affective responses to actual events cannot be called genuinely emotional. Surely, genuine emotional responses need not always prove terribly harrowing or enduring. The average newspaper or news program is replete with stories of the suffering and death of strangers, and our reactions of distress upon their contemplation are usually neither intense nor prolonged. I do not think that the momentary nature of an affective response to a newspaper article about a distressing incident must indicate that the response cannot be genuinely emotional. I could finish a tragic article or biography and go off to play with my dog, as Cassie played with her cat. Would this necessarily mean that I was not saddened by a real person's plight? Is it impossible to be sad unless one's sadness has some specified duration? Moreover, as Walton indicates, our psychological participation in a work may be extended beyond the moment during which we peruse a book or watch a film: "One may ponder the events of Anna Karenina's life for days or even years after finishing the novel."[12]

Our affective reactions to the plights of strangers are not always lasting, but our lives are frequently not affected by what happens to strangers. There is a distance involved in our contemplation of the affairs of strangers, just as there can be a distance involved in our contemplation of fictions. The degree of affective response depends to a great extent on how much information we have about the real or imaginary situation that we are contemplating. Frequently, we have more information about fictional entities than we do about real persons mentioned in a newspaper article, especially since fictions can make us privy to the thoughts of characters. We remain at a distance, however, in the sense that both the

---

12. Ibid., 254.

fiction and the article can involve the contemplation of events we cannot change and that cannot affect our lives except insofar as our thoughts, beliefs, and attitudes may be affected.

It might be held that we do not positively revel in the contemplation of actual events that arouse our pity and distress, that we do not take the kind of pleasure that Cassie did in her novel when we contemplate real events. Yet our contemplation of the plights of strangers is not always free of a certain excited interest. When one considers the O. J. Simpson trial, or the lurid and distressing subject matter favored by certain talk show hosts, the word *reveling* seems almost apposite in a description of viewer response. The reaction of some of my less sensitive students to Operation Desert Storm was (and I quote): "Let's make some popcorn and watch the war." However, it does not follow that regarding an event with excitement and interest must inevitably preclude any possibility of being saddened by certain aspects of it. When avidly following news reports of a disaster, we can enjoy having our curiosity satisfied despite the fact that we feel great pity for the victims of that disaster.

Questions about taking satisfaction in tragic or frightening fiction constitute the topic of Chapter 7. For the moment, however, it is worth noting that some philosophers claim that we can on occasion enjoy negative emotions. Would riding a roller coaster be as much fun if the element of fear were entirely removed? We can also take pleasure in the incisiveness and eloquence of an editorial that describes harrowing events and still be horrified by the events described. We might find the appearance of a fire that consumes a building beautiful, even though we are distressed by the consequences the fire has for the building's former occupants. We might even feel a certain satisfaction in our sadness, to the extent that we take it to demonstrate moral sensitivity or responsiveness. We may, as has been mentioned, be interested in and excited by newsworthy events even if we are distressed by the situations of people who are involved in those events.

It therefore seems that neither of Bouwsma's two conditions is necessary for emotion, unless we are willing to banish many of our seemingly unproblematic affective responses to actual events from the realm of the emotional. It is also worth noting that responses to fiction can sometimes meet these criteria. Reactions to fiction can sometimes be long-lasting, and it is possible to be suitably harrowed or depressed by fictions without reveling in the experience (as in the case of my own response to some of the films of Ingmar Bergman).

What of Walton's contentions about the behaviors, motivations, and desires typically lacking in our reactions to the fictional? First, there are actual events to which we respond emotionally but about which we can

do or change absolutely nothing: historical events.[13] Walton acknowledges that "Emily Dickinson, being an actual person, can be the object of
actual pity. One may really feel disgust for Ivan the Terrible or empathize
with Julius Caesar."[14] Yet our feelings about historical persons and historical events, while they are accompanied by existentially committed beliefs,
cannot involve much in the way of the kind of motivational force Walton
associates with genuine emotion. If we know we can do nothing about the
plights or actions of historical persons, our behavior and desires will be
accordingly circumscribed, as they are circumscribed in the case of fiction. Since we can do nothing to change either the historical or the
fictional incident, even though we often wish we could, we are confronted with something that is, from our perspective, unalterable. Yet I can
weep over a fictional tragedy just as I can weep over a tragic biography. My
wishing that the subject of the biography had not met her tragic fate is not
so unlike my wishing that a death described in a fiction could somehow
have been averted: both can be most easily described in terms of counterfactuals, an approach to desires that I take up later in this chapter.

While behavioral response to a contemplation of historical incidents is
atypical, it is possible that I could decide to make a donation to an organization dedicated to helping the victims of tragedies similar to one discussed in a historical description I had perused. However, a fiction could
inspire me to do the same. Unless what we feel about historical events
cannot constitute emotion, requirements about behavior, motivation, and
desire cannot demonstrate that our affective responses to fiction are not
emotions.

It has been argued that, with the possible exception of desire,[15] the four
conditions presented do not constitute necessary conditions for emotion.
In the case of some conditions, it even appears that responses to fiction
can meet them while responses to actual events can fail to do so. The
preceding also suggests that behavior, motivation, desire, and duration of
the affective response are not contingent on existential commitment, a

---

13. R. T. Allen makes a similar point in "The Reality of Responses to Fiction," *British
Journal of Aesthetics* 26 (1986): 66–67. He maintains that emotions are not necessarily
connected with desires, and he states that fiction is, in several respects, like vividly retold
history. I agree with Allen's contention that we can feel without simultaneously acting (or
being disposed to act), though I think that a counterfactual approach can be adopted in the
treatment of desire.

14. Walton, *Mimesis as Make-Believe*, 252.

15. The exception of desire is contingent on the adoption of a counterfactual analysis.
Such possibilities will be discussed in "Addressing Fictions and Expressing Desires," later in
this chapter.

claim a proponent of the first condition might be tempted to make. There appear to be no conclusive reasons for accepting the claim that our affective responses to fiction are not genuine emotions.

Construals of fictional situations may indeed be characterized as imaginary. Perhaps it could be maintained that one merely imagines making them, and so only imagines an emotional response. Yet if the cognitive components of genuine emotions need not be existentially committed, the force of such a line of argument is lost. Our construal is a thought entertained in imagination (e.g., the thought that someone's situation is perilous) but there seems to be no compelling reason for accepting the claim that this thought cannot be the cognitive constituent of a genuine emotion.

Walton has acknowledged that real emotions might on occasion be unaccompanied by existentially committed beliefs. He has also acknowledged that we can be genuinely moved by historical persons and incidents, concerning which our desires and behavioral inclinations and motivations must be severely constrained. It therefore appears that genuine emotional response to fictional events and entities is not entirely ruled out, for we can feel real emotion in the absence of some existentially committed belief about its object and in the absence of the motivational force and behavioral inclinations typically associated with reactions to occurrent events. Walton would probably maintain that at least one of these conditions would have to be met if an affective reaction were to be considered genuinely emotional. However, since he offers no explicit argument for a disjunctive characterization of his criterion for emotion and appears to incline more toward a conjunctive requirement than otherwise (the belief-desire complex mentioned earlier), I will take it that Walton has not conclusively demonstrated that affective responses to fictional characters and events cannot be emotions.

MAKING-BELIEVE

Kendall Walton likens our interactions with fiction to games of make-believe and characterizes our attitudes toward and reactions to fictional states of affairs in terms of make-believe. That is, certain of our attitudes and reactions are incorporated into a fictional world: that of a game based on a work. Walton offers a series of parallels between our encounters with fiction and such games, pointing out that they share several significant features. I will contend that the analogy is not strong enough to warrant the claim that all or most of our responses to fiction are imagined or made believe. I will also argue that the types of affective responses to which Walton's examples most frequently allude are either not representative or are open to interpretations that present alternatives to Walton's own analysis. Let us begin by considering an example that has many features in common with those Walton employs.

When I was an undergraduate, I purchased an ancient, allegedly portable black-and-white television set at a garage sale. It cost five dollars. I lugged it back to my apartment, stopping frequently to wipe my brow and utter heartfelt curses. Having gone to all this trouble to provide an alternative to studious endeavor, I investigated the entertainment possibilities and discovered a program called *Night Gallery*. Late one weekday evening my roommates and I gathered in the living room to watch it. The picture was grainy, but we were content to find an excuse for putting off German grammar.

I do not know how many recollect the notorious Zuni fetish doll episode of the program. I remember neither title nor author, though I recall that Karen Black starred. From a vantage point of twenty years, the premise on which the story was based seems ludicrous. A repressed young woman, effectively squashed by her domineering mother, receives a mysterious package in the mail. It contains an African artifact, a wooden doll perhaps a foot and a half high. The doll's expression is ferocious, and most of its head is occupied by a set of jagged teeth. The doll comes alive and pursues our heroine around her apartment, snapping its teeth in a highly unpleasant and suggestive manner, poking and feinting with its sharp little spear.

By the middle of the program, Jackie, Linda and I all had our feet off the floor and tucked up on the furniture. I spent the majority of this time behind sofa cushions, requesting progress reports from irritated roommates. The penultimate scene of the drama featured the heroine's imprisonment of her toothy foe in the oven. Leaning on the oven door, against which the Zuni fetish doll smashes repeatedly, she sets the dial to "incinerate." The thumping in the oven finally quiets. We and the heroine sigh in tentative relief. Then she . . . Wait! What is she doing? "No!" I shriek from my point of vantage behind the sofa cushion, watching with only one eye. "Don't do it! Don't open the . . ." Of course, the wretched little piranha had merely been playing dead, and leapt forth in flames for the heroine's throat. During the somewhat disappointing two-minute *denouement*, we gathered that the attack had effected a transformation. The heroine was last seen awaiting her mother's arrival, fitted out with a knife or spear and a formidable set of razor-sharp dentures. Electra lived.

The three of us chuckled weakly and scattered to prepare for bed. We were all in different parts of the apartment when, in a bizarre coincidence, we flicked off every light in the place simultaneously. Panic. Pandemonium. Screams. We ran up the electric bill that night without an iota of compunction.

Though there was much embarrassed laughter, there had also been a response that at least resembled fear, despite our full awareness that the Zuni fetish was a particularly outrageous and silly fiction. But why did we react as we did, and what was the nature of our reaction? We experienced quasi fear, according to Walton. The experience I have just recounted resembles his paradigm case of quasi fear in many respects.[16] Examples such as these can make the characterization of our encounters with fiction as games seem extraordinarily convincing.

Walton has an interactive view of these encounters and emphasizes their similarity to children's games of make-believe. Just as I screamed during the games of monster I played as a child, so I screamed during (and after) the program. Just as my pulse rate rose and my breath grew short during the game, just as I shivered, so the identical physical symptoms and sensations afflicted me during the film. Just as I shouted warnings to my sister that the monster (my father making growling noises) was coming, so I warned the character on the screen. I even hid behind sofa cushions in both cases. I got the giggles in both cases. I initiated the experience in both cases, knowing roughly what to expect. And in both cases I knew there was no monster.

Walton maintains that the same rules for participation operate in games of make-believe and encounters with fiction, that both are participatory in a fundamental way. His account of make-believe provides us with a nested set of fictional worlds. There is, first, the world of the work, comprised of the states of affairs described or depicted therein and perhaps of other states of affairs entailed by these. It is true in that world, for instance, that there is an animated doll. Then there is the world of the game, which encompasses both the world of the work and our responses to the states of affairs that are true in that world. Thus, my attitudes about and reactions to fictional entities and situations are make-believedly true of me. They are true of me only in the world of the game. Just as I imagine that there is a Zuni fetish doll that pursues a woman, so I imagine or make-believe that I fear for her. The construal of the woman's situation as dangerous takes place, as it were, in imagination. It takes place within the confines of the

16. I refer, of course, to the case of Charles and the ubiquitous slime, which made its first appearance in Walton's "Fearing Fictions" in 1978.

game, within the confines of a set of conventions that enables us to take
fictional events and situations *as real* in imagination. Because my construal
of the heroine's situation as dangerous is imaginary, my emotion is also
imaginary: it is quasi fear rather than genuine fear.

This presents a very attractive view of our encounters with fictions: they
are interactive and participatory. We get down, in a manner of speaking, to
the fiction's level. We are no longer on the outside of the fictional world
looking in. Rather, we are participants in a fictional or imaginary world: the
world of our game of make-believe, which encompasses the world of the
work. This view is made particularly plausible by the presentation of
examples like that of the ravening Zuni fetish, for the case in question
appears to involve some level of interaction between the audience and a
particular fictional character. There is a difference between self-regarding
and other-regarding emotional attitudes. For instance, one may pity oneself or others, fear for oneself or others, be angry on one's own or another's
behalf. It would seem to undermine a thoroughgoing interactive view of
our emotional encounters with fictions to claim that our affective responses were never on behalf of ourselves but only on behalf of fictional
entities (or were only responses to fictional situations not imagined to
affect us). This would appear to place our point of vantage *outside* the
imaginary world; it would make us more like observers than participants.

This could be one reason for the use of examples similar to that of the
Night Gallery episode. There seems at least a suggestion that, make-
believedly, my roommates and I feared for ourselves. Why else would we
tuck our feet up on the furniture? Why else scream when the lights went
out? And if we imagined ourselves in danger, then perhaps we imagined
the Zuni fetish creature taking up a threatening stance toward *us*. Indeed,
Walton's own paradigm case, the case on the basis of which he sometimes
generalizes about others, makes this explicit. In a horror film, a slime
monster, having eradicated all the fictional persons in its vicinity, decides
to pursue an ontological variation in its meal plan. It turns to face the
camera and lurches forward, creating the illusion that it is headed for the
audience. Charles, Walton's hypothetical moviegoer, shrieks and yells a
warning to the occupant of the neighboring seat. Here, it is said to be
make-believedly true that the monster is attacking Charles and make-
believedly true that Charles feels personally threatened.

Such examples are ideally suited to make Walton's case for two reasons.
First, if fictional entities can be held to take up various attitudes toward
readers and viewers, the interactive view would be established by pointing
to a two-way response. We would no longer be mere lookers-on, for
fictions could, in a manner of speaking, have a look at us. As Alex Neill puts

it, cases like that of the slime suggest that Charles's "perspective on the game is not [exclusively] external, but internal."[17] Second, few would wish to admit that they felt genuinely and *personally* threatened by a fiction. Fearing *for* characters is one thing: one's point of vantage may still be located outside the fictional world. But genuine fear *of* characters? It seems laughable, and Walton's "quasi" or imaginary fear is ushered in as the obvious explanation.

However, cases in which it is true in the fictional world that characters rise up to address or threaten the reader or viewer are the exception rather than the rule, as Walton himself acknowledges, so there are grounds for not generalizing from such instances of response to fiction.[18] Scenarios like *Peter Pan*'s "Do you believe in fairies?" are rare. It is seldom that a part in a fiction has been scripted for the audience. There are also excellent reasons for thinking that neither fear nor quasi fear *of* the fictional monster is felt in many situations such as these.

Walton states that Charles "experiences quasi fear as a result of realizing that fictionally the slime threatens him."[19] I will maintain that it is unlikely that Charles could have experienced a number of the physical symptoms and sensations typically associated with fear solely as a result of imagining that the monster was headed in his direction (or as a result of believing this was fictionally the case). That is, while the filming technique in question does make it fictional that the monster is after the spectator, I do not think that Charles's awareness of what is fictionally true is what produces those symptoms Walton would associate with quasi fear for oneself. I acknowledge that a first-generation filmgoer may well have had a panicked response to such a cinematographic tactic. Camera angles creating the illusion that trains were bearing down on or that guns were being pointed at the audience were notorious for the panic they produced in viewers wholly unused to the medium. Succeeding generations, however, have grown accustomed to the medium and no longer respond in this way.[20]

Consider a more current example of a medium with which present-day spectators may be unfamiliar. My students inform me that movies during which one dons 3-D glasses can produce certain reactions, such as ducking when an object depicted on the screen appears to be hurled in the audi-

---

17. Alex Neill, "Fear, Fiction and Make-Believe," *Journal of Aesthetics and Art Criticism* 49 (1991): 52.

18. Walton, *Mimesis as Make-Believe*, 237.

19. Ibid., 245.

20. Theodore Roszak, "When Movies Ruled Our Lives," *New York Times*, 30 June 1991, sec. 2, H18.

ence's direction. I believe that such effects may be due to the hitherto unexperienced optical verisimilitude of this medium. I also suspect that spectator reactions may be involuntary and that they do not proceed from beliefs about what is fictionally the case. Presumably, a film of an actual Little League game (with 3-D effects) that included a similar shot would have similar effects on the audience. Such cases seem to involve a momentary illusion rather than make-believe or imagination. If the ducking response involves thoughts at all, it seems more likely that it would involve a momentary or fleeting belief that something *was* the case (e.g., that an object was hurtling toward one's head) rather than a belief about something being fictionally the case.

Why, then, did Charles scream? Why did my roommates and I shriek? We were not wearing 3-D glasses, and all of us were well-acquainted with the medium of film. I think that the likeliest explanation is that we were startled rather than afraid,[21] a reaction that is sometimes not classified as an emotion. Scenes from films like *Jaws* and *Alien* have elicited shrieks often enough at the sudden leap of the shark from the water or the malevolent alien from its egg. I suggest that Charles's fictional slime may have lunged suddenly toward the camera. In these cases, it does not seem objectionable to claim that this very suddenness is responsible for the shrieks. Being startled is in many respects, especially physiologically, like being afraid, and we often mix our terminology when describing such a reaction after the fact. In response to an obnoxious younger sibling who sneaks up and grabs us when we least expect it, we are quite likely to snap, "You nearly scared me to death!"

Startle reactions are responses to sudden and unexpected changes in one's sensory experience. These are sometimes characterized as primitive physiological reactions like "the reflexive withdrawal from something hot."[22] It could be maintained that such reflexive responses were unaccompanied by thoughts or beliefs. Consider the scene in *Jaws* in which the enormous shark leaps from the water when we least expect it. An almost identical scene could startle if it appeared in a National Geographic special (provided that the audience did not receive prior information about what they would see). Walton states that imagining oneself in danger, or believing it is make-believedly the case that one is endangered (by the monster, for instance), is as necessary for the experience of quasi fear as the experience of the physical symptoms. Yet it does not seem that any of the startle

---

21. Alex Neill suggests this also, in his "Fear, Fiction and Make-Believe," 55.
22. Robert C. Roberts, "What an Emotion Is: A Sketch," *Philosophical Review* 97 (1988): 203.

responses being discussed were to the monster *qua* monster, even if it were permissible to characterize them as construals of objects. It seems more likely that they were responses to abrupt shifts of image on the screen, or abrupt changes in what was being filmed, or (in the case of the post-*Night Gallery* episode) abruptly finding oneself in total darkness. That is, if the responses under discussion may be characterized as intentional, their objects seem to be extrafictional and altogether outside the province of make-believe.

Thus we might maintain that one who is startled by the sudden lunge of a screen monster does not respond to what he believes is fictionally the case. One responds not to what one is imagining but to a sudden shift in sensory inputs. If we hold that startle responses are reflex reactions rather than genuine emotions, this gives no support to the contention that responses to fiction that do incorporate cognitions cannot be genuinely emotional, and it confirms the claim that there was no fear or quasi fear *of* the fictional monster as such. Alternatively, if we maintain that such a response does involve a construal of some kind (presumably unarticulated and prereflective), that construal would seem to be more closely allied with surprise and shock than with fear. It could be more readily linked to the construal of a change in sensory stimuli as sudden or unexpected than to the belief that, fictionally, one was endangered. That is, the startle responses were not *to* fictional events or entities and so could not be classed as quasi fear according to Walton's own stipulations.

But why did Linda, Jackie, and I tuck our feet up out of the reach of gnashing Zuni teeth? Does this not indicate some conception of a threat to ourselves? Certainly, it had nothing to do with being startled. I think that such actions are a response attributable in part to empathetic imagination, a topic I take up at length later in this book. While not entirely involuntary, as would be an empathetic wince in response to seeing a friend cut himself, our behavior had a good deal to do with entering into the heroine's plight. A part of empathizing with someone involves imaginatively entering into his or her situation, imaginatively adopting a certain perspective, in this case on the fictional world.[23] There was the heroine, with a refugee from some macabre version of the *Nutcracker* snapping and scrabbling at her ankles. The scene, moreover, played on genuine fears of rodents and large scuttling insects, which made entering into the heroine's perspective even easier.

---

23. So Bijoy H. Boruah claims in *Fiction and Emotion: A Study in Aesthetics and the Philosophy of Mind* (Oxford: Clarendon Press, 1988), 108–15.

There is, in fact, experimental evidence that our observation of others in nonfictional contexts involves subliminal muscular activity and motor mimicry, something that Robert Gordon ties to our ability to empathize.[24] Consider observers of televised sporting events, who not only shout advice to athletes who cannot hear them but mimic some of the players' motions and gestures. It is not unusual to see an armchair-bound sports fan give an imaginary ball an extra push. So I maintain that our response to the *Night Gallery* episode was predominantly empathetic and that our fear, whether imaginary or genuine, was for and on behalf of the heroine. We just imagined her plight a little too vividly to keep our feet on the floor.

Granted, the kind of empathizing I have described seems to involve the interactive imagination. But the couch potato's fear that his favorite player will miss a shot is genuine according to Walton's own criteria. He does not imagine that he himself — although a good deal older than the athlete and in imperfect condition — precipitates the ball in the desired direction, though he may imagine being the player. He does not imagine that the ball is in contact with *his own* nicotine-stained, potato-chip laden fingers rather than those of the player. Similarly, I will maintain that my roommates and I did not imagine or make believe that the Zuni fetish was lurking beneath the living room couch waiting for a snack.

I acknowledge that we may have imagined believing we were the objects of the monstrosity's pursuit in the course of our identification with the heroine (just as the couch potato may have imagined being a young, healthy athlete engaged in a game). This, however, would not amount to transporting the threat into the context of our own lives. The heroine's (fictional) life is the point of vantage from which the Zuni fetish might be imagined to threaten (just as the athlete's experience is the point of vantage from which the ball may be given an imaginary push). While our responses may have been silly, perhaps even irrational, for all kinds of reasons, and while we may have imagined ourselves in the heroine's place, we did not imagine that anyone *other* than the heroine was at risk. Our empathy would have involved imagining we *were* the heroine. To imagine that persons aside from the heroine were at risk would not be consistent with what was true in the world of Walton's game.

It is true in the fiction, hence in the game, that only one person is at risk at the relevant moment: the heroine. At no point in the film does the Zuni fetish lunge at the camera, something that would make the spectator

---

24. Robert Gordon, *The Structure of Emotions: Investigations in Cognitive Psychology* (Cambridge: Cambridge University Press, 1987), 153.

appear to be (fictionally) at risk. Thus it cannot be true in the world of my game that I am threatened unless it is true in the world of that game that I am the heroine. It does not appear that I could import into the world of the game a threat to someone *external* to the states of affairs comprising this work's world. Yet empathetic responses are seldom continuous. I fear *for* the heroine as well as with her, which makes it true in the world of the game that the heroine and I are distinct. Walton would probably eliminate any such potential inconsistency by maintaining that our empathetic emotional reactions and imaginings could not be part of a game authorized for this work but simply occurred along with that game.[25] Imagining we were the heroine might constitute part of an authorized game if, for instance, the camera had briefly posed as the eyes of the heroine.

There is a reason for my dwelling at such length on cases of what Walton might call quasi fear *of* a character. I think cases that can be so characterized, whether in terms of quasi or genuine fear, are open to alternative characterizations and explanations. That is, I have difficulty believing we feel quasi or genuine fear *of* fictional entities on account of believing it is fictionally the case that they threaten *us* rather than characters (as when a camera angle makes it fictional that a monster lunges toward the spectator), though I acknowledge that this may be because I have never had such an experience. Affective reactions that involve imagining one is endangered are frequently attributable to the empathetic imagination. Other reactions that might be characterized as fear for oneself or quasi fear for oneself may not occur as a result of what is believed fictional but may instead result from sudden shifts in sensory stimuli or (less frequently) optical illusions.

Finally, it is also worth mentioning that a lot of emotion-like reactions experienced during and after the contemplation of works of horror and thrillers can be reactions to what—at that moment—is regarded as a genuine possibility. The branches rustling against one's window can begin to sound suspiciously like a glass-cutter wielded by a homicidal maniac or denizen of outer darkness on sabbatical. In cases such as these, however, it is not a fictional entity to which one responds. Rather, I think that a discomfited subject might entertain the dark suspicion that predatory and unpleasant entities *like* the character could exist (and could be lurking outside the window). Such suspicions are weird, and often irrational, but the object of the response is regarded as possible (even if unlikely) rather than fictional. It is not the thought of a character that is regarded fearfully.

---

25. Walton, *Mimesis as Make-Believe*, 255.

The thought of a remote possibility is fearfully entertained. Indeed, Walton calls fear of this sort genuine, since it does not feature the complete lack of existential commitment and motivational force he associates with quasi fear. It is described as a fear of "suspected actual dangers" (202).

It is my contention that examples such as that of the slime fail to establish the assertion that some interactive feature of our encounters with fiction warrants a characterization of them in terms of games of make-believe. I happily concede a conviction that many of our experiences of the fictional are indeed participatory, but I believe that this is due to patterns of thinking, feeling, and interpreting typical of the empathetic imagination, which can be directed toward the actual as well as the fictional.

Empathy with a character differs from empathy with an actual person in that the beliefs and experiences we imagine having are those we imagine the character has rather than those we believe a person possesses. However, empathy with real people also involves imagining rather than believing that one has certain beliefs and experiences. Walton agrees, stating that empathy or identification with real people "involves imagining oneself in the shoes of the person identified with" (255).

Walton appears to consider that empathy with persons in whose existence we believe can constitute a genuine emotion, for he closely associates genuine emotions toward real people with empathy: "One may *really* feel disgust for Ivan the Terrible or empathize with Julius Caesar" (252; emphasis mine). His distinctions between fictional and actual empathy bear this out.[26] Yet the construal associated with an empathetic response is an imaginary one. If I empathize with Spike, who is threatened by vicious dogs or tenure committees, the cognitive constituent of my empathetic fear is the thought of being threatened by vicious canines or academics, and this is clearly a thought I entertain in imagination (assuming no dogs or academics are after me at the relevant moment).

Neither can empathetic emotions be held up as unproblematic sources of behavioral inclinations, motivations, or desires, for an empathetic stance involves the imaginative adoption of the perspective of another. Thus, the behavioral inclinations, motivations, and desires inherent in that perspective are not believed to be our own and are hardly likely to be applicable within the context of our own lives. That is, the cognitive constituent of my empathetic fear for Spike—the thought of being attacked or threatened—is entertained from a first-person perspective. Any

---

26. For example, such a distinction is made in ibid., 361.

inclination to act associated with this cognition (an inclination to beat off the offending parties with a stick, say) only pertains to the experience I *imagine* having.

Of course, I may feel an urge to rescue Spike from his persecutors because I believe they may injure him. Notice, however, that this belief cannot be associated with *empathetic* fear, for the situation has not been evaluated from Spike's perspective. In believing Spike endangered, I fear *for* him but not *with* him. My fear is only empathetic if I entertain the thought of the threat from Spike's point of vantage rather than my own. To empathize would be to imagine being in Spike's situation and to imagine having his beliefs and desires concerning that situation.

Consider an example Walton offers early on in *Mimesis as Make-Believe* when he describes the powers of the imagination. To understand how the member of a minority can feel about discrimination, "one should imagine *experiencing* discrimination. It is when I imagine *myself* in another's shoes (whether or not I imagine *being* him) that my imagination helps me to understand *him*" (34).[27] To empathize with another is to imagine experiencing what one believes that person experiences. It is "imagining from the inside," imaginatively adopting a first-person perspective (30-34). If I feel empathetic fear on behalf of Spike or empathetic resentment on behalf of the member of the minority, I make the construal *they* would make: the construal of certain objects or situations as threatening-to-me or unjust-to-me, rather than the construal of these as threatening or unjust to some third party (these latter cases could not involve a distinctively empathetic response).

However, Walton also describes his hypothetical appreciator of fiction as someone who imagines experiencing things, and imagines this from the inside (247). In fact, there are remarkable similarities between empathetic responses to real people and affective responses to fiction, similarities that go beyond the familiar fact that we can be said to (whether fictionally or actually) identify with characters. Both empathetic response and response to fiction involve the imaginative adoption of an alternative point of vantage, based either on what is believed to be fictional or on what is believed to be experienced (by another). The fact that we can empathize with people we believe exist cannot justify the classification of such responses as genuine while responses to fiction are classified as fictional. Cognitions associated with empathy for real people cannot be beliefs, and

---

27. While this is not explicitly identified as an example of empathy, Walton uses exactly the same terminology in describing empathy and identification in a later passage. He employs a reference to imagining oneself in another's shoes (255).

any inclinations or desires we may have to, for instance, aid the member of the minority group from the preceding example, require a third-person perspective that precludes associating such inclinations or desires with an emotional response that can be considered genuinely empathetic.[28]

Given the similarities between affective response to fiction and empathy with real people, and given Walton's acknowledgment that empathy with real people can involve genuine emotion, we have additional reasons for maintaining that affective responses to fictional entities and events can be genuinely emotional. Empathetic emotions involve imaginative construals that are not existentially committed, just as fictions do. Like reactions to fictional events and historical incidents, empathetic reactions cannot be said to exhibit features like motivational force or inclination in any intelligible way (i.e., in a way that would make them consistent with what one believed of oneself and one's own circumstances rather than what one believed of the circumstances of another). Here, we have an example of a reaction Walton considers genuinely emotional but that fails to meet *both* of his conditions for emotion (in other words, it fails to satisfy the disjunctive criterion I speculated that Walton might wish to employ).

By working through such requirements and stipulations about what can constitute a genuine emotion, I hope to have demonstrated that Walton's characterization of our affective responses to fictional events as quasi emotions is not the only legitimate alternative open to us. That is, it has not been demonstrated that such responses cannot be genuinely emotional.

ADDRESSING FICTIONS AND EXPRESSING DESIRES

I have, however, ignored one of Walton's most convincing parallels between the fictional and the make-believe. Walton's theory seems most applicable to my act of (perhaps self-consciously) taking it upon myself to address a character. I think we may be engaging in some variety of make-believe in such circumstances, perhaps making it fictional that a warning has been issued. Yet this sort of activity seems to involve an element of conscious pretense. We may imagine that we issue a warning, but do we ever imagine it will be heard? It should be noted that Walton does not equate making-believe with play-acting or self-conscious pretending (242).

---

28. Chapter 6 is devoted to the subject of empathy, and further questions and considerations are raised then.

So quasi fear is not merely a play-acted or faked reaction. It differs from genuine fear only in certain of its cognitive and behavioral components and concomitants, not necessarily in how it feels to the subject. Walton's game is the sort that requires a fairly thorough imaginative immersion. However, given that, my make-believe warning seems a bit too self-conscious to fit into the world of the game in the way Walton would want. Moreover, the occasional uttering of make-believe warnings and suggestions does not lead inevitably to the conclusion that all our affective and other responses to fictional entities and events are of precisely the same character.

Indeed, warnings that are addressed to characters—like "Look out!" and "Don't do that!"—may be taken at least in part as expressions of our desires. A comparable case in a nonfictional context might involve my erstwhile couch potato's bellowing "Take the shot!" during a televised game. Obviously, it is likely that my sedentary friend *wants* the player to take the shot. Given that he is not in a position to be heeded and is aware of this, his vocalization can be taken to express what he would tell the player to do if it were possible to communicate. Since issuing commands is usually an attempt to orchestrate another's actions, it does not seem a very great stretch to assume that the individual in question *wishes* those actions to be orchestrated in a certain way. Thus, I think it is possible that a cry of "Look out!" during a movie might express a desire that caution be exercised, and "Don't do that!" a desire that risky activity be avoided. Walton would probably claim that these were imaginary desires, because they lacked the kind of motivational force tied to inclinations to act or to intervene. It might be held that an emotion like pity cannot be genuine when it is impossible to offer aid, since we cannot be inclined or motivated to do what we know is impossible.

However, it may be possible to give an account of desires in such a context without characterizing them as wholly imaginary or as by-products of making-believe on account of their lack of motivating force. Desires are often characterized as dispositions to act. It is nonetheless clear that there are actual situations in which we may be said to have a desire even though no action is possible. We can desire that an armed conflict or potential accident be averted even when we are not in a position to influence these events. Moreover, we often wish things had happened differently than they actually did: that we had not made disparaging remarks about deconstructionists during an interview with someone who was later discovered to be a sympathizer or, more seriously, that atrocities of the past had not occurred.

These are all cases in which we cannot aid those whom we pity or punish the objects of our indignation. In other words, there can be no impetus to action when action is believed impossible. Yet no one has suggested that our reactions to such impervious objects cannot be real emotions. Indeed, it may even be possible to offer a characterization of desire applicable to examples of this kind. If desires can be said to be involved in such cases at all, they would seem to be hypothetical ones, as William Charlton has proposed.[29] For those who believe that desires are behavioral dispositions, which are usually described in terms of stimulus-response conditionals, or that desires are necessarily associated with such dispositions, a counterfactual characterization could be employed.

Desiring that some past incident had not occurred could be represented in the following way: "If it were the case that X had not as yet transpired, I would attempt to prevent it" or "Were it the case that X had not as yet transpired, would that I might prevent it." However, I have doubts about whether what we desire need always involve some hypothetical personal conduct or intervention. If I helplessly watch a news video in which a disgruntled postal worker holds innocent persons at bay with an assault rifle, I will wish this individual had been disarmed before he took people hostage, but I may also believe that I am ill-suited to make any such attempt myself. That is, I may wish the hostage situation had been prevented ("Were it the case that an armed maniac were about to go postal, would that he could be prevented from doing so") without wishing that I had done so ("Were it the case that an armed maniac were about to go postal, would that I were endowed with the strength and combat skills of the hero in an Arnold Schwarzenegger movie, so that I might prevent this manic from causing harm without sustaining serious injuries myself").

I do not think that desire need be circumscribed and held applicable only to some hypothetical sphere of personal influence. We can wish that something had not transpired without this fact necessarily justifying various suppositions about our own conduct in hypothetical situations. We can wish for world peace or that wars had been averted, but unless these desires are translated into suppositions about what we would do if we were virtually omnipotent (and this appears questionable in itself), it does not seem appropriate to restrict the consequent of the counterfactual in question to some hypothesis about the conduct of the person whose desire it is taken to represent.

Whether or not desires ought to be associated with behavioral disposi-

---

29. William Charlton suggests such an approach specifically with regard to fiction in "Feeling for the Fictitious," *British Journal of Aesthetics* 24 (1984): 206–16. However, he offers this as an analysis of the whole of one's response to fiction.

tions (and I acknowledge that the preceding discussion is speculative), we now have alternative characterizations of desire that are applicable to cases in which we cannot influence events whose outcomes our desires may nonetheless concern. Future-oriented desires, often associated with issuing warnings of the sort described earlier, could also be associated with the following: "Were it the case that a hostile attacker lurked in an innocent individual's vicinity, would that this individual refrain from behavior that could put him at risk or that the attacker were dissuaded." Characterizing desires in a way that links them to behavioral dispositions might yield the following: "Were it the case that an attacker lurked in an individual's vicinity, would that I could warn this innocent person or otherwise avert the attack."[30] Note that these characterizations could be associated with responses to both actual and fictional events.

One might object that a desire that actual events had gone differently is quite distinct from a desire involved in a response to fiction. The former, after all, is in some way based on what we believe occurred in the world, whereas the latter is based on beliefs about what is fictionally the case. This is true, of course, but a desire that things had happened otherwise than they really did (which would presumably be associated with a genuine regret) *is* counterfactual in a fundamental way. It is a desire for something that we believe impossible, so the object of the desire is one to which we cannot be existentially committed. The only motivational element that can be associated with such a desire (barring time machine scenarios) will concern some hypothesis about what we would do or would want to have happen, were a particular set of circumstances to obtain. The broader the construal of the incident in question, the broader the scope of hypotheses about possible actions or preferences, given certain kinds or types of situations.

But is it appropriate to characterize, for instance, my desire that Ripley not be caught by the alien in counterfactual terms? Would my description of fictional incidents eliminate references to science fiction aliens and to Ripley herself (as in the example of the warning)? What warrants such generalizing? I have been characterizing desires in terms of counterfactuals because this seems the only available way to characterize the desire that things had happened otherwise. Such desires resemble those associated with responses to fiction: both concern incidents it is impossible to affect. Of course, desires can make explicit reference to entities we imagine: "Were it the case that a spaceship officer named Ripley found herself

---

30. Charlton develops an account of this sort in his "Feeling for the Fictitious."

trapped aboard a space vessel with a hostile alien being of extraordinary power and ferocity, would that her death at the mandibles of this being be averted" (or ". . . would that I might warn her so as to avert . . .").

My proposal that both historical and fictional incidents could be characterized in broad terms was prompted by the greater scope this could afford in associating behavioral motivation or preference with responses involving such objects. Consider my outrage toward the selfish corporate moguls described in the film *Alien* (they are referred to rather than depicted in the first film of the series). The fiction indicates that they consider the crew of Ripley's ship expendable, so intent are they on obtaining the alien for purposes of military research. My outrage may involve a desire for justice or for punishment. When the fictional incident is broadly construed, we might get the following: "Were it the case that people in positions of power risked the lives of their employees when it profited them to do so, would that these individuals be punished and removed from power, would that they not profit from their action" (or ". . . would that I might expose them to public censure").

Compare this to a broad construal of the case in which one regrets having fatally offended the deconstructionist: "Were it the case that my future quality of life depended on another's good opinion, would that I might exercise caution in giving voice to my own views so as not to offend that individual inadvertently." Note that this is quite different from a very explicit construal of the incident, which could make reference to places and dates. It is the very general description of fictional and historical incidents that permits us to consider the question of motivation or preference in a broader range of cases and that may provide at least some insight into behavioral inclination. Generalizations of this kind would presumably have to be made with reference to the more global beliefs of the subject.

However, let us consider more carefully the desire that things had gone differently. Would such desires not, in the case of fiction, amount to the desire that the story had gone differently? Does distress about Desdemona's plight after it has befallen her suggest the wish that Shakespeare had written a different play? In attempting to answer these questions, it is first important to note that the counterfactual corresponding to the relevant desire might be rendered as follows: "Were it the case that jealous and deluded persons were intent on destroying the former objects of their affection, would that they could be dissuaded" or, more specifically, "Were it the case that a jealous and deluded man named Othello . . ." This need not be taken to express a desire for a new play or story.

We usually do not feel any burning inclination to rewrite Shakespeare or improve on his plays. I do not believe we wish *Othello* were other than it is. At least in the case of literature (as opposed to what Fay Weldon would call "just fiction"), the work may afford insights into human nature and perspectives on the human condition that would be unobtainable without precisely those fictional events that produce the greatest distress and aversion. It is certainly possible to wish that events in a story had been different, gratuitous violence being a case in point. The claim here is merely that this is not always the case and, indeed, that it is very unlikely to be the case when we value a work of fiction. I will discuss the satisfaction we may take in fictions that lead us to experience distress and aversion in Chapter 7.

To entertain the thought of Desdemona's death with aversion or regret is not to wish that the play were other than it is. Neither aversions nor negative emotions signify any such wish, for a wish about Desdemona is a wish about something I imagine, and what I imagine is a person. The play is not something I imagine. Neither the fictional world of *Othello* nor the world I imagine contains cues or stage directions or casts of characters. The play does. Therefore, it is not clear that a wish for Desdemona's rescue is a wish that the play be altered. More to the point, even if something is a necessary condition of what I wish for, that does not necessarily mean that I wish for *it* in wishing as I do. One of my students may wish to receive an "A" in my course, but this is not an inevitable sign of a desire to study.[31]

To return to the subject at hand, it can be conceded that we engage in some variety of make-believe when we address characters, just as persons addressing screen images of athletes or politicians may engage in a kind of make-believe when they address them. This need not, however, suggest that all of our reactions and attitudes toward fictional entities are likewise made believe. The kind of making-believe involved in such cases does not always resemble that described by Walton and can be closely allied with conscious pretense. Moreover, make-believe warnings may suggest the involvement of hypothetical desires that need not be characterized as imaginary any more than desires concerning historical incidents are. Neither involves existential commitment, though both may be weakly associated with some species of motivation or preference. This militates against a thoroughgoing characterization of our desires about fictional states of affairs as fictional. Though what we want can involve an imagined state of affairs, this need not be thought to render the wanting itself imaginary.

Of course, a definition of desire as an inclination to act in some particu-

---

31. Alex Neill makes a similar point in his "Fiction and the Emotions," reprinted in Alex Neill and Aaron Ridley, eds., *Arguing About Art: Contemporary Philosophical Debates* (New York: McGraw-Hill, 1995), 190.

lar way toward the object of one's affective response rules out the possibility of desire as a concomitant of response to fiction. However, it will be ruled out in the case of affective response to historical people and situations as well. Thus, if we can feel genuine emotions toward historical figures or on account of historical happenings, desire (on this narrower characterization) cannot be necessary for emotion.

PLAYING INCONSISTENT GAMES

The rules of Walton's game operate more or less according to convention. There are, for instance, clear restrictions on behavior, and doing something like wresting Desdemona from the clutches of the jealous Othello would violate the rules for participation in a game based on a stage production of *Othello*. More important, there seem to be rules about what is included in the world of the game, about what counts as make-believedly or imaginarily true. Everything that is true in the world of the work (e.g., that a Zuni fetish doll is chasing a woman) is true in the world of the game. Since we are said to take such events as real in the world of the game and on account of this to respond to them in certain ways, such responses also are taken to constitute part of that world. Thus, it is said to be true in the world of the game that, for instance, I fear for the woman threatened by the Zuni fetish doll. On the other hand, I do not think it would be true in the world of the game that my seat was uncomfortable or that my neighbor had spilled popcorn in my lap, for these things have nothing to do with what is being imagined.

However, it is still not wholly clear to me how we are to delimit the boundaries of such a world. Let us go back to my various attitudes vis-à-vis the Zuni fetish doll. I fear for the heroine on account of it. Walton would say that this is quasi fear, that my awareness of fictional states of affairs coupled with my affective and physiological responses make it fictional, or imaginary, or make-believedly true that I fear for the woman. But this does not establish the status of the rest of the relations between myself and the fictional. If it is make-believedly true that I am aware of the Zuni fetish doll's appearance and actions, is it true in the game that I *see* the doll and *observe* its actions? Does that make it make-believedly true that I am a witness of these events or that I occupy the same spatiotemporal region as that which I observe? In the fiction, it is true that the heroine is isolated and that no one else knows of her plight, which makes it true in the world of a game based on the work. However, that suggests it is true in the world of the game *both* that no one but the heroine and the Zuni fetish knows of or observes the heroine's plight and that I know of it and observe it.

For a further example, imagine a film version of Mary Shelley's *The Last Man*. The fictional states of affairs are these. Lionel Verney is the lone survivor in a world ravaged by plague. In the final scene, Verney embarks in his boat along the shores of a deserted earth. Walton would say that, make-believedly or imaginarily, the viewer will feel pity for Verney, at least some sympathy. But how can it be true in the world of the game that I pity the last and only existing human being? What exactly am "I" in the world of this game? What is it that can pity in the world of the game when it is true within it that all things that can feel pity save Verney have ceased to exist?[32]

Walton regards all such questions as "silly."[33] Nevertheless, he offers possible answers he believes defuse such apparent paradoxes and inconsistencies. These are answers initially employed in his response to a different set of questions whose silliness he considers comparable: questions about the potential apprehension of inconsistencies among the states of affairs in a work's world (I discuss such subjects in Chapters 4 and 5). Consider, for example, a work in which a career militarist without much education or literary expertise continually exhibits eloquence and linguistic sophistication: *Othello*. "How Othello could have uttered a verse worthy of Shakespeare is not a question of focal interest . . . nor is it an . . . intrusion on the appreciator's experience, indicative of a blemish in the play. From the perspectives of appreciation and criticism, it is just silly."[34] Of course, individually innocent fictional truths can sometimes become uncomfortably paradoxical in combination, says Walton. But a principle of charity should (at least in some cases, certainly that of *Othello*) be at work to block or de-emphasize troublesome fictional truths. These may, after all, stem from features of the work intended by its author to enhance audience access or appreciation rather than to produce fictional paradoxes.[35]

Walton's principle of charity expands to embrace the world of the game as well as the world of the work. The solutions to my own set of silly questions are as follows. First is the possibility of declaring one of the conflicting fictional truths de-emphasized. Second, we can declare it not to be generated at all. Third, we can declare that, while each of these

---

32. I am grateful to Professors Catherine Lord and Jose Benardete for suggesting this example.

33. Walton, *Mimesis as Make-Believe*, 239.

34. Ibid., 176.

35. Ibid., 183.

propositions is fictional, "the conjunction of these propositions is not fictional."[36] That is, while it is fictional that I witness the Zuni fetish doll's pursuit of the heroine and it is fictional that no one witnesses it, it is *not* fictional that there are and that there are no witnesses of the pursuit. We seem to have consistency by fiat.

I understand and share much of Walton's motive for bringing such regularizing principles to bear on inconsistencies among states of affairs in the world of a work or among those states of affairs and others inferred on their basis. We would probably want to tell a spectator who fixated on questions about the improbability of Othello's linguistic facility instead of focusing on the performance that he had missed the point—the point of going to the play in the first place, the point of what it was for. Such questions can be silly because they are in a fundamental way irrelevant to what should be going on. These are not the questions an appreciator should be attending to. (Some works make this attention virtually unavoidable, of course, just because they are flawed. However, these are probably not the works to which Walton wishes to extend his principle of charity.)

I take it that my set of questions is presumed misdirected for similar reasons. If I am caught up in Lionel Verney's plight or riveted by the wicked machinations of the Zuni fetish, the questions I have raised will not matter to me. Imaginative engagement does not involve some deliberate and orchestrated procedure whereby one calculates how and when particular fictional truths are generated. Such questions are irrelevant to my appreciation of the fiction, they are irrelevant to my involvement in it, and they are irrelevant to literary criticism as well. I do not, however, think that they are necessarily irrelevant to the assessment of a theory that purports to describe the mechanisms underlying that engagement, involvement, and appreciation.

Let us review once again the structure of the world of Walton's game. As has already been indicated, a given work generates fictional truths and, over and above this, spectators or readers of that work generate fictional truths about themselves in the course of their imaginative engagement and response. Any statements a participant makes that refer exclusively to what is imagined rather than what is believed (e.g., "There goes the slime," rather than, "The slime depiction moves across the screen"), any thoughts about or attitudes toward what he imagines rather than what he believes, are classified as fictional, as true in the world of the game.[37] Uttering a

36. Ibid., 239.
37. Statements and propositions could be true in both worlds, of course, as with the contention there is gravity.

sentence like "I'll bet the slime eats that guy with the Uzi next" makes it fictional that one is referring to real monsters and real people.[38] Similarly, having a certain affective response to a fictive depiction of the slime's pursuit of some person can make it fictional that we fear for a real person. Our fear is as imaginary as the slime or its victim, though the possible intensity of such experiences is not denied.

There are restrictions on the games that spectators and readers play that shift emphasis from physical to psychological participation. The appreciator belongs to the fictional world but has "usually, a rather 'sketchy' or 'ghostly' presence in the world of his game, in light of the restrictions on his role in it and the indeterminacy that often results from them."[39] Such restrictions would prohibit making-believe that one intervened in the course of events when involved in a game based on a stage production, as in the example of rescuing Desdemona. Presumably there might also be restrictions on imagining inconsistencies.

My own concern is about the shift from having an attitude toward or about something we imagine to imagining we have the attitude or its being fictional rather than true that we have it. I do not think that these are interchangeable. While I absolutely agree with Walton that we construct a world in imagination and contribute to it in various ways, I do not think it follows from this that we render imaginary our attitudes about what we have imagined. It is this difficulty that has led me to raise my questions, whose silliness I believe is incommensurable with the silliness of questions about inconsistencies in the worlds of works. The proposal of the game of make-believe is far more radical than that of the world of a work. Again, I agree that no appreciator of fiction could contemplate my questions during the course of an engagement with fiction without being seriously misguided and missing the whole point of the enterprise. However, this does not mean that a philosopher who is wondering whether we can really be held to imagine our own attitudes on account of having imagined the objects toward which those attitudes are directed is likewise misdirected.

When Walton speaks of the principle of charity and of the decision to disallow certain fictional truths, when he speaks of our declaring them de-emphasized or not generated at all, he may be considering what it is that the competent appreciator (i.e., an appreciator who does not fixate on irrelevancies) *does*. However, though it is clearly true that competent appreciators do not fixate on the kinds of inconsistencies at issue here,

38. Walton, *Mimesis as Make-Believe*, 220–24.
39. Ibid., 237.

it need not follow from this that the appreciator must be engaged (subliminally or automatically, perhaps) in the aforementioned procedure of blocking and de-emphasizing fictional truths.

The failure of the appreciator to focus on inconsistencies could be as readily explained by the contention that there were none, because some truths were not fictional or imaginary in the first place. So it could be held that the problematic fictional truth that the appreciator pities Lionel Verney and no one pities Lionel Verney was suppressed or de-emphasized, *or* it could be held that there was no fictional truth about the appreciator's pity to begin with, because his pity was not imaginary. The distracting inconsistency is eliminated in both cases. Thus, Walton's answers to my questions, whether those questions are silly or not, do not explain why it is we should accept an account whose assumptions appear to lead to the generation of fictional inconsistencies that need to be glossed over or suppressed, when we have an alternative available to us that does not seem to generate such inconsistencies at all.

Walton would say that it is make-believedly true that I fear for a heroine, because I make-believe a certain kind of woman is in danger (and this produces certain characteristic sensations and physical symptoms). I would say that I imagine an endangered woman, just because I imagine the instantiation of properties or characteristics that I believe are sufficient for being endangered. My imagining an endangered woman can amount to my entertaining the thought of a woman in a certain kind of situation fearfully. To say that I imaginatively construe the heroine's situation as dangerous is not to say that I imagine my own fear, for it has not been conclusively shown that the cognitive constituents or consorts of genuine emotion cannot be thoughts to which we are existentially uncommitted, and it has not been demonstrated that affective reactions lacking what has been referred to as "motivational force" cannot be genuine emotions. To claim I imagine my own fear is to confuse the content of a thought I entertain in imagination with the *way* I imaginatively entertain it.[40]

---

40. Richard Moran makes a similar point in "The Expression of Feeling in Imagination," *Philosophical Review* 103 (1994): 93.

CONCLUSION

In this chapter, I have attempted to show that the grounds for regarding our affective responses to fictional events as quasi emotions are not conclusive. It has not been demonstrated that existentially committed beliefs are requisite for genuine emotion, nor is it clear that desires are requisite when characterized as straightforward inclinations to act in a certain way toward the object of one's emotion. The stipulation that genuine emotions must meet at least one of these two criteria eliminates empathetic response from the category of genuine emotion, and that is a category in which it has been acknowledged that empathy belongs. I think, therefore, that fiction can move without deluding us about what it is we feel, and that what we feel for and about the fictional need not be regarded as fictitious.

While the approach of this chapter has been predominantly critical, I want to stress that I agree with and admire a great deal of what Kendall Walton writes in his book. In particular, I think that his whole idea of the experience of fiction as an imaginative exploration of worlds is exactly right. The only discordance stems from my belief that, when we so explore, we do not surrender our emotions to the worlds we apprehend but retain them in the very quality of that apprehension.

3

Objects of Emotion
and Emotional Imagination

In the first chapter, construals and evaluations were described as the cognitive constituents of emotion. At the end of Chapter 2, construal was characterized as a manner of thinking or imagining. The present chapter attempts to discuss and clarify this characterization in terms of one particular kind of response to fiction. It is my contention that our emotions can take any of several objects in the course of our interactions with fiction. Once these intentional objects are canvassed, an adverbial account of emotional response to fictional events and entities will be attempted. The first few sections of this chapter will for the most part retain conventional terminology that makes of an emotion an attitude held toward a particular object. This will change in the final sections, which offer an analysis of emotion not in terms of attitudes held toward objects but in terms that reflect how thoughts with a certain content can be entertained.

The first three sections are intended to provide a selective survey of recent literature on the objects of those emotional responses that are experienced in the course of encounters with fiction. These are many and various. Indeed, a typical reaction to the contentions of Colin Radford and Kendall Walton has involved attempts to discover more ontologically correct intentional objects. If one responds to an object that one believes to exist, then one of Walton's conditions for genuine emotion is fulfilled and Radford's criterion for rational response can be satisfied. This may in fact be the central motivation behind some of the approaches that will be discussed.

Candidate intentional objects have taken various guises. I will discuss three of the most typical candidates. Barrie Paskins, Peter McCormick, and Jerrold Levinson have proposed that we (at least on occasion, in the case of McCormick and Levinson) respond emotionally to real people, experiences, and events, and that these are (or can be) the objects of our response when we are said to respond to fictions. A different option is considered by B. J. Rosebury and Peter Lamarque, who maintain that the object of our emotional response to fiction can be characterized as a thought (Rosebury) or the content thereof (Lamarque). Finally, Don Mannison and Harold Skulsky suggest that potentialities or logical possibilities are the objects of our emotion in fictional contexts. I think that all of these accounts capture important facets of our experience of fiction, but that most have not captured the entire picture, and only one has established the key point about what it is to pity, hate, or admire a character.

RESPONDING TO ACTUAL PEOPLE AND EVENTS

What is it to hate a character? One of the more loathsome objects encountered in my own experience of fiction is the character called Sergeant Hartman in the film *Full Metal Jacket*. A sadistic drill instructor, Hartman humiliates and tortures a recruit to the point of madness. The extent of my own emotional response to the film became evident when I disgraced myself utterly in a room full of politically correct colleagues by cheering loudly and uttering cries of encouragement when the crazed recruit killed Hartman. The word "bloodthirsty" was bandied about more than once by my disapproving fellows. If I was bloodthirsty, however, whose blood did I want to see spilled?

According to an account proposed by Barrie Paskins, my hatred of Hartman is a hatred of those actual persons, if any, who perform the same kinds of deeds and have the same character defects. It is a hatred of actual persons who instantiate the characteristics whose instantiation I imagine when I watch the film. My pity for the recruit would be described as pity for those who are in the same bind as the character.[1] Colin Radford's response to this analysis of what it is to feel pity or anger toward a character is one with which I concur in part. I agree with Radford's

---

1. Barrie Paskins, "On Being Moved by Anna Karenina and *Anna Karenina*," *Philosophy* 52 (1977): 346.

contention that, since the character and those real people who are in the same bind are distinct, we cannot conclude that feeling something for or toward a character amounts to *nothing more* than feeling something for or toward real people.[2] I also agree that our own experience seems to bear this out: to hate Sergeant Hartman seems to involve a focus of attention on very particular incidents and behaviors. I may, in fact, hate all actual persons who are unregenerate bullies. But I also hate this particular one: the one who looks and acts a particular way and who performs the uniquely reprehensible actions depicted in the film. This is just the point that Paskins does not allow for. His theory does not seem to permit a *specific* pity or hatred. Our responses must be global, on his account of fictions. They cannot be responses to particular things. As Radford says, our experience does not seem to confirm this.

On the other hand, I do think that we may be led to feel for people who, as Paskins puts it, are in the same bind. I think that this could occur in the course of our feeling something toward a character. Certainly, I think that if we are moved, we will believe it is possible for people to be in that kind of bind. We will believe that some of the characteristics whose instantiation we imagine could actually be (or could actually have been) instantiated. Beliefs in possibilities such as these will be discussed at length in the next chapter. At present, it is important to ask whether we can pity or loathe real people in the course of responding to fictional ones.

Radford contends that we do not, perhaps cannot, pity or hate persons of whose individual existence we are unaware when we respond to characters.[3] If Radford simply means that we cannot *identify* pitying a character with pitying people in similar situations, then I agree. But he seems to go further than this and to imply that, in the course of reading or viewing a given work, we never pity strangers whose circumstances resemble those of the character. Radford cannot mean that we cannot pity those with whom we are unacquainted, for he emphatically denies William Charlton's claim that we can feel for real people only if we know who they are: "This is simply not true. The sinking of the Belgrano moved many people to tears, grief and rage about what had happened to hundreds of Argentinean sailors, all of whom were quite unknown to them. Human sympathy is freer and wider ranging than Charlton can imagine or will allow."[4]

---

2. Colin Radford, "The Essential Anna," *Philosophy* 54 (1979): 390–91.

3. Colin Radford, "Replies to Three Critics," *Philosophy* 64 (1989): 94.

4. Colin Radford, "Charlton's Feelings About the Fictitious: A Reply," *British Journal of Aesthetics* 25 (1985): 381–82.

Perhaps Radford, in his response to Paskins, means to imply that we cannot pity people of whom we have not *heard*, of whose *individual* existence we are entirely ignorant. But it is not clear what degree or kind of knowledge is sufficient in this case. An awareness of the sailors' plight need not be characterized as an awareness of particular individuals with unique histories. One could be aware of the sailors only as the experiencers of a particular plight described in one's newspaper. My difficulty here concerns a distinction that may motivate this disagreement, a distinction between believing of certain people that they instantiate certain properties (those relevant to the emotion) and believing that certain properties are instantiated by people. These are not equivalent formulations. I can believe there are people who cheat on their income tax without believing of any particular people that they cheat on their income tax.

Pity for the sailors could be closely associated either with believing of sailors that they experienced a certain plight or believing that the plight (conceived as that of being a sailor aboard a sinking ship) was experienced. Radford's contentions might be held to suggest that he has the first formulation in mind while associating Paskins's claims with the second. If this is indeed at the core of the difference at issue, I am not sure that Radford could legitimately employ the first formulation. He has acknowledged that the object of a rational emotion can be one that does not actually exist but is merely believed to exist — in other words, that rational emotions take epistemic objects.[5] Thus, grief would be associated not with people whose existence was a given and of whom something was believed but with the belief that there were people who had a certain experience.[6]

Yet one can construe the relevant experience in very broad terms. One can believe that there are people who have experienced racial discrimination or starvation or suicidal feelings without having a particular incident or time and place in mind. Perhaps Radford would require such particularity and would want the relevant belief to concern an incident associated with certain spatiotemporal coordinates. What disinclines me to accept

---

5. Radford suggests that false beliefs can inspire emotion as readily as true ones, that finding that one's belief is false puts a halt to one's emotion, and that belief is necessary for rational or coherent emotional response: "How Can We Be Moved by the Fate of Anna Karenina? (I)," *Proceedings of the Aristotelian Society* 49, suppl. 6 (1975): 67–80.

6. Note that this does not affect the argument in Chapter 1 concerning cases like that of the stuffed tiger. Case 1 could be reformulated to concern what one believed to be true of an object one believed to exist, and this could be contrasted with what one imagined of the object that one believed to exist. The distinction between such a case and that of a response to fiction remains, for in the latter case nothing is imagined of what is believed to exist.

such an approach is that there are no guidelines available to delimit the requisite degree of particularity. Between the particularity of a belief about a friend's being subject to discrimination on account of her race and the generality of a belief about people's being discriminated against for such reasons throughout human history, there lie countless intermediate beliefs: about discrimination in the United States; about discrimination in the United States during a particular century, a particular decade, a particular year, a particular day. What degree of specificity is it that makes compassion possible?

I do not believe that there is any easy answer to this question. Moreover, I do not believe that the particularity of an object is as central to pity as the degree of concern or seriousness with which we regard the thought of a given kind of experience and the degree of attention we devote to thoughts of what it might be like to have it. Ultimately, there seems no conclusive argument against the claim that our pity can be global, that it can embrace people known to us only as the instantiators of certain characteristics or experiences.

To return to the primary focus of the discussion, consider a fiction that includes among its characters a victim of AIDS, such as Tony Kushner's *Angels in America*. Most of us know something of AIDS and know something of what is suffered by its victims, even if we are not acquainted with any sufferers. That is, I know that real persons have, could, and do suffer from AIDS. Let us assume that I find the fiction moving, that I entertain the thought of Prior Walter and his plight with pity and distress. Could I not feel for real people in the course of feeling for the character? Indeed, would my being moved by the fiction not make it all the more likely that I would be moved by the plight of actual AIDS victims (people in the same bind as the character)? If there is nothing odd about weeping for the victims of a sinking ship, why should it not be possible to weep for the victims of an illness? One can be aware that both calamities have occurred and that both have led to suffering and death. I may not have heard of the plight or experience of any *particular* AIDS victim, I may only have been privy to generalities, but this would not make my sympathy impossible in and of itself. My not being acquainted with the names and specific circumstances of AIDS victims should not draw objections from Radford unless he has changed his mind about how freely the bounds of human sympathy can range. Pitying the fictional character, regarding the thought of his plight with pity, can involve or lead to pity for people believed to be similarly placed.

Thus, being outraged by the way Sergeant Hartman treats the tortured recruit, entertaining the thought of this treatment with outrage, can also

involve being outraged by the notions of proper training that I believe
certain members of the military still espouse. I think that we frequently do
feel emotion toward real people when we entertain the thought of a
character's actions or plight with emotion. I therefore conclude that the
emotions experienced during our contemplation of fictional events can
take actual objects.

Peter McCormick has taken a somewhat different approach to the
question of the intentional object. He indicates that "in responding imaginatively to fiction, we judge [a character] . . . and ourselves, we feel for
[a character] . . . and ourselves."[7] According to McCormick, "part of
what we come to be at home with in [a] . . . fictional world . . . is
nothing more than a horizon of a virtual world we already inhabit."[8] The
feelings that fictions arouse are described as the extensional referents of
the contents of the reader's emotions.[9] This suggests that feeling for a
character can involve feeling for oneself. McCormick indicates that a part
of what can move us about a fiction is what, for instance, the characters'
fictional sufferings can refer to, "and this may well be the real sufferings of
our own families, our friends and ourselves."[10] That is, the experiences of
characters are taken to refer to our own, similar, experiences or to those of
others about which we have knowledge, though it is not clear what degree
of resemblance is required. Perhaps the fictional and actual experience
need only be similar in a very general way.

In his discussion of the place of real emotion in our responses to fiction,
Jerrold Levinson has suggested an analysis along the same lines. Emotions
we have previously experienced toward real objects are said to be "tapped
into and reactivated, by those aspects of the story and characters that
resonate with them."[11] It is notable that Levinson's approach is more than
compatible with recent research in neurology, which indicates that emotional response involves some evaluation of an occurrent experience in
terms of one's previous experiences. It is believed that emotional memo-
ries are permanently stored.[12] Indeed, philosophers like Ronald de Sousa

---

7. Peter McCormick, *Fictions, Philosophies, and the Problems of Poetics* (Ithaca:
Cornell University Press, 1988), 145.

8. Ibid., 144.

9. Ibid., 142.

10. McCormick, "Feelings and Fictions," *Journal of Aesthetics and Art Criticism* 43
(1985): 381.

11. Jerrold Levinson, "The Place of Real Emotion in Response to Fiction," *Journal of
Aesthetics and Art Criticism* 48 (1990): 79.

12. Sandra Blakeslee, "Tracing the Brain's Pathways for Linking Emotion and Reason,"
New York Times, 6 December 1994, B5, B11.

ally emotions with paradigm scenarios drawn from early experience and suggest that these scenarios can govern the nature and focus of an occurrent response.[13]

Levinson also suggests that a fiction "may end up evoking my sadness at the death of children, my pity for starving people, my anger at racial prejudice, my contempt for politicians. . . . And these things . . . do actually exist. . . . our emotions toward social phenomena or situation types or categories of persons may quite intelligibly be engaged by the course and particulars of fiction."[14] One of the things that the preceding quotation suggests is that, as indicated by Paskins, fictions can lead us to feel for real people. What Levinson and, I suspect, McCormick have to say about some of our responses to fiction is this: fictions — when we are moved by them — resonate with our own experiences and knowledge of the world and may lead us to feel for others or for ourselves on account of what we and they have experienced or could experience. Insofar as fictions do resonate with our experience in this way, they may change the way we see the world and ourselves, may change what we believe and what we notice. In addition, something that McCormick suggests in his discussion but never quite spells out is that a part of our emotional response to fiction is due to empathy with characters. If we imagine what it is like to have certain beliefs and experiences — a certain outlook on the world — then perhaps a character's experiences might become, as McCormick puts it, virtually our own. Empathy is the topic of Chapter 6.

How might fictions resonate with one's own experience? Consider my response to the film *Full Metal Jacket*. As it happens, the bullying personality of Sergeant Hartman bears an uncanny resemblance to that of someone for whom I and several of my friends used to work years before I saw the film. Perhaps, in McCormick's words, the resentment of the recruit victimized by Hartman became virtually my own. Perhaps, as Levinson has it, my emotions toward my former employer were tapped into and reactivated by the aforementioned resemblance. My imaginative empathy with the recruit is likely to have involved something of the sort.

Yet to say that my pity was *only* self-pity (or perhaps pity for those at the mercy of bullies) and that the object of my anger was only my former employer (or perhaps all persons who derive satisfaction from bullying those in their power) does not seem to afford a complete story of my emotional experience of the film. It may be that I feel these things, but it

---

13. Ronald de Sousa, *The Rationality of Emotion* (Cambridge: MIT Press, 1990), 182–90.

14. Levinson, "The Place of Real Emotion in Response to Fiction," 79.

also seems that I pity the recruit and detest Hartman. If I have been imaginatively empathizing with the recruit and to some extent making his experience my own, then it would seem that his tormentor would also, in imagination, be mine. It once more appears that the characters are in some very direct way the targets of my emotion, something the preceding treatment does not entirely allow. As was indicated with respect to Paskins's hypothesis, it does not seem that the particularity of my response to fictional entities can be analyzed away.[15]

What of "situation types or categories of persons"?[16] When Levinson suggests that these are sometimes the objects of our response, he appears to refer to the kind of global emotion with which I have associated Paskins's contentions. These emotions would be directed toward people or situations that were believed to exist and to instantiate certain proper-ties. Here, the people and situations might be identified exclusively as the instantiators of such characteristics rather than in any more specific way.

Ronald de Sousa describes the paradigm scenarios he identifies with emotion as constituted in part by situation types, which are allied with the characteristic objects of certain emotion types. The other component of such scenarios consists of sets of characteristic responses. A situation type is a part of something *in terms of which* an object or event is construed or taken. The designation *situation type* might be thought to delimit the objects an emotion can take according to the characteristics those objects instantiate. (In the case of fiction, we could presumably speak of imagining the instantiation of certain characteristics.) Thus, the situation type/response set exhibits the familiar connection between certain properties (e.g., danger) and certain responses (e.g., fear).

De Sousa further suggests that emotional responses to fiction might be exceptions to the rule that paradigm scenarios go back to infancy. He thinks that they can "constitute emergent emotional structures which bear witness to our capacity for fresh emotional experience, built on, but

---

15. Levinson is aware of this, since his discussion of genuine emotions is intended merely to supplement Walton's account of quasi emotions rather than to replace it. Indeed, he thinks that recognition of two sources of genuine emotion that underlie our involvement with fiction "may help reconcile us to the fact that our emotions for them as such remain, at base, make-believe" (ibid., 80). I, for one, am not reconciled, as has been indicated in the preceding chapter. I am more than willing to reiterate my conviction that we are frequently moved by the state of the world and by aspects of the human condition in being moved by fictions. What I am not willing to acknowledge is that this is all there can be to *genuinely* pitying or loathing a character, or that this is the only kind of object (genuine) emotions can take in the course of an experience of fiction.

16. Ibid., 79.

not out of, preexisting emotional repertoires."[17] Paradigm scenarios (situation type/response sets) are projected onto particular situations in the course of an emotional response. Taken together with the preceding, this indicates that fictions may sometimes provide us with new scenarios that can be so projected. De Sousa's comments about fiction suggest that fiction may provide us with a lens through which we can see the world, offering us a way to regard the world that makes certain aspects of it more salient than others. I think this is true, and some implications of this will be taken up in the next chapter. I will also maintain in Chapter 4 that beliefs about universals or situation types can govern the focus of attention in emotional response and that such attentional foci can transcend the boundaries between the fictional and the actual.

As de Sousa's account confirms, the link between universals or situation types and emotions can involve more than emotions regarded as "global." We often say that we, for instance, dislike a certain kind of person (one with certain traits), and this can be taken to convey dislike of those who instantiate these traits. However, the statement that one dislikes or is distressed by people or situations of a certain kind could also be interpreted as a statement about who or what one *would* dislike, were certain traits to be exhibited or certain characteristics to be instantiated. This might be presented as a way of formulating de Sousa's situation type/response set, though it reads more as an explanation of what may motivate the evaluating that is tied to emotion than it does as an example of an evaluation. A more accurate parallel might be found among beliefs that concern characteristics or properties whose possession is sufficient for inclusion in a category or "type" analytically linked to a certain emotion. Such an approach will be pursued in Chapter 4.[18]

How might the preceding apply to fiction? When we pity a character, we can be said to entertain the thought of a certain kind of person in imagination or to imagine the instantiation of certain characteristics. This boils down to imagining something quite specific: imagining a ship's officer named Ripley being chased by a homicidal space creature, for example. The thought I entertain in imagination is not of a kind or type. It is of a woman with certain characteristics. Those characteristics may be classified in certain ways, making it correct to say that I imagine a courageous

---

17. De Sousa, *The Rationality of Emotion*, 263.
18. I use the term *parallel* rather than *interpretation* because de Sousa rejects the characterization of belief as a component of emotion (ibid., 165). I agree that the "component" analysis is problematic, since emotions are experienced as unified. However, I think that a good deal depends on which particular view of what constitutes a belief one adopts.

kind of person or an endangered kind of person. That is, I imagine the instantiation of characteristics whose possession I believe is sufficient for the possession of courage, or whose instantiation I believe is sufficient for being endangered.

B. J. Rosebury offers an explanation of our responses to fictions in terms of universals. He begins with an idea already accepted here, that of entertaining the *thought* of some entity or event, to allow for our awareness of fictional events in the absence of existential commitment to them.[19] The question of universals is raised when he goes on to propose an account of our beliefs predating but quite similar to Bijoy Boruah's account of the evaluative beliefs associated with our emotional reactions to fiction.[20] I concur with the view that our responses to fiction are accompanied by beliefs about universals, about how given acts, attributes, or events are to be classified. This could be said of my belief that to humiliate and bully people in one's power (as Sergeant Hartman did in *Full Metal Jacket*) is despicable and wrong. For Rosebury, this is a belief about how events of a certain kind are to be classed. It is one's *thought* about a particular fictional entity or event, however, that is described as the object of one's emotional response, as is indicated in the next section.

THOUGHTS AND THOUGHT CONTENTS
AS INTENTIONAL OBJECTS

There is a dual advantage, Rosebury claims, in proposing that we merely entertain the thought of a fictional event. Not only does this explain how we can entertain a proposition without believing it, it also gives us something to be committed to: namely, the thought itself. He goes on to characterize the content of that thought (thought contents and mental images seem to be interchangeable here) as one of the thought's attributes. Just as we can be aware that a cloud is shaped like a lion without any existential commitment to airborne felines, so having a certain content (deriving from the contemplation of fictional events) becomes the property of the thought, an object less ontologically problematic than are fictional entities and events. Rosebury even mentions a belief in the "man-shapedness of this thought" and compares the belief that "the man-

19. B. J. Rosebury, "Fiction, Emotion, and 'Belief': A Reply to Eva Schaper," *British Journal of Aesthetics* 19 (1979): 125.

20. Ibid., 128. Bijoy H. Boruah, *Fiction and Emotion: A Study in Aesthetics and the Philosophy of Mind* (Oxford: Clarendon Press, 1988), 102–3.

shapedness of this thought is frightening" to a belief that the lion a cloud is shaped like is roaring.[21] My thought of Sergeant Hartman would be said to possess attributes describable by reference to the idea of a certain complex personality.

What attributes could these be? Can a thought bully, or rant, or be six feet tall? Can it be a member of the military? These do not seem to be attributes of the thought at all but of what the thought is about. Presumably, Rosebury would want to deal with such features as attributes of content (this thought has the property of being *about* thus-and-such, or has the property of having thus-and-such content). However, this still leaves us in difficulties, for the kinds of properties tied to our feeling an emotion toward an object (dangerousness for fear, suffering for pity) are not the kinds of properties that thoughts are typically said to possess. We do not pity thoughts themselves, because thoughts do not suffer. Talk of attributes of thought content does not solve the problem. A sentence might have the attribute of being about a possible war, but if it stimulated fear, that fear would be of a war, not a sentence. Similarly, a thought or belief about someone's suffering could cause us to feel pity and distress, but we would not pity the thought. Rosebury does not provide an intentional object that makes sense of our emotional reactions to characters.

There is obviously some causal or necessary connection between thinking a situation is dangerous and feeling fear, for it is not clear that one could feel fear in the absence of any thought or belief about danger. I believe that having such a thought is necessary for experience of the emotion. Yet the causes or the conditions necessary for an emotion can clearly be distinct from its object. One could claim that a thought of or belief about a threat to one's well-being was a causal factor in one's experience of fear or was in fact necessary for the experience of that emotion but that it was not the thought itself that one feared. The intentional object of fear would instead be associated with the content of that thought, with what the thought or belief was about.

Peter Lamarque offers some insight into the intuition that may be at the core of Rosebury's account. He describes the objects of our emotional responses to characters and fictional situations as thought contents characterized by fictional descriptions or depictions.[22] Thoughts may involve imaginings, mental images, or fantasies. We can be frightened *by* thoughts (that is, certain thoughts can cause or constitute conditions necessary for our fear), though we are not usually frightened *of* them (in other words,

---

21. Rosebury, "Fiction, Emotion and 'Belief,'" 126.
22. Peter Lamarque, "How Can We Fear and Pity Fictions?," *British Journal of Aesthetics* 21 (1981): 293.

they are not the intentional objects of our fear). Thus, we do not fear thoughts, but they can be frightening. The account as Lamarque presents it has many advantages. Our thoughts, to which existential commitment is unproblematic, can be graded according to the level and kind of attention we give to them. This is particularly helpful in the development of an adverbial account of emotional response (discussed later in this chapter), for it may enable us to identify an emotional response to a character with the way the thought of the character is entertained and the way one's attention is focused.

The idea of attending to one thought rather than others, the idea of focusing one's attention, also has explanatory value in other respects. When I find a film or novel gripping, my attention is focused on the thought of fictional events rather than on the thought that the events are fictional.[23] It is in such circumstances, of course, that I am most likely to be moved. I am far less likely to be moved when I am not attending to the thought of fictional states of affairs with any degree of exclusivity. If I am worrying that my actor friend will forget her lines, my imaginative involvement in the play in which she performs will naturally be less, and my being moved by the thought of fictional events will be correspondingly less likely.

Different responses to the same fictional event can, on such an approach, be accounted for by considering differences between the thoughts that agents entertain or by noting differences in the focus of the agents' attention.[24] Take, for instance, two readers of William Makepeace Thackeray's *Vanity Fair*. Both entertain a number of thoughts about Becky Sharp and some of her more nefarious machinations. Both hold roughly the same evaluative beliefs: for instance, that to lie persistently in order to further one's own interests at the expense of others is improper, and that schemes of the sort in question are indeed nefarious. Why, then, does one reader regard Becky with grudging admiration while another despises her? The answer might be found by putting the normative repertoires of both readers under review, but we could also claim that each reader focused her attention differently. One might entertain the thought of the sheer cleverness of the nefarious scheme admiringly while the other entertained the thought of Becky's treachery with distress and disgust.

---

23. David Novitz has also made this point in "Fiction, Imagination and Emotion," *Journal of Aesthetics and Art Criticism* 38 (1980): 281.

24. This is also suggested by Michael Stocker, although he does not discuss our response to fictions specifically, in "Emotional Thoughts," *American Philosophical Quarterly* 24 (1987): 59–69. Stocker's approach will be discussed later in this chapter.

To return once more to the question of the intentional object, Peter Lamarque's account suggests that talk of fear or pity for characters involves an internal perspective and a response to *what* we imagine. The response is not to thoughts themselves but to what they are about. That is, what I loathe when I loathe the alien in the film of the same name is an imagined being. As Noel Carroll has recently put it in describing the object of our response to horror fiction, "the thought content of the relevant mental representations is derived from the propositional content of the descriptions in the text. This propositional content concerns the properties of horrific monsters. This supplies us with the properties we contemplate as instantiated in the monsters of our mental representations."[25] Is it at all intelligible to cast thought contents as the objects of our pity and fear? It might be claimed, for instance, that my pity for Desdemona and your pity for Desdemona could never have the same object, since our thoughts are necessarily distinct. But while our thoughts are distinct, their content may not be. Two people can entertain the thought of the same state of affairs in imagination.

Yet questions may remain, for it is not clear that what I imagine when I read Shakespeare's *Othello* bears any but a general resemblance to what you imagine when you read it. Lamarque acknowledges this difficulty and does not deny the "genuine indeterminacy in some of our claims to be responding to *particular* fictional characters and events." He acknowledges that the imaginative reconstruction we put on fictional states of affairs might issue in mental representations "far different from those directly, or logically, related to the propositional contents of fictional sentences."[26] This is hardly tidy, but it seems true to the nature of our experience. We can indulge in a lot of imaginative supplementation of fictional states of affairs by means of inference or outright invention, and this is capable of creating divergences among the contents of the thoughts of different readers or viewers. Thus, we do not respond to the fictional state of affairs proper but to the state of affairs we have imagined. The upshot of this is not that my pity for Desdemona and your pity for Desdemona never have the same object but only that they do not *necessarily* have the same object.

A further and more serious objection to the adoption of Lamarque's analysis involves the question of whether imaginary people and events, mental representations of people and events, mere thought *contents*, can

---

25. Noel Carroll, "Disgust or Fascination: A Response to Susan Feagin," *Philosophical Studies* 65 (1992): 90.
26. Lamarque, "How Can We Fear and Pity Fictions?," 301.

constitute proper intentional objects at all. After all, we do not even believe that Desdemona or Ripley or Sergeant Hartman exist as *people*. They are merely the inventions of authors, and perhaps of actors.

In clarifying this objection, it should be noted that there are two distinct senses in which we can speak of Desdemona, as the work of Peter Van Inwagen and Nicholas Wolterstorff suggests.[27] First, just as a Cartesian would say that I do not *have* the property of being five feet, three inches tall (since being a certain height cannot be predicated of an immaterial substance), but animate a body that has or exemplifies this property, so, Van Inwagen indicates, Desdemona does not *have* the property of being a woman or of being unhappy. Being a woman and being unhappy are properties *ascribed* to Desdemona in Shakespeare's *Othello*. However, Desdemona *has* such properties as being a character in a play, being a theoretical entity of literary criticism (in the same way as are plots and themes), and having been created by Shakespeare.

Nicholas Wolterstorff describes characters as person-kinds or universals and makes a similar distinction. Universals clearly cannot possess the same properties people possess. Thus, a character could only *have* properties like having been invented by an author. However, Wolterstorff sees characters as kinds or types of persons that are set before us by the author. Thus, he speaks of properties *essential within* a person-kind. These properties are "held" rather than "possessed" and would include those properties ascribable to people.

It is the set of properties *ascribed* to characters, which they are said to *hold* but not to possess, that is relevant to our emotional response. We pity neither an authorial construction nor a theoretical entity, since neither can suffer. The properties ascribed to Desdemona in *Othello* — that of being unfairly maligned, that of undergoing a painful experience — are the ones relevant to our pity. It is true in the world of the work that Desdemona possesses such properties, and it is also true in the world we imagine. Thus, we (in imagination) entertain the thought of a woman who undergoes a painful experience when we entertain the thought of Desdemona pityingly.

Yet we know there is no such woman. How, then, could the mere act of imagining a woman provide us with an intentional object for our emotion? The key objection here is that, while Lamarque's proposal seems accurate enough (i.e., it appears true that it is what we imagine that is most closely related to our emotion), thought contents seem to constitute *improper*

---

27. Peter Van Inwagen, "Creatures of Fiction," *American Philosophical Quarterly* 14 (1977): 299–308. Nicholas Wolterstorff, *Works and Worlds of Art* (Oxford: Clarendon Press, 1980), 144–49.

intentional objects. My response to this contention is to rehearse the arguments already presented in Chapters 1 and 2. What are the grounds for thinking that the intentional object of an emotional response is improper or unacceptable? As I maintained in Chapter 2, it has not been demonstrated that emotions must of necessity involve existential commitment to their objects. If emotions are to be characterized as cognitive, then they require some kind of thought in the role of cognitive constituent. However, nothing appears to mandate conclusively that this thought be an existentially committed belief. It has also not been demonstrated that a response to what is believed fictitious must inevitably fall a prey to irrationality. The reasons for this contention have been discussed at length in Chapter 1. Nothing, therefore, militates conclusively against the adoption of Lamarque's approach.

It should be further noted that even emotional responses that are in general deemed unproblematic need not be associated with actual objects. The first two chapters should have made clear, given the extended discussions of existential commitment, that the intentional objects of unproblematic emotional responses could be described as *epistemic* objects. For instance, intentional objects associated by Walton with genuine emotion could be considered objects that are merely *believed* to exist or to have occurred, not objects that do in fact exist or that must have occurred. Most philosophers would concede that, for example, a fear felt on the basis of a false but justified belief was a rational and genuine fear.

So when Scott is told by a hitherto reliable source that there is a plan for cutbacks at the plant where he is employed and when this information is corroborated by articles in the local newspaper, Scott's fear that there are plans to lay him off is rational and genuine. This can be accepted even when it later transpires that both Scott's source and the newspapers were completely misinformed. Here, the threat does not exist but is only believed to exist. Even these unproblematic cases involve thought contents in much the same way that Lamarque says our responses to fiction do. It has been held that we can identify the intentional object of the relevant emotion only by considering what is thought to be the case, only by considering the content of a thought or existentially committed belief. Anthony Kenny maintains that "the description of a formal object of a mental attitude such as an emotion, unlike a description of a non-intensional action, must contain reference to a belief."[28] Although I contend that the cognition in question need not be a belief, Kenny's

---

28. Anthony Kenny, *Action, Emotion and Will* (1963), excerpted in Cheshire Calhoun and Robert C. Solomon, eds., *What Is an Emotion? Classic Readings in Philosophical Psychology* (New York: Oxford University Press, 1984), 284.

association of belief with an emotion's object bears out my point. Any difficulty that could attach to identifying an emotion's object with thought content is by no means restricted to emotional response to fiction.

Finally, the possibility of alternative and perhaps more accurate locutions should also be considered. Where the content of a thought that is entertained emotionally has no external referent, it may be preferable to employ an adverbial account. To fear for Ripley could be described in terms of entertaining the thought of Ripley's plight fearfully. Such an approach will be discussed in the last two sections of this chapter.

Thus far, Lamarque's theory appears to provide the most viable candidate for the role of intentional object in cases where responses are specifically to the fictional. It may be possible to take his insightful treatment of thought contents a step further and to demonstrate that to pity an imaginary person is to entertain the thought of a certain kind of person (i.e., a person with certain properties) pityingly. In terms of what is true in, for instance, the fictional world of *Othello*, Desdemona is a woman who suffers. The access that we have to this world is by means of the imagination. We imagine such a world and such a woman, and so it must be that, if we do pity Desdemona, we pity what it is we imagine. That is, we imagine a suffering woman pityingly. The mental representations Lamarque speaks of are described as thought contents derivable from the senses of fictional descriptions and from depictions. Insofar as these can be identified as imagined people and events, Lamarque offers what seems the most accurate description of what it is to respond emotionally to characters.

POSSIBILITY AND POTENTIALITY AS OBJECTS OF EMOTION

However, as I have said before, emotional reactions produced during encounters with fiction can have more than one kind of object. I think that we can be saddened by the plights of real people in the course of being saddened by the plights of fictional ones. I also believe that empirical possibilities can sometimes be the objects of emotional responses inspired by fiction. Harold Skulsky has made suggestions along these lines, though he speaks of logical rather than empirical possibilities. He proposes that, when we are saddened by the thought of a given fictional state of affairs, the thought is a belief that the state of affairs is logically possible.[29] That is,

---

29. Harold Skulsky, "On Being Moved by Fiction," *Journal of Aesthetics and Art Criticism* 39 (1980): 11.

we respond with pity to what we take to be a case of logically possible suffering — suffering in a possible world.

Skulsky refers to a belief about the logical possibility of a given state of affairs as a modal belief and uses the following example to demonstrate that such beliefs can lead to emotional responses: "I respond with un-feigned horror to the belief that if the trolley conductor had not been signalled by passers-by, he would have ridden me over. . . . The shudder is perfectly spontaneous . . . nor need the emotion be attenuated by the fact that the object of my pity is an individual concept and not an indi-vidual: the same thing is true of my fear of the mugger who may be hiding along the dark street I am about to enter."[30] Elsewhere, Skulsky speaks of the object before the mind's eye of the novelist, not as a woman, but as the concept or mental representation of one — perhaps (though this is my own interpretation) a concept or representation of a way a woman could be.

I agree with Skulsky's contention that when we respond emotionally to fictional states of affairs we believe that states of affairs of that *kind* are possible. I am not entirely convinced, however, that we believe the *precise* state of affairs we imagine is possible. I also agree that beliefs about what might have been the case (but now cannot be) can move us. On the other hand, Skulsky's example of the mugger is a little troubling, for it is not clear that fear of a possible person is involved. Instead, I think one fears the possibility of there being a person lying in wait. That is, I do not think one fears a person who may or may not be there. I think one fears that a certain type of unpleasant event could take place.

It also appears difficult to accept that we can fear or pity a concept, though the problem here may only involve terminology. Skulsky allies concepts with mental representations, and his discussion suggests that what the mental representations in question actually represent are ways people can be — in other words, logically possible people. None of this is incompatible with those aspects of Lamarque's account that have been adopted, for that is what our thoughts or imaginings seem to be of or about. An imagined person is a logically possible one, if logically impos-sible people (e.g., married bachelors) are unimaginable.

I wonder, however, about treating fictional worlds as possible worlds. Nicholas Wolterstorff objects to the identification of fictional and possible worlds on the grounds that a possible world is a state of affairs that is maximally comprehensive: "A state of affairs S is *maximally comprehen-sive* = df for every state of affairs S*, S either requires or prohibits S*." No

---

30. Ibid., 12.

matter how voluminous and comprehensive a fictional world is — considered as a single, highly complex state of affairs — such a world will never be such that it requires or prohibits any state of affairs whatsoever. The fictional world of *Macbeth* includes the state of affairs of Lady Macbeth having given birth to a child but neither requires nor prohibits the state of affairs of her having given birth to exactly one child.[31]

Despite the treatment of fictional worlds as possible ones, Skulsky's account hints at many interesting avenues, some of which are never quite explored. For instance, we can be led to entertain thoughts of (what we regard as) empirical possibilities by entertaining thoughts of fictional states of affairs. We may even respond emotionally to the former in conjunction with the latter. This may suggest that our belief that a certain kind of event could occur can be tied to an emotional response that has as its object just such an empirical possibility. Consider that, for example, in reading Margaret Atwood's *The Handmaid's Tale*, I pity some of the characters and am distressed by the oppressive and dictatorial regime described in the novel. I believe that there could be a regime of this sort: a system in which censorship prevailed over free speech on allegedly moral grounds, in which the laws were based on fundamentalist religious principles. Because I believe this, I may be led to contemplate certain empirical possibilities having to do with the opinions and policies of various members of the U.S. Senate, or the consequences of the U.S. Supreme Court's decisions on issues involving abortion, privacy, and freedom of speech. That is, the distress I feel in reading Atwood's book may not just have imagined events as its objects. Distress may be directed toward empirical possibilities as well.

In his "On Being Moved by Fiction," Don Mannison speaks of potentialities rather than possibilities.[32] In a step that might be disputed on phenomenological grounds alone, Mannison concedes that we do not pity characters, because he does not wish to claim that we pity a state of ourselves.[33] As has been indicated earlier, the claim that what one pities can be an imagined person need not lead to the conclusion that one merely pities a state of oneself. Certainly, a thought is a mental event, but this need not make it true that it is a thought one pities. Pity is tied to what the thought is of or about. Mannison hopes to explain what we call our pity for characters by translating it into a case of our being moved by their plight.

He takes a leaf from Michael Weston's book in expanding on this, and

31. Wolterstorff, *Works and Worlds of Art*, 131-32.
32. Don Mannison, "On Being Moved by Fiction," *Philosophy* 60 (1985): 71-87.
33. Ibid., 82.

echoes some of the ideas offered in Skulsky's account. Weston has indicated that what we respond to in being moved by a character's plight is "a possibility of human life perceived through a certain conception of that life. I am not responding to *events* that have happened or are likely to happen, for the 'possibility' here is not an expression of prediction. Such responses are part of a conception of what is important in life."[34] Mannison is intrigued by this notion of nonpredictive possibility and cashes it out in terms of Aristotelian "potentiality"—what he calls "the sort of possibility that constitutes the *actual* nature of the kind of thing under consideration." Mannison's examples suggest that potentialities are distinctly human capacities to behave in certain ways or to have certain experiences. Our emotional responses to fiction, then, are not responses to empirically unlikely possibilities but to human potentialities. Accordingly, "to be moved by the fate of a tragic hero or heroine is to acknowledge one's recognition of how it must be for at least a certain sort of human being in such a situation."[35]

As I have already stated, Mannison wants to analyze what we call pity for a character into distress at the plight of a character, to reduce thoughts of people to thoughts of events. This is his first step. The fictional event, says Mannison, can "present us with a picture" of distinctly human potentialities.[36] Yet if potentialities *are* human capacities for action or experience, then what we respond to in responding to fiction is just a "picture" or representation of them. That is, the very difficulty that Lamarque confronts (I think successfully) and that Mannison attempted to avoid—the difficulty of distinguishing between a thought and what it is about—seems to reemerge here as a difficulty in distinguishing between a fiction and what it is about. A fiction like *Full Metal Jacket* may be held to present a picture of the human capacity for a cruelty that disguises itself as an enforcement of discipline. It does so, however, only in the behavior of its character. The capacity is still fictional because it is a fictional entity's capacity, because the "picture" with which we are presented is a fictional film rather than a documentary.

Mannison may be engaged in yet another reduction, of course. Perhaps, just as our pity for characters was reduced to our distress in imagining a character's having a certain experience, the latter could be once more

---

34. Michael Weston, "How Can We Be Moved by the Fate of Anna Karenina? (II)," *Proceedings of the Aristotelian Society* 49, suppl. 6 (1975): 86.

35. Mannison, "On Being Moved by Fiction," 84, 87. I do not disagree with this contention, but I am more inclined to associate it with the empathetic imagination.

36. Ibid., 84.

reduced to distress at the (real) human potential to have or undergo such experiences. It could be that fictions are considered in terms that evoke not just events we believe imaginary but potentialities we believe real. I am certainly not willing to deny outright that part of my outrage at the sergeant's behavior in *Full Metal Jacket* involved outrage or distress at the human capacity for cruelty. But there is nothing in this contention that conclusively demonstrates that this is all there can be to my loathing of the drill instructor. Surely it can be true both that I am outraged at the human capacity for cruelty and true that I detest Sergeant Hartman and those who bully people in their power.

As must have been obvious during the course of the chapter thus far, I think that the emotions we experience as the result of contemplating fictional events and entities can have a wide variety of intentional objects. In pitying a character, I may entertain the thought of an individual who is in pain or distress pityingly, but I may also pity actual people (including myself), feel distress at the human capacity for cruelty, feel fear about that to which such capacities could actually lead. These reactions and objects are not mutually exclusive. It is my contention that emotional responses to or on account of fictions can be multifaceted and complex. There is no need to say that we can feel emotion toward only one kind of object in such circumstances or that it is only the thought of one kind of object that can be entertained emotionally.

EMOTION, IMAGINATION, AND ATTENTION

I owe some explanation of my characterization of emotional construal as a manner of imagining and of how this fits with Peter Lamarque's account, especially in light of my preceding identification of construal with property ascription. Talk of imagination and what it involves tends toward the confusing and convoluted, so I will simplify for the purpose of clarity. For our present purposes, imagining will be treated simply as a mode of thinking that does not necessitate doxastic or existential commitment. To entertain the thought of a person can be to imagine a person. Further, one may entertain both the thought *of* a person or the thought *that* there is such a person in imagination. The former is not, I think, just the creation of a mental image. It does not rely mainly on the phenomenological. It can involve the contemplation of a way a person could be in a variety of respects. I stress this because a lot has been made of metaphors like "vividness" and "envisioning" in attempts to convey the seriousness or intensity with which it may be possible to imagine a person (rather than simply to entertain a proposition that there is one). The difficulty with such metaphors is that they convey little more than the notion of a mental picture or visual image.[37]

It should be noted, however, that to imagine a person, and to do so with the degree of interest and concern that emotional responses to fictions seem to involve, is to do more than picture physical appearances, however vividly. I do not for a moment believe that the philosophers who use terms like "envisioning" and "vividness" intend anything of this sort by them, but I do think it is useful to emphasize that picture thinking is *not* the only alternative to propositional thought content. Visualizing can play a role in what we imagine, especially in the case of literature, but it does not constitute the whole of it. We can imagine how things would seem to a person, what his ethics were, what he wanted and believed, how tired he was, in a way that was not exclusively propositional or exclusively phenomenological. To consider a nonfictional example, one can contemplate a proposed governmental spending cut and imagine or believe that it will cause distress in a certain quarter (where this is entertained as a mere possibility), but this is not the same as imagining that distress. Thus, we can imagine a character's distress in addition to imagining that he is distressed, and this is often done by making assumptions based on the states of affairs described in the work or by making assumptions based on empathetic response to characters. These topics will be taken up in later chapters.

At present, it is worth noting that two kinds of imagining have been distinguished. There can be, as Richard Moran suggests, the imaginative entertainment of a proposition. There can also be the kind of imagining that provokes "the mind to *do* various things (relating, contrasting, calling up various thoughts). . . . What is meant by 'liveliness' in such contexts is a matter of both spontaneous and directed mental *activity*. Both vividness and the emotional engagement with fictions should be seen as, irreducibly, aspects of the *manner* of one's imagining, and not as part of the content of what is imagined."[38]

Meanwhile, let us consider construals as modes of imagining. I think that our construals involve patterns of attention and, moreover, that they can depend on the content of what is imagined, without themselves constituting part of that content. To repeat an example, the states of affairs that

---

37. Richard Moran suggests this in "The Expression of Feeling in Imagination," *Philosophical Review* 103 (1994): 75–106. These concerns will be addressed at greater length in Chapter 5.
38. Ibid., 89.

comprise Thackeray's *Vanity Fair* offer plenty of scope for a wide variety of construals of the character of Becky Sharp. The states of affairs in the world one initially imagines are numerous, varied, and complex; they involve a multitude of characters and their adventures and experiences. To construe Becky as, say, selfish and unkind is to attend to this complex of states of affairs selectively. It is to focus attention on certain events and actions rather than others: Becky Sharp's manipulation of people, her continual dishonesty, her complete disregard of Amelia's feelings and fortunes. The attention gives prominence to those features of the contemplated states of affairs that are taken to demonstrate selfishness and mistreatment of others. I do not believe that such a pattern of attending is usually undertaken with conscious purpose. I do think, however, that someone who feels contempt for or disapproval of Becky has indeed focused his attention in this way and that, in the world he imagines, Becky Sharp *is* selfish and bad. Most probably this person has an evaluative belief that identifies certain *kinds* of behavior as immoral: manipulation, self-interested lying, betrayal of one's friends.

I hasten to add, however, that there are imaginary worlds in which Becky Sharp is not all bad. Mine, for instance. Admiration of Becky Sharp (albeit tempered by an awareness of certain unadmirable traits) involves attending to entirely different features of the world of the work, attending to the state of affairs of Becky's having survived and gotten the better of a thoroughly difficult childhood, her intelligence (she's smarter than anyone else in this world), her talent, her wit, her ability to survive disasters, the sheer cleverness of some of her more nefarious schemes (also the fact that most of those whom she wrongs are themselves either thoroughly unprincipled or thoroughly stupid, but taking this into account would involve us in too many construals). Here the attention is once again focused selectively; different qualities are salient. If Becky Sharp is admired for at least some of her qualities, that admiration would involve a pattern of attention such as this. I have exaggerated, of course, but I do think we can say that there are a few people who imagine a sometimes admirable Becky. I should again emphasize that a lot depends on the reader's normative beliefs in this case. For some, to be admirable is to be without certain enumerable defects, and these persons would probably be disinclined to attend with any particular care to the many demonstrations of Becky's shrewdness that occur in the world of *Vanity Fair.*

I should also note that exhibiting such patterns of attention is a *way* of imagining the world of a work, a way of attending to it (i.e., selectively), and also a way of developing it. As has been shown, attending in different ways to the same fictional world can involve us in adding to that world and constructing a world in imagination. I agree with Walton's suggestion of a private kind of participation built on the powers of the imagination. But, to reiterate, it does not follow from a claim that I imagine a sometimes admirable Becky that I have imagined my own admiration. My admiration involves a *way* of imagining Becky, a focus of attention on her feats of shrewdness (and a failure to attend to some of her other actions) that can sometimes amount to contemplating her admiringly and can sometimes import an admirable Becky into the world I imagine.

Discussion of how we may imagine fictional worlds is reserved for Chapter 5, but it should be clear that whenever we read a novel or see a film we make a plethora of inferences and assumptions and extrapolations to fill in the story for ourselves. Obviously these are imaginative, but just as obviously, some will be based on general normative judgments and on the *way* we imagine the fictional world, on what draws the focus of our attention, on what is salient for us.

I should probably mention the reasons for my fairly dramatic shift in examples from space opera and horror to Victorian literature. Some fiction, and this is typical of films, manipulates our attention in such a way that making certain construals (say a construal that Ripley's situation is dangerous) is virtually a foregone conclusion. The plots of many films simply consist of a series of attempts on the protagonist's life, occasionally alleviated by the odd attempt on the protagonist's offspring, spouse, or family pet. In other words, a pattern of attention focused on the potential for bodily harm in various situations is guaranteed, since those are the only situations we get, and there is little else to attend to.

In fact, fictions frequently focus our attention *for* us in other ways, repeatedly dwelling on some particular aspect of a character's mental state or repeatedly detailing some series of difficulties a character encounters. This is one of the reasons why it may be plausible to think of some fictions as construals in themselves. They can, for instance, continually draw a reader's or viewer's attention to a particular kind of experience *as* painful (for instance, being the member of some minority or bearing the brunt of others' expectations) by including states of affairs detailing aspects of those experiences that may have been hitherto unconsidered.

Normative judgments and evaluative beliefs have been mentioned more than once. These are, I think, usually part of the grounds for both imaginative and existentially committed construals. For instance, construing Becky Sharp as admirable in one respect or another would probably involve a universal evaluative belief about it being admirable to possess such characteristics as intelligence and ingenuity. I am wary, however, of the further claim that the previous possession of such beliefs is necessary for the construal. Any hypothesis about the moral impact of fictions on ourselves and our lives must surely make reference to new ways of construing human situations. Hence, the possibility of additions to one's doxastic repertoire must be taken into account. I think that our construals may be determined or guided by the evaluative beliefs we already possess, though this very guidance can on occasion lead to a process of thinking that eventually adds to or alters our beliefs by building on our existing repertoire. Examples of how such a process might occur are offered in Chapter 4.

To say that construal is a manner of imagining is to link it to the patterns of attention we exhibit when engaged in the contemplation of a situation, whether that situation is real or imaginary. I may, while ascending an extremely rickety twelve-foot ladder to effect the rescue of a cat my dogs have treed, attend to the instability of the ladder (rendered even less secure by scrabbling and leaping dogs) and the probable demonstrations of ingratitude on the part of the feline in question. Such a pattern of attention would involve my construal of my situation as precarious. I would doubtless contemplate my situation with some degree of trepidation.

Alternatively, I could contemplate the experience of the beleaguered cat, who is young and inexperienced in the ways of bored Labrador Retrievers whose willingness to behave in a manner calculated to earn the sobriquet "Mandibles of Death" in a feature film is seldom followed by any action more aggressive than a merciless licking of the victim about the head and shoulders. I could, that is, attend to the aspects of the situation that include the young cat's panic, its abortive attempts to climb back down, its plaintive cries, its shivering. I could construe the cat's situation as extremely unpleasant and contemplate the cat's plight with pity.

One interesting consequence such an example suggests is that some emotional responses are in principle controllable.[39] If my emotional response depends on or is identified with *how* I attend to my situation, on the selectivity of my attention, then by refocusing my attention I might mitigate or prevent the response. Consider that the less I dwell on, for instance, the probability of injury to myself and the more I dwell on the cat's unpleasant situation, the less likely I am to regard my situation with trepidation.

The analysis becomes more complicated when we consider the ex-

---

39. As Robert C. Roberts indicates in "What an Emotion Is: A Sketch," *Philosophical Review* 97 (1988): 183–209.

amples of irrationality in emotion discussed in Chapter 1. The individual who fears the stuffed tiger focuses his attention on certain aspects of it: its enormous bulk or its fangs, perhaps. His construal may have reference to some of his beliefs about dangers inherent in close proximity to wild animals, but I think that Hume's alliance of habitual associations with such cases is very much more to the point. Habitual associations are linked to the imagination, and it may be at the door of such associations that the misconstrual can be placed.

I have said that the child who fears the stuffed tiger imagines of the stuffed tiger that it is dangerous. What would that involve? Well, perhaps the subject attends to those features of the stuffed tiger he would believe dangerous in other contexts (glistening fangs, sheer bulk) and imaginatively entertains the thought of these in such contexts. Just as Hume's man in the cage was troubled by imaginings of swift descent even though he knew himself safe, our subject might be troubled by imaginings of snarling and pouncing, even though he knows the tiger is stuffed. He is not, I think, imagining the stuffed tiger magically re-animated. Rather, the features of it to which he attends are taken out of one context and placed in others. Somehow, in (not improperly) construing these imaginary situations as dangerous, he also (quite improperly) construes the actual sharer of the features central to his imaginings as dangerous. An alternative explanation is that our subject may simply imaginatively abstract the features to which he attends (teeth, claws, and so on) from their natural context and construe *them* as dangerous (more or less in the same way that someone would construe a weapon as dangerous: it would be dangerous if used). Thus, he imagines of the stuffed tiger that it is dangerous.

Smith's irritation with his computer could be described in a similar way. Those aspects of the computer's performance Smith attends to (unreliability, with serious negative consequences for Smith) lead him either to imagine other cases of unreliability (perhaps unreliable people) or to abstract this feature and contemplate unreliability or being "let down" out of context. It may be, if Smith contemplates other cases of unreliability — for instance, cases in which he was let down by people upon whom he had counted — that he construes *these* agents as culpable and consequently construes the computer's performance as just another instance of the culpable unreliability he imagines. Alternatively, perhaps these features of the computer's performance are imaginatively abstracted from their context and construed as culpable in isolation.

In either case, I have tied imagination to the construal because of the abstraction of selected features of the performance (those that are attended to) from their natural context. Smith imagines of the computer that it is culpable, rather than believing it. Since Smith does not believe that inanimate objects can be culpably obstructive, our only option is to suppose that Smith has taken unreliability or obstructionism out of the context of any belief about machines and imaginatively contemplated it either in isolation or by associating it with other examples of culpable unreliability or obstructive behavior. Whether it is a case of guilt by imaginative association or not, the misconstrual is clearly linked to the imaginative entertainment of certain features of one's experience out of their natural context, and this maintains the distinction between such cases of irrational response and our response to fiction.

A different and more complex example should also be considered. Cheshire Calhoun describes patterns of attention and associations that operate at a prereflective level as the cognitive constituents of an emotion that she says may be at odds with an intellectually held belief.[40] The kind of case she considers is ideally suited to explain a variety of racist, sexist, xenophobic, and homophobic reactions, though I am not sure that the emotion/belief conflict she uses such examples to illustrate is as clear as those in the preceding examples. Consider a subject S, who was raised to fear and despise members of group X. As a child, S is taught that Xs are inferior and dangerous. Newspaper stories about crimes perpetrated by members of X are dwelt on by members of S's community and are taken as irrefutable evidence of the base nature of all who are X. Jokes about members of X abound and are considered the height of wit. Later, S begins to study philosophy and comes to believe, after much consideration, that he has no adequate evidence or justification for any belief in the inherent inferiority, criminality, brutishness, or defectiveness of members of group X.

However, when S is forced to interact with someone who is X, he cannot help focusing his attention in ways that he does not ordinarily focus it. He attends to features of the X individual's appearance, speech, or mannerisms with which he has negative associations. If S fears X, he may attend particularly to the individual's size and potential to inflict harm, to any hint of aggressiveness in the individual's demeanor. If S feels contempt for X, S may, for instance, attend to minor flaws in pronunciation or grammar that he would overlook in other cases, to any aspect of X's demeanor or appearance that could be regarded as a defect or potential defect.

---

40. Cheshire Calhoun, "Cognitive Emotions?," in Cheshire Calhoun and Robert C. Solomon, eds., *What Is an Emotion?*, 327–42. Though he does not offer a detailed analysis, Robert C. Roberts uses a comparable example of a racist reaction in illustrating a conflict between emotion and judgment in "What an Emotion Is: A Sketch," 195–97.

While most would consider S's contempt for any particular member of X whom he encounters perverse, note that such a case need not demonstrate an outright conflict between belief and emotion. S could believe that Xs are not *inherently* inferior but also believe that poor grammar is a sign of intellectual inadequacy in some particular person. There is no outright inconsistency between these beliefs, though the second is allied with S's contempt. It is the fact that S's attention is focused exclusively on flaws and defects *only* when he is confronted by a member of X that leads us to suspect S of X-ism. The difficulty need not involve any imaginative projection onto X of some property X does not possess. Rather, it could involve a disregard of any features of X that could be seen as laudable or advantageous, plus a focus on qualities that S believes are or can be defects. The problem, then, seems to involve habit and habitual patterns of attention rather than outright misconstruction. Exhibiting these patterns of attention only when responding to members of X, having such a habit of evaluation, *could* yield a belief inconsistent with the belief that members of X are not inherently inferior. It could do so if generalizations were formed on the basis of individual evaluations that constituted this habit of response.

I have used the preceding example because it illustrates a case of emotional response that many would be inclined to consider unjustified. The problematic nature of this response can be most readily explained *not* in terms of unjustified belief or property misascription, but in terms of patterns of attention typical of emotional response. On the present account, emotions are characteristic ways of attending to the content of our experience. Attending exclusively to the features of a person one believes could constitute defects amounts to regarding the person contemptuously.

IMAGINING EMOTIONALLY

Thus far, I have been speaking mainly of different ways of contemplating persons, properties, and states of affairs. The work of Michael Stocker can help to elaborate such an account, for he makes the important point that what is really involved in such contemplation is the way in which the thought of a given state of affairs may be entertained. Although his focus is not on the fictional, Stocker has developed an analysis of emotion that allies it with *how* one can have a thought. To take a thought (which can, but need not be, a belief) with emotional seriousness is to take it emotionally.[41] "How" one has the thought in question is a matter of the serious focus of one's attention on a particular thought with particular content.

In the earlier example of my attempts to rescue the terrified feline, there are any number of thoughts I could have focused on. The extent to which I felt fear or trepidation involves the extent to which I focused serious attention on the thought of the unsteadiness of the ladder, the thought of the insecurity of my position, or the thought of a possible fall. To take the thought of a possible fall seriously (even if one does not believe it likely) can be to entertain the thought fearfully, provided one believes falls from ladders can be painful or lead to injury. In the case of the film *Alien*, my serious attention is not focused on thoughts of how Ripley looks, thoughts of the spaceship's layout, or beliefs about films and actors. My serious attention is focused on the thought of the risks to life and limb with which a certain kind of woman's situation is fraught. To seriously focus attention in this selective way can be to imaginatively construe the situation as dangerous and to think of the situation fearfully. Here, the serious focus of attention on a *particular* thought — the thought of a situation of the kind that I believe involves danger — is necessary for taking that thought fearfully. That is, the content of a thought, whether it is a thought about the probability of physical injury or a thought about someone's pain, can explain why the thought is entertained fearfully or pityingly.

This may provide a direction in which to take Lamarque's account of our emotional responses to fiction. To say that I pity an imaginary person is to say that I entertain the thought of a person pityingly or compassionately. The difference in the way we respond to beliefs, as opposed to thoughts entertained only in imagination, does not involve the difference between the rational and the irrational or the difference between genuine and pseudo-emotion. The question of emotional response here depends not on existential commitment to the object or content of one's thought but on how that thought is held.

My adverbial analysis of emotional response to fiction is motivated by several additional factors. Just as some adverbial accounts of sensing were in part intended to avoid reification of the content of sensory experience (i.e., to avoid positing sense-data as existents),[42] so an adverbial account in the present context could help us to avoid reification of thought contents (i.e., to avoid speaking as if we were positing imaginary objects as exis-

---

41. Michael Stocker, "Emotional Thoughts," 59–69.

42. For adverbial analyses of sensory experience see, for example, R.M. Chisholm, *Perceiving: A Philosophical Study* (Ithaca: Cornell University Press, 1957), and B. Aune, *Knowledge, Mind and Nature* (New York: Random House, 1967).

tents). We can take advantage of the commonly held and philosophically respectable view that imaginings cannot exist without imaginers so as to reconstrue statements that apparently refer to imaginary persons or events as the objects of emotional attitudes into statements about the manner in which a thought (a much less ontologically problematic object) is entertained. This analysis is not intended to replace a characterization of emotion as (or in terms of) construal. Rather, it is intended to suggest that construals may be considered from both internal and external points of vantage and that the description of a construal may depend on the perspective adopted.

R. J. Hirst points out that it is a pervasive and distinguishing aspect of any conscious activity that it has two aspects.[43] The inner aspect, reflecting what is experienced by the person concerned, involves an act/object mode of awareness. The outer aspect is said to reflect a correlator's point of view concerning that experience. From that perspective, "it is a mode of experience of the person, a way in which he experiences; it is adverbial because no distinction of act [or agent] and object can be made from without." While Hirst's main interest is in perceptual consciousness, he believes that "almost all mental activities are adverbial in this way — feeling a pain, thinking, having mental imagery, or dreaming. And yet in all of them there is . . . a content which we can but describe as distinct from a subject — whether we call it an object or image."[44] From the outside, as brain activity, imagining (and thinking in general) may be characterized as adverbial, though from the inside it is the experience of a content distinct from oneself.

It may be a failure to distinguish between two such points of vantage that has led some philosophers to identify pity for a character with pity for a state of oneself. The point in making a distinction of this kind in the present context, however, is to acknowledge that act/object terminology is applicable from a distinctively *internal* point of vantage. This is a perspective from which our pitying and the object of that pity are regarded as distinct. From an external perspective, an adverbial analysis may be found more apposite. From that point of vantage, we may speak of someone's entertaining a thought pityingly. It is only the inner perspective of the experiencer that the act/object separation can be held to reflect.

Obviously, I have not taken my analysis to extremes, nor have I proposed as comprehensive an adverbial reconfiguration as that suggested by

43. R. J. Hirst, *The Problems of Perception* (London: Allen and Unwin, 1966), 294.
44. Ibid., 289, 294.

Hirst's treatment of the outer aspect of any conscious activity whatsoever. Such a step would appear to necessitate cumbersome and infelicitous locutions like "imagining woman-pursued-by-alien-ly," insofar as the content of the thought would be transformed into a mode of the thinking. Instead, I have taken the thought that is entertained in imagination as basic and unproblematic. Most would agree that we can have thoughts about nonexistents, and can have them without thereby standing convicted of irrationality or of some inauthenticity in our thinking. In the context of discussions concerning fiction and emotion, the difficulty appears to arise when we ask what a given emotion is "of" or "for" or "about." In particular, many become exercised over the proposal that merely imaginary events and entities can nevertheless be considered the intentional objects of emotions.

Accordingly, I have attempted to suggest a way to avert the dilemma. Since no objections have been raised in the course of this particular debate to the treatment of thoughts as existing (if psychological) objects or to the claim that thoughts are held or entertained, I have proposed that emotions can be characterized as ways of entertaining or experiencing thoughts (those thoughts whose contents stand in an analytic or logical relation to the emotion). That is, instead of an emotion being characterized as an attitude held toward a certain thought's content, the emotion is reconstrued as a way of having, holding, or entertaining that particular thought.

Here, emotions are treated as selective ways of attending to the content of one's thoughts. Emotions become modes of attending, each of which is governed and informed by a different conception of salience and each of which involves a focus on a different set of characteristics. Thus, attending to the content of one's thoughts fearfully involves a focus of attention on the content of some thoughts rather than others: thoughts about the possession of characteristics whose instantiation is believed sufficient for being endangered. A specific thought can be described as one that is entertained fearfully when the attention isolates its content *as* a content that instantiates characteristics believed sufficient for danger. An inner perspective would, of course, allow us to describe our experience of fiction in act/object terms as fearing for or pitying an entity we have imagined. An external perspective would describe us as agents who entertained thoughts (of people in dangerous or painful situations) fearfully or pityingly.

As Peter Lamarque has recently pointed out, in the case of fictions what we are afraid *of* is not what we are frightened *by*: "We can think of the 'of' locution giving us the intentional object of the emotion (in the fictional case something non-existent) and the 'by' locution the real object (in the fictional case something existent but psychological)."[45] What emotional attitudes toward the real and the fictional have in common, then, is what Lamarque calls their "real" objects: thoughts (either beliefs or thoughts entertained in imagination). The content of the thoughts we imaginatively entertain explains our emotions, because it can explain how it is those thoughts are entertained.

CONCLUSION

In this chapter, I have attempted to establish that the emotions we feel during the course of our encounters with fiction can take any of several objects, including objects we believe exist. Emotional responses to fictional events and entities in particular can be characterized as ways of entertaining thoughts in imagination. Pitying Desdemona involves seriously and attentively entertaining the thought of an undeservedly suffering woman in imagination, entertaining that thought compassionately. To translate talk of how a thought is entertained or had to talk of what the thought is about leaves us with an imaginary sufferer as the object of our pity. Clearly there are less problematic objects, though I do not think that there are conclusive grounds for holding that such an intentional object is wholly improper, for the act/object distinction could be held to apply only to the inner perspective of the experiencer or imaginer. In the case of pity for actual sufferers, both the adverbial analysis and the analysis that requires a specific epistemic object appear appropriate. The case of our imaginative encounters with fiction does not appear dissimilar, once we take into account the content of thoughts seriously and attentively entertained in imagination. We may be led to have these thoughts by reading books or watching actors, but we pity neither the books nor the actors, neither the mental images nor the thoughts themselves. Indeed, from an external point of vantage, we can simply be held to entertain thoughts of people described in books or depicted by actors compassionately.

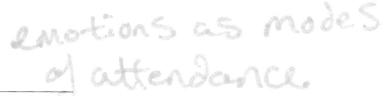

emotions as modes of attendance.

---

45. Peter Lamarque and Stein Haugom Olsen, _Truth, Fiction, and Literature: A Philosophical Perspective_ (Oxford: Clarendon Press, 1994), 105.

4

Fiction, Emotion, and Morality

T his chapter asserts that fictions can be, and frequently are, morally significant for us. First, many emotions are linked to evaluative beliefs that can be regarded as normative. While it is certainly not always the case that an emotional response is a moral one, emotions experienced on account of fiction can sometimes involve changes in and challenges to our repertoire of normative judgments. In the course of our encounters with fiction, we can be led to apprehend such judgments as newly challenged or substantiated. Fictions can invite us to imaginatively consider ways in which life could or should be lived. We can imaginatively enter into attitudes fictions explicitly or implicitly endorse.

It is my contention that the role of evaluative beliefs in imaginative response to fiction may also explain incidents of imaginative disengagement, for we may be disinclined or unable to enter into a construal implicit in a work. I suggest that the part played by evaluative beliefs in our emotional reactions to fiction may indicate the involvement of still other beliefs: beliefs about possibility, whose role in our imaginative engagements and disengagements will be discussed. These investigations will lead to the development of a tentative set of necessary conditions for emotional response to fiction.

EMOTION AND NORMATIVE JUDGMENT

I am working at home, both dogs ensconced in the kneehole of my desk, when the telephone rings. Tripping over canine body parts, I make it to the phone before the answering machine picks up. "Yes?"

"Hi!" It sounds like a voice-over in a commercial. "Have *you* got a Katzenjammer Home Security System in *your* home?"

"Huh?" I ask incisively. I am still thinking about quantification over opaque contexts.

"*Every* home needs a Katzenjammer Security System, guaranteed to halt potential miscreants and machete-wielding maniacs in their tracks. And just this week, only for a few very *special* customers, we are offering our introductory package at the *incredible* price of $999.99 — "

"No. Look. I have two dogs, OK? They like to pretend they're Rottweilers. I don't — "

"You'd put your personal safety, your very *life* and the lives of your loved ones, into hands of your *dogs*?"

"They don't have hands. What's wrong with dogs anyway? They make more noise that ten car alarms put together."

"Well, ma'am, I can tell that you, like some other ladies I've spoken to, have just been too darn busy to watch the news lately. Why only the other day, an entire family was dismembered and sold to a dog food company for twenty-nine cents a pound before they discov — "

"I saw that movie. I don't *want* a home security system. I don't want — "

"But for a mere $999.99, you too can rest secure in the knowledge that Katzenjammer Safe-T Window Guillotines and Tiger Pits(TM) are primed and ready to protect both you and your loved ones!"

"You don't get it. I'm not interested. What I *am* interested in is getting you off the — "

"Why little lady, do you have any *idea* how many of your *very own* neighbors have had Katzenjammer Safe-T Tiger Pits(TM) installed in their *very own* — "

Click.

I am sure that the actual conversation I had with the annoying telephone solicitor could not have been this surreal, but I do recollect that it was peculiar. I only attended to it sporadically, and my recollection of conversations I conduct when my mind is on something else is not very dependable. However, I distinctly remember my irritation. I was annoyed at the interruption and at having a sales pitch inflicted on me. The slur on my dogs was irritating. The scare tactics were contemptible. Being addressed as "little lady" pushed me over the edge. I seldom hang up on people.

While this example is not particularly serious, the call occurred as I was about to begin this section, and it does capture a garden-variety annoyance that nearly all of us have experienced. In such cases, our annoyance can usually be tied to a series of normative judgments. A lot of us believe that it ought not to be permissible for salespersons to hound us in the privacy of our homes. More of us find it irritating that telephone solicitors seldom take no for an answer. There is a tendency to ignore all refusals, however firm, and to blithely continue reciting the sales pitch (I always imagine that telephone solicitors are equipped with cue cards). This is annoying because most of us believe that it is rude, indeed an insult, to ignore or effectively discount the responses of a person one has addressed. In other words, we may believe that people ought not to treat others in this way.

Some tend to regard the telephone solicitor's motivations as wholly self-interested. We are aware that these people work on commission and that their paychecks reflect the extent of their ability to convert potential customers into actual ones. Given this, most of us would distrust the authenticity of the security system salesman's concern for our welfare. Indeed, many assume that product descriptions themselves may be a tissue of lies, especially given the continual exposure of fraudulent solicitation schemes in the newspapers. That is, whether fairly or not, we often construe telephone solicitors as insincere and dishonest. This is clearly grounded in some set of normative appraisals. We might believe that people ought not to behave in that way, or at least ought not to attempt to deceive or dupe *us*.

The scare tactics sometimes employed by salespersons can elicit contempt either because the tactics are transparent (contempt for incompetence and irritation that the salesperson assumes I will fall for this) or because we may believe there is something particularly unsavory about exploiting someone else's private worries in order to further one's own ends. There is also something very frustrating about being forced to exhibit the very rudeness or dishonesty of which one disapproves and to which one resents being subjected in order to free oneself of it. One must usually resort to interruption, cutting the monologue off by hanging up, or telling some lie (e.g., "I'm a starving graduate student") calculated to make the solicitor give up.

As has been suggested before, many emotional responses are linked to evaluative beliefs that can only be considered normative. Indeed, some philosophers identify them with such beliefs outright, stating that my being angry at some person *entails* my believing that she or he has somehow wronged me or others,[1] that anger is a judgment that someone (usually oneself) has been wronged. Many theorists go so far as to draw necessary connections between the emotional response and an estab-

---

1. Robert C. Solomon, "Emotions and Choice," in Cheshire Calhoun and Robert C. Solomon, eds., *What Is an Emotion?* (New York: Oxford University Press, 1984), 312.

lished moral order, tying the acquisition of culturally appropriate normative construals to the acquisition of habits of emotional response.[2]

I wish to maintain here that particular normative judgments very frequently accompany emotional responses and that even imaginative construals can depend on more general normative assessments. As has already
been demonstrated, anger, irritation, annoyance, contempt, and resentment can usually be tied to a negative appraisal of a behavior or the person
who exhibits it, to entertaining the thought of this behavior angrily or
contemptuously. These emotions are also sometimes tied to the evaluation
of actions or people as incompetent and foolish, but this has its own
normative edge. For example, any philosopher would tell her students
that they ought not to indulge in fallacious reasoning.

Roughly, what I intend to indicate is that it is the serious entertainment
of a thought about the kind of behavior one *believes* unfair, unjust, or
incompetent (or the kind of act one believes will usually have harmful
consequences) that can be entertained angrily — rather than pityingly,
enviously, or fearfully. If I believe that discrimination on the basis of
gender (all other things being equal) is unjust, then I can entertain the
thought of such an act with anger or disapproval. My evaluative belief, a
general belief about *kinds* of acts rather than some particular act, can lead
me to attend to the thought of a particular instance of gender discrimination angrily. It can be my evaluative belief that leads me to focus attention
seriously on this thought about this particular act rather than on other
thoughts about the act. That is, it is what I believe to constitute unfairness
or injustice that sets the stage for an emotional response of anger.

Pity involves, for the most part, an evaluation of someone's experience
as painful or unpleasant, but this is often accompanied by some assumption that the experience is undeserved. As the nostalgia of *Pygmalion*'s
Alfred Doolittle for the status of the undeserving poor suggests, the undeserving are more free from the concern and interference of others. I may,
on occasion, pity someone whose situation I believe to have come about as
a result of his own actions. However, my pity tends to be mitigated
according to my assessment of the extent of the individual's culpability in
other respects. I am more likely to pity someone whose life has been
blameless than I am to pity a sadistic killer. Self-pity also involves an
assessment of one's experience as undeservedly painful. It is often linked

---

2. This approach is typical of social constructionism, as for instance in Claire Armon-
Jones's "The Thesis of Constructionism," in Rom Harre, ed., *The Social Construction of
Emotions* (New York: Basil Blackwell, 1988), 32–56.

to the (sometimes inaccurate) belief that one's share of burdens is unfairly or disproportionately large and that this ought not to be the case.

Here again, my beliefs about what constitutes suffering and what constitutes just desert can focus my attention on one thought rather than another, sometimes providing the groundwork for an emotional response. Different beliefs can lead to different responses. Consider the state of affairs of a wealthy individual who feels that a parent she did not visit during the course of an illness has become unfairly cold to her and indifferent to her concerns. One could contemplate this woman's plight pityingly if one believed that rejection was a dreadfully painful experience or if one believed that the indifference of parents could cause terrible psychological damage. On the other hand, one could contemplate the woman's plight with equanimity if one believed that material comfort could mitigate or abolish suffering or if one believed that to ignore a relative's illness was selfish and unkind. Note that different thoughts become the focus of attention in each case. Focusing attention on the thought of parental rejection leads to a different response than would attending to the thought of material comforts or the thought of selfish behavior.

Jealousy, guilt, pride, and admiration usually involve evaluations of our own actions or those of others. Guilt and pride can involve a negative or positive normative assessment of one's own actions. For instance, if one believes a certain kind of act is wrong and one entertains the thought of having performed just such an act, one can entertain the thought of one's action guiltily. Envy can involve some belief about inequity or unfairness. Even euphoria and depression might sometimes be linked to assumptions about the way life ought or ought not to go.

To tie emotions to cognitions and to assessments of situations is, first, to render them liable to the ascription of rationality and irrationality, warrantedness and unwarrantedness. To tie them to normative, often moral, judgments is significant in other ways. It suggests that an emotional response can bring one's repertoire of normative beliefs into play and *bring it to bear* (justifiably or not) in fairly unmistakable ways. For instance, if I entertain the thought of Sergeant Hartman's treatment of the young recruit (in the film *Full Metal Jacket*) angrily and disapprovingly, then I do so in part because I believe that certain kinds of behavior (bullying, abuse of power) are cruel and unjust, or because I believe these behaviors to be wrong when they have worse consequences than the alternative courses of action that are available to agents. This has particularly interesting implications for fictions. If our emotional responses to fiction can be genuine, if they are not irrational, and if they further depend on our repertoire of moral and evaluative beliefs, then many fictions can no longer be characterized as trivial or frivolous but might be thought to constitute an important adjunct to moral reasoning and intuition.

Martha Nussbaum stresses the connection between ethical significance and emotional response in her discussion of the connection between literature and ethics. For Nussbaum, emotions are cognitive, involving "beliefs about how things are and what is important."[3] According to Jesse Kalin, Nussbaum further identifies emotions with disclosures of and responses to value.[4] This view might lead one to draw close parallels between Nussbaum's hypotheses and those of Max Scheler, since he ties the moral significance of emotion to its disclosure of value. However, in Scheler's account, feeling is a perception of value entirely distinct from intellectual cognition, a view I cannot think Nussbaum intends to support.[5] The associations she makes between belief and emotion have persisted, reemerging in her most recent work.[6]

Nussbaum's elaborated view of the connection between emotion and fiction is in some respects reminiscent of Ronald de Sousa's speculation that emotional reactions to art can constitute emergent emotional structures, providing us with fresh paradigm scenarios in terms of which we respond to situations.[7] She stresses that stories that enable us to learn what our society and culture value "first construct and then evoke (and strengthen) the experience of feeling."[8] Fiction has frequently been linked to moral education and development. Not only do philosophers emphasize that stories can provide an understanding of society and its expectations, but many go on to emphasize the importance of characteristic "storytelling categories" in our understanding of human actions and our assessment of moral responsibility for those actions.[9]

Further, as Edward Sankowski has pointed out, a great many of our ascriptions of blame in fictional contexts appear to have the same grounds as our ascriptions of blame in nonfictional situations.[10] I propose that such

---

3. Martha C. Nussbaum, *Love's Knowledge: Essays on Philosophy and Literature* (New York: Oxford University Press, 1990), 41.

4. Jesse Kalin, "Knowing Novels: Nussbaum on Fiction and Moral Theory," *Ethics* 103 (1992): 40.

5. For example, see the discussion of Scheler in *What Is an Emotion?*, 217.

6. See Christopher Hitchen's review of Nussbaum's *Poetic Justice* (Boston: Beacon, 1996), entitled "Stuck in Neutral: The Place of Feeling in Law and Politics," *Times Literary Supplement*, 15 March 1996, p. 9–10.

7. Ronald de Sousa, *The Rationality of Emotion* (Cambridge: MIT Press, 1990), 263.

8. Nussbaum, "Narrative Emotions," in *Love's Knowledge*, 294.

9. As does Edward Sankowski in "Blame, Fictional Characters, and Morality," *Journal of Aesthetic Education* 22 (1988): 57.

10. Sankowski, "Blame, Fictional Characters, and Morality," 49–61.

grounds can involve our more general normative judgments. Existentially uncommitted construals, especially those involved in a response to fiction, can be grounded in universal or general normative judgments, as can existentially committed construals. When watching the film *Alien*, I can construe the fictional corporate policymakers whose decisions endanger the personnel on Ripley's ship as self-interested, short-sighted, and sleazy. I can and do make similar construals concerning actual corporate policy-makers whose decisions lead to the exposure of their personnel to hazard-ous waste and of the public to toxic pollutants. Both of these construals are grounded in a repertoire of universal judgments about responsibility, accountability, and, generally, what it is wrong to do to others. My sincere contempt for persons of this kind spans both the actual and the fictional, on roughly the same evaluative grounds. That is, one can regard the thought of such people and actions with anger and contempt, whether they are fictional or not, in part because one believes what one does about these kinds of actions.

The beliefs under consideration here need not be well-established or fully articulated, nor need they be thought unalterable. Evaluations estab-lished by past experience have been said to guide our reaction and atten-tion, but they could also guide it in a way that leads to the alteration of our doxastic repertoire. A hitherto unconsidered thought might prompt us to call a belief into question or to expose conflicts between one norma-tive judgment and others, leading us to alter or add to our fund of evalua-tions. Thus, I do not wish to maintain that emotional reactions to fiction are wholly determined by preexisting evaluations, for fiction can afford unique and sometimes transformative opportunities for insight into our normative appraisals.

Indeed, it has even been held that fiction can sometimes enable us to achieve *more* in the way of universalization from particular to general cases, and more in the way of recognizing the universal in the particular, than can many of our everyday experiences of real objects. Fiction is intended to convey meaning and, ideally, to place the nature of certain kinds of human capacities and experiences into sharp relief. Its form is compressed; it is not intended to encompass the extraneous. Leo Hickey argues that this is what we turn to fiction for, what allows us to take it *as* meaningful, whereas this is not necessarily an attitude we will adopt toward an unrelated sequence of incidents in our lives.[11] Fiction's capacity

---

11. Leo Hickey, "The Particular and the General in Fiction," *Journal of Aesthetics and Art Criticism* 30 (1972): 327–31.

to enable us to recognize the universal in the particular seems evident when the connection between belief and emotion is considered.

I have referred to the general evaluative beliefs that can ground emotional response to fiction as existentially uncommitted because they are beliefs about universals. They are not about any particular state of affairs but about how certain states of affairs are to be classified. There is some commitment here, I think, to the possibility of states of affairs of the kind the belief concerns, but not to any actual state of affairs. In contrast to responses to actual events, which involve existentially committed beliefs about particular situations, reactions to the fictional have been associated with universal judgments. As Peter Lamarque and Stein Haugom Olsen point out, Aristotle's contrast between poetry and history exhibits this distinction, associating the poetic with the universal and the historical with the particular. Lamarque and Olsen indicate that descriptions of the fictional can be used to describe the actual and that fictions invite us to imagine that there are, for instance, people who instantiate certain characteristics.[12] Characterizations, or sets of characteristics, can also be instantiated in the actual world. We can believe that the characteristics whose instantiation we imagine are, could be, or could have been, actually instantiated.

We also have beliefs about the properties whose possession may be contingent on the instantiation of such characteristics, in particular, the evaluative beliefs I have just described as beliefs about universals. These are beliefs that certain characteristics, when instantiated, can be classified or categorized in certain ways. Thus, my angry response to the corporate moguls of *Alien* involves my imagining that the characteristics of greed, self-interest, and disregard for others are instantiated in certain people. I believe that to possess such characteristics (to perform those kinds of actions or to be that kind of person) is contemptible.[13] That is, I believe that if an individual were to possess or instantiate such characteristics, that person would be contemptible. This belief is instrumental in my entertaining thoughts of *Alien*'s corporate money-grubbers contemptuously. Further, my imagining contemptible people is contingent on my entertaining the thought of people who instantiate characteristics whose possession I believe to be contemptible.

---

12. Peter Lamarque and Stein Haugom Olsen, *Truth, Fiction, and Literature: A Philosophical Perspective* (Oxford: Clarendon Press, 1994), 121, 96–101.

13. As has already been indicated in previous chapters, Bijoy Boruah maintains that similar evaluative beliefs accompany our responses to fiction: *Fiction and Emotion: A Study in Aesthetics and the Philosophy of Mind* (Oxford: Clarendon Press, 1988).

The relationship between what is imagined and what one believes is far more complex than this, for we are not possessed of a set of ready-made and concrete judgments applicable to every conceivable combination of characteristics whose instantiation we may imagine, nor do we always consciously attend to such judgments in the course of emotional response. However, many of our beliefs can be said to be held dispositionally, for we certainly cannot be consciously aware of all the things we believe at a given instant. Some of our beliefs may also never have been fully articulated, in the sense of having been acquired by a process of conscious deliberation or conscious acceptance (e.g., the belief that one is aware of black marks on paper at this moment). Such beliefs may nevertheless guide the focus of our attention and influence our response.

LOVE'S BEST GUESS: THE MERELY FICTIONAL

I doubt she's read a novel since an overdose of Georgette Heyer made her marry your father. Books can be dangerous.
Fay Weldon, *Letters to Alice on First Reading Jane Austen*

This is not a book exclusively about Literature, whose capital supports and warrants the kind of reverence to which other philosophers have already done justice.[14] This is a book about fiction, some of which is bad and more of which is not considered art at all, at least according to the criteria put forward by innumerable aestheticians. Yet it has been suggested that fictions may constitute construals of the human condition in themselves. Martha Nussbaum proposes that literature can present us with distinctive ethical conceptions of life and how it should be lived.[15] Does this apply to *all* fictions, to the trashy as well as the sublime?

Clearly not all fictions convey anything as intellectually taxing as an ethical conception of life, unless such conceptions extend to the extraordinarily simplistic. "Winning is good" hardly constitutes a conception of life, let alone an ethical one. It is not about life as a whole but about particular competitive situations that may arise in the course of it. It is not about what one believes should be the case or about what one believes should be done but about what one may value or desire. "One ought always to act so as to fulfill one's desires or so as to obtain what one values"

---

14. As has Martha Nussbaum in her essays in *Love's Knowledge*.
15. Nussbaum, *Love's Knowledge*, 26–27.

is, on the other hand, a normative conception. The latter, however, is less likely to be conveyed by the works presently under consideration. There are films that offer us little more than comic books with special effects, those multimillion-dollar effects usually providing the stimulus for affective response. One need look no further than Aristotle's *Poetics* for a commentary on such tactics: "Pity and fear may be aroused by spectacular means; but they may also result from the inner structure of the piece, which is the better way, and indicates a superior poet. . . . To produce this effect by the mere spectacle is a less artistic method, and dependent on extraneous aids. Those who employ spectacular means to create a sense not of the terrible but only the monstrous, are strangers to the purpose of Tragedy."[16]

Films of this kind frequently rely on eliciting the startle response and on shocked reactions of revulsion to or withdrawal from visual stimuli. The startle response seems less a reaction to fictional objects and events than it does a response to a sudden change in one's perceived environment. It is not clear that instinctive responses such as these *can* involve any construal that specifically concerns fictional events or objects. Indeed, I think that a few apparently genuine emotional responses to such movies owe more to the musical score than the fictional states of affairs depicted in the film. Whatever the status of affective responses to music may be, and I will not belabor Plato and Aristotle on that point, this makes it even less likely that it is exclusively the fictional event that moves us in such cases.

There are also, I think, novels that resort to the spectacular by dwelling lovingly on explosions, gun duels to the death, and acts of extraordinary violence. They cannot startle in the same way a film can, of course. Yet, to the extent they are intended to arouse shock and excitement by the spectacular nature of what is described, they too depend, as Aristotle puts it, on creating a sense of the monstrous rather than the terrible. My point here is that the reaction to reading such scenes is frequently not one of concern for the protagonists (fear or pity for them) or distress at their situation. Instead, it can frequently be a reaction of distress or shock at the very *idea* of something. This is especially true of novels like Bret Easton Ellis's *American Psycho*. In this case, I wonder whether the events described are still contemplated in the context of the world one imagines. The kind of outrage at the author of *American Psycho* that such shock and distress have involved demonstrates that it is not invariably directed toward the fictional. That is, it may be the thought (a belief) of the author's

---

16. Aristotle, *Poetics* XIV, 1–2, trans. S. H. Butcher (New York: Hill and Wang, 1961), 78.

attention-getting tactics and ideas that is entertained emotionally, rather than the thought (imagined) of the villain's machinations.

In any case, none of the points made here preclude a genuine emotional response to these kinds of fictions, though my suggestions may demonstrate that these can be less frequent than one might initially assume. There are also examples of books and films that resemble comic books yet do not resort either to the spectacular or the shocking. The supermarket shelves are filled with works whose plots and characters are formulaic and stereotypical. Few of these offer any but simplistic conceptions of human life or experience. If they endorse some particular value it is often that which is assumed to be held by the lowest common denominator evidenced among members of the buying public. Such works may move us to entertain the thought of a beleaguered heroine pityingly or to contemplate with trepidation what awaits an adventurous undercover officer, but they seldom provide us with a new way of looking at our lives or ourselves. That is, they seldom lead us to change, add to, contest, or even consider our repertoire of evaluative beliefs. Judgments from which such emotional responses stem are frequently as formulaic as that to which we respond, a catechism of the obvious (e.g., to murder innocent people for one's own entertainment is bad). Such fictions may describe or depict events and people we have not experienced in life, but these are seldom events or people that we attend to seriously enough to produce reflections on or assumptions about life or the human condition. They do not typically call our attention to hitherto unnoticed facets of human nature or experience.

The question of form and style will be dealt with in later chapters, though it is worth noting that these affect the impact fictions have on us in most cases. I speak of most cases rather than all, because the kind of symphonic harmony between form and content typically associated with excellence is no more instrumental to our being moved by a fiction than an imaginative engagement and intimacy that may select unprecedented or unusual objects. For now, it is simply worth noting that the ascription of moral significance to fiction is fully warranted neither by affective reactions during the course of its contemplation nor by an occasional emotional response that is grounded in some commonly held normative judgment few would think to dispute. Fictions are morally significant for us when our responses to them call our existing judgments into play: when we become newly aware of these judgments as challenged or substantiated, or when we add to their number. For instance, normative generalizations to which we may have (consciously or unconsciously) adhered may be challenged in the course of entertaining the thought of an exception to such a generalization. Fictions can have moral significance when what they depict or describe (and what follows may be a function of the quality of the depiction or description) affords a construal of human life and experience that goes beyond the particular fictional objects and events that demonstrate it.

This does not depend, of course, on whether the fiction in question is considered literature or art. I think that the spectacular and the formulaic make the kind of response described in the preceding paragraph less likely. However, the ultimate determinant of anything we can honestly call moral significance must rest on how one takes the fiction, not on whether the fiction takes the critics aback or by storm.

The provision of a morally significant construal of human life or experience need not involve explicit ethical endorsements of, say, one mode of living and behaving over another. Even implicit endorsements or condemnations may not be involved. A work could simply demonstrate the way that one particular perspective on life and how it should be lived could play itself out, without either explicit or implicit editorializing. The fact remains, however, that such editorializing is common enough to raise certain questions. A lot has been written about the difficulties we experience with works that endorse an ethical perspective drastically different from our own, and this is the topic of the next section.

MORAL CONFLICT AND THE LIMITS OF THE IMAGINATION

Can we imagine a world in which some particular act is blameless when we take that *kind* of act to be reprehensible in most contexts? Can we imagine as right the kind of act that we believe is wrong? Hume raises such questions in his essay "Of the Standard of Taste" when he considers cases in which viewers of a play or readers of a novel are confronted with the endorsement of conduct they would typically think immoral.[17] It is his contention, one with which I will in part concur, that such a work can fail (imaginatively or emotionally) to engage the viewer or reader.

Such endorsements are taken to constitute deformities and to disfigure the work. It should be made clear at the outset that Hume is not advocating legal moralism or espousing a form of aesthetic evaluation that harks back to Plato's *Republic*. I will argue that Hume's point is not about which

---

17. David Hume, "Of the Standard of Taste," in *Of the Standard of Taste and Other Essays* (New York: Bobbs-Merrill, 1965), 21–22.

works it is proper to enjoy, but about human psychology. Further, I will contend that Hume's observations grant to literature a moral import and human significance that militate against attempts to trivialize all fiction as nothing more than a form of occasionally exalted recreation. Hume characterizes beauty and deformity as sentiments and sees sentiment as the ultimate source of morality and moral judgment. Neither morality nor taste are thereby relativized. They become not radically subjective but *inter*subjective, in that Hume suggests our faculties are constituted so as to respond in a like manner to like interpretations of phenomena. I believe that it is the connection between emotions and our repertoire of moral judgments that may motivate Hume's contention about our imaginative capacities.

The claim about resistance presently under consideration is not the same as that made by Stanley Cavell in "The Avoidance of Love: A Reading of *King Lear*."[18] For Cavell, a reader's resisting a text can be like Lear's resisting human engagement: it can be or embody a failure to acknowledge truths about oneself.[19] Certainly, this can sometimes be true of a reader's experience. Indeed, the contention resonates with many of the claims of Peter McCormick that were discussed in the preceding chapter, for McCormick suggests that the experiences of characters may ultimately refer to our own. However, the resistance with which Hume concerns himself, while equally personal, is differently focused. Hume's claim could be grounded in an assumption of the viewer's incapacity to enter imaginatively into an endorsement made by the work, the inability to *imagine* right the kind of act that one *believes* is wrong.

It is seldom (with the exception of moralizing authorial narration such as that of Thackeray in *Vanity Fair*) that ethical assessments of actions and behaviors are *explicitly* presented as true in the world of a work. A character's assessment merely makes it fictional that someone holds a certain moral belief, not that this belief is true. Yet we all understand the problem of which Hume speaks. An implicit endorsement of behavior can seem to be made when no apparently upright character finds it objectionable or when a protagonist endowed with heroic virtues exhibits it. There may be implicit condemnation when the behavior appalls every character save the apparently villainous or when it is shown to have terrible consequences. What Hume is asks whether we can enter into the perspective of the endorser. The connection between normative assessment and emo-

18. Stanley Cavell, "The Avoidance of Love: A Reading of *King Lear*," in *Must We Mean What We Say? A Book of Essays* (New York: Charles Scribner and Sons, 1969), 267–353.
19. Ibid., 312–13.

tion is not difficult to see. If it is true that normative assessments accompany certain kinds of emotional reactions, then it appears that responding with outrage or indignation to fictional conduct involves or incorporates some belief that to behave in the way the character has, or to instantiate the characteristics the character does, is to be blameworthy in some respect. When Hume suggests that we cannot imagine as right the kind of act that we believe is wrong, he may be indicating that we cannot believe that the characteristics we imagine could make an act permissible, were those characteristics to be instantiated. Conversely, to enter into a work's endorsement could be to regard a depicted action with approval and to make a corresponding judgment about that *kind* of action. It could be to imagine the instantiation of characteristics whose instantiation one believed sufficient for permissibility or acceptability.

One might object that while fictions certainly move us, they do not inspire belief unless we are deranged. Instead, fictions lead us to entertain thoughts in imagination without thereby assenting to them. The propositions that could be held to express these thoughts can be ludicrously false, as in the case of horror films. If we do not balk at imagining vampires, space aliens, and other entities in whose existence we do not believe, why should the imagination boggle at imagining the rightness of an act? As Kendall Walton inquires, "There is science fiction; why not morality fiction?"[20]

Two points should be made in response to this. We can of course know *why* someone might believe an act permissible, why the morals or manners of another age would dictate values to which we do not adhere. Yet this is not to imagine the rightness of an act. Imagining an act's rightness does not simply involve imagining a character regarding the act approvingly, nor is it the mere entertainment of the hypothesis that something morally acceptable has transpired. Rather, it may involve imagining the instantiation of characteristics we believe sufficient for moral acceptability.

Further, the resistance Hume describes appears to involve more than a fear that one's imagining will somehow lead to the adoption of views with which one disagrees or that it will play havoc with one's ordinary moral orientation. Kendall Walton suggests these as possible interpretations but goes on to consider a third. Perhaps, he indicates, what is involved is one's inability to understand how the relation of dependence between moral

---

20. Kendall Walton, "Morals in Fiction and Fictional Morality (I)," *Proceedings of the Aristotelian Society*, suppl. 68 (1994): 37.

properties and those natural properties upon which one takes them to supervene could *differ* from what one thinks it to be.[21] However, Walton is uncertain about whether this can fully explain our imaginative resistance in the kinds of cases that Hume describes. I think that an explanation that links our general normative assessments to the emotional reactions involved in our imaginative engagement with fictions may go some way toward providing such an explanation, for Hume himself states that morality is determined by sentiment.

Consider a film or story in which the protagonist effects the rescue of another character. If the scene moves us to admiration, then we have focused attention on certain of its aspects rather than others: the protagonist's courage in the face of danger, her acumen in dispatching the villains. If we did not consider courage and acumen of this *kind* laudable—the kind instantiated in the scene we contemplate—we would not entertain the thought of the heroine's actions admiringly or approvingly. It is the belief that certain *kinds* of acts (or acts that have certain *kinds* of results) are admirable and the focus of imaginative attention on those aspects of the fictional states of affairs that involve the instantiation of relevant characteristics (e.g., courage) that can elicit an emotional response. The evaluative belief in question is not existentially committed but universal, a belief about kinds of acts or consequences rather than specific ones, a belief about how certain characteristics can be evaluated.

I should stress that our imaginative capacities are wider-ranging than the preceding analysis would at first seem to allow. Consider an example that appears to involve just the sort of departure from one's normative repertoire that Hume describes. Jane Austen's Fanny Price, ensconced in *Mansfield Park* as its unheeded conscience, is a font of moral sensitivities whose ethical forebodings are inevitably verified. Her disapproval of the staging of a play is justified retroactively by the unpleasantness consequent on the staging effort. Thus, the views of Fanny seem to be endorsed. Fanny's pious propriety would appear inaccessible to modern audiences, if considered in terms of her specific moral valuations. Could a case be made for an outright conflict of judgment? I love amateur theatricals, and many of my other convictions are opposed to Fanny's. Surely, then, I could not wholly enter into the ethical perspective of *Mansfield Park*. On the face of it, it does not seem that I could entertain the thought of the play with disapproval.

Thankfully, neither Austen's perspective nor our moral engagement

---

21. Ibid., 46.

with fiction is that simple. There is a distinct ethical perspective in Austen's writing, but it cannot be extracted by examining the moral sentiments of the characters themselves out of the context of the work. We see
repeatedly in Austen an affiliation of the moral with the personal and
emotional. The wrongness of putting on the play is a wrongness of bringing together certain personalities in a certain context. There is a wrongness in how these people will feel about themselves and toward each
other. This is perfectly possible to imagine: the guilt of some, the distress of
others, the damage these do. In this sense, it is possible for someone who
approves of playacting and questions obsolete proprieties to imagine the
wrongness of putting on the play. Indeed, Austen herself questions out-
dated proprieties that have no ethical basis. It is perhaps the unique ethical
perspective her works afford that makes them more accessible to us than
others of the same period. We are not bludgeoned with a series of normative assessments in her work but are imaginatively placed in situations
where we can make them ourselves. Fiction, at its best, rehearses our
normative repertoire by leading us both to make judgments and to become
aware of judgments we have already made.

I return to Hume to find a demonstration of conflict with ethical construals inherent in a work. What of a work "where vicious manners are
described, without being marked with the proper characters of blame"?[22]
What comes forcibly to mind is a scene from the film *Gone with the Wind*,
which my feminist students inform me has been discussed in their wom-
en's studies courses. This scene features an apparent prelude to a forcible
rape, an act which is depicted as having no negative consequences, since
the heroine is shown to be retroactively delighted by the incident. This is
disturbing for several reasons. First, the story is a historical romance, and
while Rhett Butler's actions are not always endorsed, it is pretty clear that
this one is not condemned. In the world of the film, no one is victimized by
this action. No one is harmed; hence, the action is not harmful; hence, it is
not (or does not seem to be) wrong in the world of the work. In that world,
I presume, Scarlett's objections are not sincere, or at least are unconsciously insincere. Yet this perspective makes of the heroine a child who
does not know what she wants and whom it is therefore permissible to
compel.

To imagine Rhett Butler's action blameless is to consider the heroine the
kind of person whom it is appropriate to coerce on account of her denial of

---

22. Hume, "Of the Standard of Taste," in *Of the Standard of Taste and Other Essays*,
21–22.

her own desires. Since few of us believe that an autonomous adult's lack of familiarity with her own desires justifies coercion, our normative beliefs could be directly at odds with construals implicit in the work. This could prevent imagining the act approvingly. Alternatively, the heroine's eventual complacence could be seen as fundamentally incompatible with the force of her initial objections. Such a perceived inconsistency could also lead to imaginative disengagement.

It may once again be objected that fictions always invite us to entertain false propositions in imagination. The fact that some incident in a fiction is *unlikely* should not boggle an acknowledged watcher of fictional monsters. Its being fictionally the case that some normative proposition is true in the world of the work should not be any more disturbing than its being fictionally true that there is a monster. These things are *fictional*. Why expect them to be true? Assumptions about what is believed possible and what is not will be addressed later in this chapter. For now, I will focus on conflict between normative judgments.

I will maintain that it is difficult to imagine true a normative judgment one believes false and that this difficulty need not impugn one's imaginative capacities. In what has gone before, I have linked emotional construals to evaluative beliefs. In the case of fictions, such construals are tied to existentially uncommitted judgments. The trepidation about playacting that I share with Fanny Price has to do with the evaluative belief that to suspend social conventions when the suspension can exacerbate vulnerabilities may be productive of disaffection and unhappiness.

What, then, about the scene in the film? Rhett Butler's actions in the scene are presented at the very least as blameless and shown not to lead to unhappiness. Indeed, it could be argued that they are construed as dashing, masterful, and romantic. Consider the construal of the behavior as romantic. Judgments tied to the imagined insincerity of Scarlett's objections and the imagined desire to have those objections ignored remain problematic. We could consider the belief that the abnegation of responsibility, not only for one's actions and decisions but for one's body and self, constitutes romance. There is, I acknowledge, some attractiveness in the denial or rejection of *all* responsibility, but it is the attractiveness of the womb, the attractiveness of being no one. A conception of romance based on any such construal has to do neither with the enjoyment of love nor the enjoyment of sex but with the enjoyment of not being accountable, either to others or to oneself. Walton might even point out that the natural properties upon which a property like "romantic" was taken to supervene could, for many persons, run counter to these and could thus make it impossible for them to imagine the act in question romantic.

Let us assume that someone denies outright any such belief about romance, and let us further assume that he or she denies the belief that it is permissible to coerce someone despite that person's objections when the sincerity of those objections is suspect. Those who reject such beliefs will experience difficulty in imagining Rhett Butler's particular actions romantic. It will be difficult to entertain the thought of these actions approvingly or admiringly, because construals of fictional situations are grounded in already existing or newly formed normative judgments whose application transcends the fictional. The reason we cannot dismiss all fictions as frivolous or trivial is that they can bring much of our normative apparatus into play; they can offer different perspectives on and construals of human experience. This particular scene in the film is one that can be taken to offer a false construal of physical coercion as romantic.

Naturally, it could be held that it was possible to regard the relationship between Rhett and Scarlett as exciting and romantic without thereby subscribing to any judgments of the sort described. In fact, I agree. However, quite different aspects of the fictional situation become salient in this case. Where the attention is focused on the imagined attraction of the characters toward one another, rather than on physical actions and verbal and physical resistance, the kind of conflict presently under discussion need never arise.

I do not claim it is the business of the reader or viewer to do the moral assessing rather than its being the business of the fiction to provide an avenue to assessment. That kind of view is based on a misapprehension, for it can be the prerogative of literature to lead us through a kind of moral reasoning by imaginatively acquainting us with its grounds and its conception of what is salient. This can lead to new and different apprehensions of the human condition, to new applications of preexisting judgments, to awareness of conflicts among existing beliefs, or simply to a standstill.

The last may occur when we encounter something we take to be a false construal of human nature or experience tied to a general normative judgment that we cannot consider other than false. It involves an inability or disinclination to make what one considers a false normative judgment, one applicable to the actual as well as the fictional. One can resist entertaining the thought of a particular act approvingly when one believes that kind of conduct is not permissible. To construe an act right is to focus attention on the thought of what are believed to be the act's right-making features. In order to imagine an act approvingly, a normative judgment about what such right-making features may be is requisite. When the imaginatively contemplated action does not instantiate features believed to conduce to rightness, one must alter one's existing judgments about what such characteristics may be if one is to enter into the construal implicit in the work. I am not claiming that our doxastic repertoire is a grim bulwark that fiction cannot penetrate, but I am claiming that what we believe and what we can be brought to believe when we engage in acts of imaginative construal and construction have a great deal to do with how it is we imagine certain states of affairs.

Yet if evaluative beliefs are the guides of an attention necessary for emotional response, how could attending to the thought of some hitherto unconsidered state of affairs cause a change in those beliefs? Any such claim seems viciously circular. In responding, it is important to note that judgments about *kinds* of acts or events could take the form of hasty or biased generalizations. Entertaining a sequence of thoughts that embodied a counterexample to such generalizations could, in principle, lead to the alteration of beliefs, if the attention were focused in certain ways by *other* beliefs one held.

Consider someone who takes an extreme stand on matters involving freedom of speech and expression. This individual believes that censorship is never justified. No circumstance, no particular content, could warrant the suppression of a speech act. Let us further assume this lover of liberty is confronted by the thought of an event (either fictional or actual) that brings John Stuart Mill's harm principle to the fore. Perhaps he entertains thoughts of a trusted media personality who begins to indulge in outrageous fabrications that his audience takes as gospel and that prompt this audience to perform criminal and violent acts.

Our hypothetical subject does not initially focus his attention on matters involving the freedom of speech but only on depictions or descriptions of a resultant harm. As he watches a film or news report, he entertains the thought of the pain and death of innocent individuals with distress. Since he believes that harming innocent people is wrong, the focus of his attention shifts to the thought of the perpetrators and their motivations. Let us assume that these motivations are presented as being based on complete misapprehensions fostered by the aforementioned media personality. The thought of the media personality may now be entertained angrily and disapprovingly. Our subject disapproves of people who intend to cause harm to others by telling lies. He believes that such actions are wrong. It is at this point that a reformulation of his doxastic repertoire is, in principle, possible. The belief that it is impermissible to suppress *any* speech act may undergo modification.

Evaluative judgments that guide emotional response and are necessary for the serious focus of attention on certain thoughts may also direct that attention in ways that call other judgments into question. My example is simplistic. Actual reassessments would have to be far more subtle and complex. Also, realistically, a brief awareness of inconsistency among one's beliefs might be ignored. However, it seems that one can claim without circularity both that evaluative beliefs guide the conceptions of salience in emotional response and that particular patterns of attention can alter evaluative beliefs. Patterns of attention can bring existing beliefs into play in new contexts and can expose inconsistencies among one's evaluations.

I am far from believing that any single encounter with a text can effectively reconfigure a reader's normative repertoire. However, I do believe that a pattern of imaginative engagement with texts, and in particular employment of the empathetic imagination, can gradually alter that to which one is inclined to attend and the manner in which one may be disposed to attend to it. Of all imaginative exercises, empathy is especially notable for its ethical significance in nonfictional as well as fictional contexts, something that adds even more weight to the contention that fictions can be morally important for us. This subject will be explored at length in Chapter 6.

I suggest that general or universal evaluative beliefs are necessary components or concomitants of emotional response to fiction—necessary, that is, insofar as they influence the attention. This would not preclude our calling such a response irrational if a case could be made for calling the evaluative belief itself unjustified. Still, the proposal accords with my view that fictions can have considerable moral significance and accords with our sense that it would be very odd indeed if someone who loathed a character on account of a particular trait should have formed no normative beliefs whatsoever about the trait itself.

The passage in Hume's "Of the Standard of Taste" indicates that we may sometimes find ourselves incapable of entering into the sentiments of certain characters, for this would "pervert the sentiments" of our own hearts.[23] Even fictional actions, then, can involve us in moral evaluation, for the requisite change in sentiment, says Hume, would involve a change in judgment. Our being moved or, indeed, our failure to respond may provide evidence that such evaluations are made. Even in a passage concerning our response to fiction, admissible variations in taste on account of personal preference are said *not* to include our moral sentiments or the judgments that are held to accompany them.[24]

---

23. David Hume, "Of the Standard of Taste," in Eugene F. Miller, ed., *Essays: Moral, Political, and Literary* (Indianapolis: Liberty Classics, 1987), 246–47.

24. Though he does allow for some degree of variation, it should be noted that Hume

Hume's association of morality with sentiment and his denial that such a union must reduce morality to a mere matter of potentially idiosyncratic personal predilection foreshadow current trends in ethics that may also be applicable to a discussion of the fictional. Feminist philosophers doing work in ethics have long decried the all too common divorce of emotion from any matter pertaining to moral judgment. It could be argued that such a schism is not only unnecessary but fundamentally mistaken. Given the propensity of ethicists for the formulation of thought experiments designed to test the applicability or effectiveness of moral principles, and in particular thought experiments intended to provide counterexamples, it would seem that the very test of a principle's validity could sometimes depend almost entirely on our responses to and sentiments regarding a single case.[25]

From the utilitarian, we hear of cases in which adherence to a perfect duty, say that of keeping a trivial promise, would prevent one from performing the imperfect duty of effecting a rescue or saving a life. From the deontologist, we hear of cases in which minuscule increases in utility could justify atrocities (e.g., two Nobel Prize–winning physicists will survive to benefit the world if they are given the kidneys of the utilitarian). Such cases are presented to appeal neither to the moral principle at issue (since examples such as these are frequently intended to bring a rival theoretician to a sense of her principle's own iniquity) nor to the principle espoused by the provider of the counterexample (since that philosopher offers the example in order to establish the superiority of his own theoretical approach and therefore cannot assume the correctness of the approach at the outset). The point of presenting such cases, surely, is to confront the listener with a case to which he or she *reacts* as wrong, in order to demonstrate the inadequacy of the principle under consideration. Since this reaction does not rest on the principle being examined and cannot properly rest on the rival principle, it may well be suggested that the response in question rests and is intended to rest on sentiment.

In view of such a significant and basic role in serious ethical disputes, it would appear inconsistent to present such cases and simultaneously to insist that sentiment can play no serious role in moral judgment. And in

takes the principles of taste to be universal in "Of the Standard of Taste," *Essays: Moral, Political and Literary*, 241.

25. Albeit in another context, Richard Moran makes a similar point about thought experiments in ethics in "The Expression of Feeling in Imagination," *Philosophical Review* 103 (1994): 75–106. Rosemarie Tong uses such thought experiments in a critique of principled accounts in *Feminine and Feminist Ethics* (California: Wadsworth, 1993), 64.

view of the significance of such thought experiments in ethics, it is not out
of the question to suggest that fiction can be and often is just such a
thought experiment — one that can challenge or substantiate the judgments to which an individual adheres or which that individual contemplates. Even if we set the question of emotion entirely aside, fiction might
be held to retain its importance. According to M. J. Sirridge, the mere fact
that thought experiments are intended to clarify philosophical hypotheses, that they are repeatedly accorded " 'quasi-evidential' status," suggests
that fictions can have a similar status and significance.[26]

A DIGRESSION ON HUMOR

It should be noted that amusement could be thought an exception to
the contention that our evaluative beliefs and normative judgments are
closely related to our emotional response to fiction. Fictions are notorious
(though not exclusive) sources of an amusement that can appear at odds
with our normative judgments. Indeed, fiction seems at times to provide
us with an opportunity to regard the thought of acts or experiences we
ordinarily believe unjust or painful with positive hilarity. However, I do not
believe that claims of this sort constitute conclusive counterexamples to
an account that draws a connection between the normative or evaluative
and the emotional.

First, if amusement is to be regarded as an emotion at all, it can be
characterized in terms of construal. It is possible to construe something as
funny or humorous, just as it is possible to construe something as dangerous. The only difficulty lies in the fact that, in the case of fear, for instance,
we can easily delimit the dangerous in terms of threats (potential or actual)
to life or health or well-being. The dangerous is tied to a particular kind of
thought that can be identified by its content. Can the same be said of
humor? It might be held that humor is not so unequivocal in its objects.

However, many theorists have offered a cognitive characterization of
humor or amusement, just as cognitive characterizations of emotion have
been proposed, and these accounts are frequently accompanied by hypotheses about the characteristic objects of amusement. In his book on
humor, P. E. McGhee indicates he "concluded that humor seemed to be

---

26. M. J. Sirridge, "Truth from Fiction?," *Philosophy and Phenomenological Research*
35 (1975): 471.

essentially a cognitive or intellectual experience, and that incongruity was a necessary (although not sufficient) prerequisite."[27] Research into humor stretches across many fields, and the connection between humor and incongruity has emerged repeatedly.[28] Even linguistic analyses of humor focus on issues that could be taken to fall under the concept of incongruity, e.g., linking the humorous to defeated discourse expectations.[29] John Morreall traces the incongruity theory of humor from the work of Aristotle, through accounts developed by Kant and Schopenhauer, and up to the present day.[30] It is the contention of Morreall and others who ally humor with incongruity that "amusement is the enjoyment of something that clashes with our mental expectations,"[31] that it involves a perception of incongruity.[32]

While none appear to hold that the apprehension of incongruity guarantees amusement (in part, because shock or puzzlement may also be responses to perceived incongruity), such an apprehension is usually regarded as necessary. Thus, the incongruity associated specifically with amusement is further associated by Morreall with the absence of tension and with freedom from practical concerns.[33] The mental jolt tied to incongruity is enjoyed when one is amused; it is not found disturbing or regarded as something about which one's understanding needs to be rectified.[34] The stipulation about freedom from practical concerns makes it more likely that incongruities will be enjoyed in fictional contexts. As discussed in Chapter 2, motivations to intervention are conspicuously absent in most responses to fictional (and historical) events. On a parallel with accounts of emotion, then, to entertain the thought of a fictional state

27. P. E. McGhee, *Humor: Its Origin and Development* (San Francisco: Freeman, 1979), viii.

28. P. Keith Spiegel's "Early Conceptions of Humor: Varieties and Issues," in J. H. Goldstein and P. E. McGhee, eds., *The Psychology of Humor: Theoretical Perspectives and Empirical Issues* (New York: Academic Press, 1972), lists twenty-four theorists who support theories linking humor to the apprehension of incongruity.

29. For instance, Elizabeth J. Pretorius offers such an analysis of one of my favorite scenes in Monty Python's *In Search of the Holy Grail*: that of the interchange between King Arthur and the Marxist peasant. This is discussed in her "Humor as Defeated Discourse Expectations: Conversational Exchange in a Monty Python Text," *Humor* 3 (1990): 259–76.

30. John Morreall, ed., *The Philosophy of Laughter and Humor* (Albany: SUNY Press, 1987), chaps. 8–9.

31. John Morreall, "Enjoying Incongruity," *Humor* 2 (1989): 1.

32. For instance, see also Giovannantonio Forabosco, "Cognitive Aspects of the Humor Process: The Concept of Incongruity," *Humor* 5 (1992): 45.

33. Morreall, "Enjoying Incongruity," 1–18.

34. Ibid., 9.

of affairs with amusement is to construe that state of affairs as incongruous. The thought entertained in imagination would be of or about the kind of incident or action regarded as benignly incongruous.

Given this, however, could it not be objected that the same thought could be entertained both with amusement and another, seemingly incompatible emotion? Consider the film *A Fish Called Wanda*, in which a novice hit man of shattering incompetence is given the mission of eradicating the key witness in a trial. The hit man is an animal lover. The witness is a crotchety woman who possesses several small yappy dogs. Unlike others, I am very fond of small yappy dogs. One of my own dogs is small and, when the spirit moves her, exceedingly yappy. I am therefore the last person in the world to find amusement in the eradication of diminutive and noisy canines. Yet whenever the incompetent and animal-loving hit man concocts an apparently foolproof plan for eliminating the witness (dropping a large object on her from the second floor, for example) it inevitably goes awry and takes a canine victim in her stead, much to the hit man's chagrin. I was not amused by the dogs' eradication. In fact I was sorry about it. I even felt sorry for the hit man, who quite sensibly preferred dogs to people. Yet the continual reversal of carefully laid plans, the continual occurrence of the least desired result, the perpetual refinement and foiling of ludicrous murder techniques, was, I will admit, hilarious. That is, I entertained the thought of the latter states of affairs with amusement and entertained the thought of the dogs' demise with regret. My amusement and my regret involved different thoughts of different states of affairs. In a manner of speaking, my amusement and my regret had different objects.

To imagine something with amusement is to focus attention on certain features of the fictional situation rather than others, on the dissonance and reversals typically associated with incongruity. It seems, then, that amusement need not preclude or replace other responses. The thought that is entertained with amusement may be a thought of or about only one aspect of a fictional incident: a feature of it the agent apprehends as incongruous. Clearly a fictional state of affairs can give rise to many thoughts about any number of its aspects. It is unclear, therefore, that amusement and more negative emotions like fear or distress must necessarily be tied to precisely the same thought. In such a case, two different thoughts may simply be entertained in two different ways.

Amusement may, of course, be held to involve extrafictional objects, even amusement felt during an encounter with fiction. The way words are juxtaposed may be found amusing, a turn of phrase or a pun may amuse us, and while its utterance may be fictional, the pun or phrase need not be so regarded. It may be fictional that a character has told a funny joke, but an audience member may regard that joke as evidence of the script writer's skill rather than the fictional person's wit. The joke might be regarded as a good joke *simpliciter*, perhaps as one the subject wants to repeat, rather than a fictional joke. That is, it could be held that the utterance of the joke is imagined but that the joke could be considered in contexts other than the fictional or imaginary. In such cases, it might be held that the agent is not responding to fictional entities or events, though his response is still based on an apprehension of incongruity.

It should also be noted that abusive humor, humor that involves making fun *of* some individual or group or involves finding amusement in people's discomfiture, may not involve an apprehension of incongruity alone. That is, it does not seem to involve that apprehension *exclusively*. This kind of humor is frequently allied with contempt, resentment, or smugness, and may rely on rendering salient those aspects of an individual's or group's characteristics or behavior that could be construed as inferior, incompetent, unattractive, or wanting in some other way. Here, some negative evaluation or attitude seems to have a subsidiary role in guiding the response. This is, I think, why so many construe certain instances of such humor as offensive: they take it to involve insults. However, there is no conflict with the account proposed in this chapter. For instance, a reaction of vindictive amusement to a scene featuring someone's discomfiture may involve not just the thought of an incongruity but the thought of the individual's deserts.

Consider a scene from one of the *Lethal Weapon* movies in which the protagonists, to their great chagrin, have been demoted to the rank of patrolman. Frustrated by their predicament and tired of the tedious routine, they accost a jaywalker. They lead him to believe — although the audience is well aware of their insincerity — that the price of his jaywalking may be death. In other words, their conduct could be regarded as sadistic. An innocent person is terrorized simply to amuse the protagonists and alleviate their boredom. Yet audiences were highly amused by this scene. Why? First, the scenario does possess features that could be classified as incongruous, the reversal of the policeman's role from that of protector to that of potential assailant being a case in point. Second, the victim of the protagonists' harassment does not take them seriously at first. His initial attitude toward the protagonists is irritated and contemptuous. He does not respect their authority. An additional incongruity in the situation might thus be found in the drastic reversal of the jaywalker's attitude toward the protagonists: a shift from irritated contempt to extreme fear. Further, negative audience attitudes toward a particular kind of person (the kind who does not take one seriously, the kind who is disrespectful) could have contributed to some assumption about desert and mitigated tendencies to respond sympathetically to the jaywalker's plight.

A lot of hostile humor appears to involve assessments ascribing a lower moral status to some individual or group. While this is disturbing, it need not inevitably suggest the presence of beliefs many of us would consider unjustified (e.g., a belief that disrespectful persons deserve to be terrorized). The patterns of attention and associations tied to an emotional response can, in cases such as these, involve a focus on negatively evaluated characteristics that leads to estimations of diminished worth unaccompanied by any determinate assumption about what treatment this may warrant.

Audience amusement would, I think, depend on some response to incongruity. However, since the apprehension of incongruity is necessary but may be insufficient for amusement, violent or harmful situations that are found humorous would seem to involve something further: a disposition to see the object upon which the harm is inflicted as lacking full moral standing. Such a disposition could be characterized in terms of an evaluation that depended on a set of associations and a pattern of attention — in this case, on negative attitudes toward or negative associations with various manifestations of disrespect. Such associations and patterns of attending, while not fully articulated or deliberate, can contribute to a critical or unsympathetic evaluation. These considerations suggest that a reaction of amusement could be thought unwarranted. They nevertheless reinforce connections drawn among our evaluations, our patterns of attention, and our emotions.

IMAGINING POSSIBILITIES AND THE POSSIBILITY OF IMAGINING

I have attempted to establish a connection between emotional responses to fiction and evaluations that apply to both the fictional and the real. The kinship between the actual and the fictional can be further elaborated when two facets of our emotional response to fiction are considered. First, an emotional reaction to a character or fictional situation is often accompanied by an emotional response to people and situations in the world. Although this may be less likely in the case of amusement (since it is based on evaluating events apprehended as incongruous or contrary to expectation), it nonetheless suggests that the application of our normative judgments can sometimes be extended to the actual when they take on a significant role in our response to the fictional. In the first section I described such beliefs as beliefs about universals: beliefs about *kinds* of acts and events, or beliefs about characteristics that could be instantiated. This also implies that the fictional event or situation is tied to a construal of how life or experience or human nature *could be*, insofar as it involves the imaginative instantiation of certain sets of characteristics. That is, there appears to be a connection between our emotional response and the recognition that the *kind* of situation or event described in the fiction and entertained in imagination (as distinguished from the *particular* event that is imagined) could occur or could have occurred. This is the topic of the present section.

"Let me imagine," says the actress playing Virginia Woolf in Masterpiece Theater's version of *A Room of One's Own*, "what would have happened had Shakespeare had a wonderfully gifted sister, called Judith, let us say."[35] I settle into my armchair to listen, attempting to dislodge from my lap a seventy-five-pound Labrador Retriever who is under the impression that she is a lap dog. I am happy, interested. The actress is wonderful, I think. Within no more than three minutes (the script can have occupied no more than two pages) I am pacing about the room in a state of emotional upheaval. I admire Judith's flouting of convention in venturing a career in that day and age. I am enraged with those who thwart her, with the theater manager who "bellowed something about poodles dancing and women acting." I am in tears over the eventual fate of Judith, who "killed herself one winter's night and lies buried at some crossroads where the omnibuses now stop outside the Elephant and Castle."[36] I am, in short, about as moved by a fiction as I can be, to the consternation of my dog, who would have preferred a peaceful evening. She is confused. What can have gotten into me?

This is the shortest of short stories, a brief excursion in a longer essay. It is also, I think, an excellent example of how fiction can be a thought experiment, of how it can explore what *could* have happened or, indeed, what could happen. Woolf leads us to consider what could, probably would, happen to an Elizabethan woman of genius who had the effrontery to attempt its exercise. Her answer: annihilation. It is a mark of the vividness and life of Woolf's prose that so brief and incomplete a sketch is capable of grasping the imagination in a way that elicits immediate sympa-

---

35. Virginia Woolf, *A Room of One's Own* (New York: Harcourt, Brace, and World, 1929), 48.
36. Ibid., 50.

thy for the character.[37] More than that, however, we believe that this kind of incident could have occurred, that the thwarting of ambition on account of gender has occurred, does occur, and could occur in the future. Because of this, a part of our emotional response can take actual objects, can be to and about the world. Entertaining the thought of Judith's plight with pity and outrage can sometimes lead one to entertain the thought of the plights of real people in the same way.

It has been suggested that we cannot, in fact, pity people of whom we have not even heard, or pity those whose individual tragedies are unknown to us.[38] Yet we have, heard of women being prevented from the exercise of their talents by absurd societal conventions and have heard of what could ensue when such conventions were defied. No one would deny that we can pity the victims of some natural disaster whose plight is described in the papers, even though we do not know either who the victims are or how many have been victimized. If there is nothing odd in pity for the nameless victims of a natural disaster, why is it so problematic to pity the victims of abhorrent societal conventions? We are aware of the occurrence of the disaster and the existence of the conventions, just as we are aware that they had victims. Surely the fact that the societal conventions in question are pervasive, that they are not restricted to a particular time and place, does not warrant the assumption that we do not or cannot on occasion pity their victims. I believe that there have been and are women whose circumstances are similar to those of Judith, who defied convention in an effort to exercise their talents and suffered for the attempt. I do not know who all of them are, but I believe that they existed in the past and exist now.

We can also, of course, be moved by the plights of people with whom we are acquainted in the course of being moved by a fiction. As has been indicated in the preceding chapter, the experiences of characters may reactivate emotional experiences of our own or bring forcibly to mind the experiences of others who are close to us.[39] This suggests that an imaginative encounter with fiction can lead us to feel for real (as well as

---

37. The significance of such stylistic elements will be addressed in Chapters 5 and 7.

38. For instance, Colin Radford argues in this way when responding to accounts that attempt to replace, for instance, pity for a character with pity for actual persons, something that my own account does not attempt. Colin Radford, "The Essential Anna," *Philosophy* 54 (1979): 390–91, and "Replies to Three Critics," *Philosophy* 64 (1989): 94. This has already been discussed in Chapter 3.

39. This subject is discussed in the work of McCormick and Levinson. Peter McCormick, "Feelings and Fictions," *Journal of Aesthetics and Art Criticism* 43 (1985): 381, and *Fictions, Philosophies, and the Problems of Poetics* (Ithaca: Cornell University Press, 1988),

fictional) people, because of what they have experienced or could experience and because of what they have done or could do.

My intention has never been to identify fictional and possible worlds. No fictional world is such that it requires or prohibits any state of affairs whatsoever, as is the case with possible worlds.[40] I bring possibilities into the discussion because there seems to be an intimate connection between an imaginative engagement intense enough to generate an emotional response, sometimes a response that embraces real as well as fictional objects, and the belief that the *kind* of event being contemplated could occur or have occurred.[41]

I propose, in fact, that the belief that a given *kind* of event (the kind depicted or described in the fiction and upon which the attention is focused) could occur may be necessary for an emotional response to fiction.[42] The evaluative beliefs that ground our construals of fictional events and dictate the focus of our attention can draw that attention to events beyond the scope of what is imagined. My anger at those who cruelly thwart Judith's aspirations simply because she is a woman involves a construal of these imagined persons as cruel and unjust. If I believe that actions of that kind (actions that instantiate the relevant characteristics) are unjust, then I may entertain the thought of such actions angrily. It is the content of the thought entertained in imagination, in conjunction with the evaluative belief, that can lead to its being entertained with anger or irritation. The evaluative belief that it is reprehensible to thwart someone's aspirations solely on account of her gender is a belief that can apply to existing women, and it does not seem that we would hold such a belief unless we believed that such a thing *could* occur. It is also my contention that a failure to believe this of the kind of situation being imaginatively contemplated can prevent our being moved.

---

142. Jerrold Levinson, "The Place of Real Emotion in Response to Fiction," *Journal of Aesthetics and Art Criticism* 48 (1990): 79.

40. See, for instance, Nicholas Wolterstorff's discussion in *Works and Worlds of Art* (Oxford: Clarendon Press, 1980), 131–32. This is also discussed in the preceding chapter.

41. Harold Skulsky, for instance, proposes that the object or cause of our emotion may be a belief that the fictional state of affairs is logically possible ("On Being Moved by Fiction," *Journal of Aesthetics and Art Criticism* 39 [1980]: 11). I would not cast the belief as an *object* of emotion (one does not fear or pity beliefs) but think believing in the possibility of the *kind* of event one contemplates is necessary for emotion.

42. Note that this is not inapplicable to cases of amusement. If a particular fictional incident involves the kind of event I apprehend as incongruous, that would not mean I do not believe this kind of event was possible. We can, for instance, believe that unexpected incidents can occur without that belief being contravened by our failure to expect any such incident.

This claim is not particularly ambitious or far-reaching. I am mainly interested in more firmly establishing the link between our imaginative construals and our normative judgments by pointing out that there is some connection here to our beliefs about what happens or can happen in the world. I am also interested in accounting for instances of imaginative disengagement (and consequent lack of emotional response) that cannot be explained by the kind of conflict among normative judgments discussed earlier in this chapter.

My claim seems, prima facie, at odds with the role of the imagination. Surely, when we contemplate fictional states of affairs involving nonexistent sisters of Shakespeare and science fiction monsters, we do not believe them possible. Should the point not be that fiction involves our imaginings *rather* than our beliefs about what could occur in the world? At what level of abstraction, given the requisite belief in a *kind* of event or action, must conviction enter on the scene?

In responding to these questions, let me return to the story of Judith. In imagination, I entertain the thought of Judith's ambitions being thwarted on account of her gender. To thwart people's ambitions exclusively on account of their gender is, generically, the kind of act that I consider stupid and unjust. I also believe that it is possible to thwart ambition on account of gender. It is not clear that I would believe these kinds of actions were unjust were I to believe that such actions could never be and could never have been performed. The level of abstraction in what we must regard as a possibility is dictated by the level of generality displayed by the normative judgment or evaluative belief. The requirement that one believe an event of a certain kind possible delimits that "kind" with reference to the evaluative belief that focuses the emotional construal.

I think that this is a question about which sets of characteristics we believe *could* be instantiated, because our evaluative belief is a universal one that concerns the classifications of certain kinds of states of affairs. The kinds of universal beliefs that I have associated specifically with emotion are beliefs about injustice or unfairness, about risk, about praiseworthiness and culpability. All seem to involve the ascription of properties that involve human capacities and a distinctively human potential for experience and interaction. The recognition of such capacity and such potential in a particular imaginative instantiation of characteristics would appear to be a recognition of authentic possibilities for human life and experience. It is therefore not required that we believe each fictional event possible. What is necessary for the emotional response is the subsumption of the characteristics whose instantiation we imagine under a category concerning which a normative or evaluative judgment has been or is being made.

Consider the problem posed by science fiction and fantasy, a problem because most people do not believe that the specific states of affairs described or depicted therein could occur. People can be and frequently are moved by such works. Why? I have suggested that to respond emotionally to a fiction, the subject must believe that the *kind* of state of affairs being imaginatively contemplated could occur. Imagine a scene from a science fiction novel someone finds moving, a scene in which a man betrays his brother and blasts him with a photon torpedo. Our reader may have no faith whatsoever in the possibility of photon torpedoes, but he may believe (and if he is moved, I think he does so believe) that treachery between siblings is possible, that one brother could kill another with a lethal weapon. The evaluative belief necessarily linked to his being moved is probably that to betray a trusting relative is treacherous or wrong. That is, the evaluative belief in question is hardly likely to feature photon torpedoes either. The characteristics whose imagined instantiation would be necessary for entertaining an imagined situation with distress would have to be those *believed* sufficient for the further instantiation of properties like "violation of trust," "instance of inhumanity," or "betrayal."

Thus, the features of the imaginary situation necessary for its being regarded with distress have nothing to do with photon torpedoes. The attention is not focused on exotic weaponry but on characteristics of the imagined act that the subject believes would classify the act as treacherous or disloyal. Photon torpedoes are far more relevant in cases of fear for the fictional target prior to his elimination. Here, the evaluative belief would delimit what could constitute danger and what could not. To entertain the thought of someone being at photon-torpedo-point fearfully would presumably involve some evaluative belief about its being dangerous to have deadly weapons aimed at one. It would involve imagining the instantiation of characteristics one *believed* sufficient for danger. Most believe that being at the mercy of someone in control of a deadly weapon is sufficient for being endangered. Again, no states of affairs are eliminated from the fictional world or the world we imagine. My point is only that the nature of the evaluative belief that informs emotional response, the fact that it is universal and that such evaluations seem always to concern the human potential for experiencing, appears to necessitate as a corollary some corresponding belief in the possibility of the kind or type of event of which the fictional event is imagined a token.

Nicholas Wolterstorff, in *Works and Worlds of Art*, indicates that those states of affairs entailed by the states of affairs comprising the world of a work (i.e., entailed by what is indicated in the work) are part of that fictional world. He states that if "Houdini's having drawn a circle" is included in such a world, then "Houdini's having drawn a mathematical figure" is included, since the first entails the second.[43] This certainly has application to my science fiction example as well as the other cases I have been discussing here, for a man's treacherous murder of his brother with a photon torpedo entails a man's treacherous murder of his brother, and the frustration of Judith's ambitions entails the frustration of a person's ambitions. The level of abstraction depends largely on what aspect of the fictional event the subject is attending to and on how he evaluates it. Part of the reason that I am moved by Judith's plight is that I believe persons were and can be prevented from the exercise of their talents by ridiculous conventions. Others might simply see Judith as a damsel in distress. If they are moved by her plight, then it is in part because they believe that this sort of distress is painful and that it could occur.

Characters can be dealt with in much the same way. Dislike for or admiration of a given character need not involve any belief that a person *exactly like that* could exist. It would, I think, only need to involve a belief that there could be a person like that—a person with certain characteristics, a person placed in certain circumstances, a person who performed certain actions. My admiration of Judith involves the evaluative belief that to flout convention in an effort to develop and use one's talents is courageous (if not particularly safe) and the belief that people could (indeed, have done and do) flout convention for such reasons.

As will be explained at greater length in the next chapter, the world we imagine when we read a novel or attend a performance derives from the fictional events that are depicted or described, what is entailed by them, and what is inferred on their basis. Our imagination is not normally constrained in such circumstances. Problems arising in the case of implicit endorsements or condemnations that carry moral weight do so because we may not be able to imagine certain states of affairs in a certain way. Works themselves often make construals concerning human experience. Whether we enter into these construals is another question, for to enter into such construals is to make them oneself. For instance, to imagine an act right and to entertain the thought of it approvingly is to imagine the instantiation of characteristics one believes are sufficient for an act's being right.

Frequently, this presents no difficulty whatsoever. When we watch the

---

43. Wolterstorff, *Works and Worlds of Art*, 119.

protagonist of an action film shooting it out with terrorists, we construe such a situation as dangerous without any omniscient narrating voice having to inform us of this. It is an inevitable imaginative inference from the fictional states of affairs. If our attention is focused in particular on the riskiness of the protagonist's situation and on the likelihood of physical injury or death, we may fearfully entertain the thought of, for instance, her being vastly outnumbered by the terrorists. We will imagine an endangered person. However, there are less obvious cases in which entering into a work's construal is not inevitable. Such cases involve some of the construals I have associated with emotion throughout this book, and that I have associated with normative judgments at the beginning of this chapter. That is, as Richard Moran suggests, we can resist imaginatively entering into a certain point of view.[44]

Another source of imaginative disengagement might involve inconsistencies or contradictions among fictional states of affairs themselves, or among fictional states of affairs and imaginative inferences drawn on their basis. The source and nature of these inferences will be discussed in Chapter 5. For now, it is worth mentioning that it is not the possibility of fictional events themselves that is at issue, for the raison d'être of fiction is to "imagine that." The difficulty arises when it is what we take to be an outright contradiction or inconsistency that we are invited to imagine.

These kinds of imagined inconsistencies might, for instance, be related to the earlier example of *Gone with the Wind*. If a viewer imaginatively inferred (justifiably or not) on the basis of the fictional assault that terrible psychological damage had been inflicted, this could be perceived as inconsistent with the succeeding state of affairs of an obviously untraumatized and undamaged Scarlett. Clearly, there can be better and worse inferences. The focus here is simply on possible reasons for disengagement, not on warranted reasons.

I do not intend to embark on any prolonged discussion of harmful fictions. Other philosophers have already treated this topic with the detail and thoroughness that it deserves. I do, however, wish to point out that this chapter's discussions show that the motive for referring to certain fictions as harmful need not involve the sometimes unreasonable claim that people are inclined to imitate the behavior of fictional characters. The account given here suggests that an emotional response to fiction is necessarily accompanied by the belief that the fictional event being contemplated is an event of the kind that could occur. The disturbing questions

---

44. Moran, "The Expression of Feeling in Imagination," 105.

that this might raise become evident when we consider the scenario from *Gone with the Wind*. To believe that it could happen that a woman wished to have her objections to an assault ignored, to believe that a woman could wish to be assaulted or that she could be grateful for and appreciative of an assault after the fact, has disturbing implications, as does the possibility that normative judgments concerning situations of this kind may be made. I find that I cannot stress the ethical import of emotional response to fiction without considering cases such as these. If fiction can sometimes affect our perspectives on and attitudes toward the world, and can on occasion lead us to contemplate new conceptions of human nature or the human condition, then there are bound to be conceptions and attitudes that some of us find repugnant.[45]

CONCLUSION

In this chapter, and over the course of the preceding chapters, conditions necessary for emotional response to fictional events and characters have begun to emerge. It is time to make these explicit. Emotions are, in this context, taken as ways of entertaining thoughts. Necessary conditions for emotional response to fiction might be as follows.

If subject S entertains the thought of some fictional event emotionally (for example, fearfully) then:

1. S entertains the thought of a particular state of affairs in imagination seriously and attentively. For instance, S imagines a woman's being pursued by a hostile and powerful alien being.
2. This state of affairs is of a certain kind, identifiable by reference to a characteristic or set thereof. Entertaining the thought of it in imagination involves imagining the instantiation of certain characteristics.
3. There exist sets of properties, each of which bears an analytic relation to a particular emotion. For example, the properties "dangerous" or "threatening" are related in this way to the emotion of fear. S holds an

---

45. The preceding is not intended to reflect any views concerning the current debate about pornography. I do not believe that hypotheses about pornography and hypotheses about fiction are interchangeable, because of the very different attitudes taken toward these media by readers or viewers. Although the research into reader attitudes is neither vast nor conclusive, some of it suggests a pervasive tendency to regard pornographic material as a species of "how-to" manual. Few regard fiction in this way.

occurrent or dispositional universal belief that the instantiation of a certain set of characteristics (those whose instantiation he imagines) is sufficient for the further instantiation of the property linked to the emotion. For instance, S may believe that instantiation of the characteristic or situation type "pursuit by powerful and hostile being" is sufficient for the instantiation of the characteristic "dangerous." S believes that to be pursued by a powerful and hostile being is dangerous.

4. S believes that the instantiation of this set of characteristics (those he believes sufficient for the further instantiation of the property related to the emotion) is possible. Thus, S believes that pursuit by a powerful and hostile being is the kind of event or experience that could occur or that could have occurred.

I do not think that these conditions are sufficient for an emotional response to fiction, unless something further is stipulated about the nature of our imaginative attention, the seriousness or concern or interest with which the attention is focused. Yet the claim that such responses seem inevitably related to normative or evaluative beliefs, as well as beliefs about the possible, strongly suggests that fiction can be, and frequently is, morally significant.

5

Imagining Fictional Worlds

This chapter draws a distinction between fictional and imaginary worlds. It considers what can be taken as true in the world of a work and goes on to contrast this with what we may imagine on the basis of such assumptions. The imagination plays an interpretive role in our contemplation of the fictional, and these interpretations comprise the content of the worlds that we imagine. Clearly, the imagination accounts for our apprehension of the fictional in the absence of existential commitment. Beyond this, however, it is the imagination that best explains the kind of world we apprehend and the quality of that apprehension. Imagining fictional events that move us involves imagining them in ways that render some aspects of those events more salient than others, something that requires a particular pattern or focus of attention.

The imagination being thus engaged, there are things to which we do *not* attend when responding emotionally to fictional events: namely, our belief that they are fictional. In the terminology of David Novitz, our explicit knowledge that we are contemplating a fiction is rendered tacit.[1] This claim is not based on assumptions concerning the suspension of disbelief. There are innumerable beliefs to which we do not attend at a given time. I believe that there is no king of France, but this is hardly likely to be in the forefront of my consciousness on most occasions. Beliefs about

---

1. David Novitz, *Knowledge, Fiction and Imagination* (Philadelphia: Temple University Press, 1987), 83.

142 What's Hecuba to Him?

camera angles when watching a film, beliefs about acting quality when watching a play, or beliefs about the author when reading a text are typically rendered tacit when one is moved specifically by a fictional event. Camera angles, acting quality, and authorial prose style all, of course, contribute to the states of affairs that comprise the world of a work. The first section of this chapter will attempt to establish which states of affairs can be taken to constitute that world.

FICTIONAL WORLDS

The states of affairs in a fictional world correspond to the propositions that are true in that world. Thus, the state of affairs of, for example, Ripley's being pursued by an alien corresponds to the proposition that Ripley is pursued by an alien. That is, this is taken to be fictionally true, or true in the work. Many philosophers employ or prefer the propositional account.[2] My reason for choosing to discuss states of affairs instead of propositions is twofold. First, Nicholas Wolterstorff has offered an equally comprehensive treatment of fictional worlds in such terms.[3] More important, most of what I have claimed about the nature of our emotional engagement with fiction suggests that it involves something in addition to the imaginative entertainment of a proposition. I do not just imaginatively entertain the proposition that Ripley is in danger. I imagine an imperilled woman (that is, I entertain the thought of an imperilled woman in imagination). There is a difference between entertaining hypothetical propositions and imagining people in dire circumstances. Since fictional states of affairs are at the heart of what we imagine when we say that we are moved by Ripley's plight or fear for her, I will speak of fictional worlds in those terms.

The fictional world can be thought of as an intricate and complex state of affairs, comprised of all the states of affairs that are explicitly described or depicted or otherwise delineated by features of performances and enactments. It also includes all the states of affairs entailed by these. As has already been mentioned, some propositions will be neither true nor false in the world of a work. That is, in the world of *Alien* it is neither true nor false that Ripley has written poetry. The state of affairs of Ripley's having

---

2. For instance, David Lewis, in "Truth in Fiction," *American Philosophical Quarterly* 15 (1978): 37–46, and Gregory Currie, in *The Nature of Fiction* (Cambridge: Cambridge University Press, 1990).

3. Nicholas Wolterstorff, *Works and Worlds of Art* (Oxford: Clarendon Press, 1980).

done so is not included in that world, nor is the state of affairs of Ripley's never having done so.

Style and technique contribute considerably to the content of fictional worlds. Performance arts in particular demonstrate this, and also pose some interesting problems. First, it seems that we can speak of the worlds of texts or scripts and the worlds of individual performances. If we consider Shakespeare's *A Midsummer Night's Dream* as written, there is no state of affairs of Puck's being taller than Mustardseed. In the world of a performance, there may well be such a state of affairs. The appearance of actors, the set, the costumes, the movements, and especially how actors play their roles make things true in the world of a performance that are neither true nor false in the world of the play as text. The worlds of the text and of the performances of *A Midsummer Night's Dream* will all include the state of affairs of Oberon's casting an enchantment on a sleeping Titania and will all include his adjuring her to "wake when some vile thing is near." Yet the world of one performance may include the state of affairs of its being said gloatingly while the world of another may include its being said angrily.

Techniques of cinematography can also contribute states of affairs to the world of a work. For instance, consider films in which the camera briefly poses as the eyes of a character who has been slipped a Mickey Finn. The shifting focus and doubling images add the state of affairs of a person's having been drugged, of a person's eyes losing their ability to focus, to the world of the work.

Prose style itself makes a major contribution. This is easiest to see in plays and films. Consider the Saint Crispin's Day speech in *Henry V*. No one needs to be convinced of the sheer magnificence of Shakespeare's prose. What this contributes to the fictional world is the state of affairs of Henry's being a magnificent orator, for it is fictional that Henry uttered just those words, made just those allusions, in just that meter. Imagine that someone translated this play into a language I will refer to for purposes of simplicity as Modern Idiomatic. ("Yo, dudes! Today is, like, the Feast of Crispin.") It would not be true in such a world that Henry was a magnificent orator. Much has been made of distinctions between style and content. Typically, only the latter is allied with fictional states of affairs. Yet the preceding example makes it clear that this distinction may not be so easy to make. The two fictional worlds I described will be comprised of radically different states of affairs, since what characters say and how they say it constitute nearly the whole of the world of a play. We may, of course, have an aesthetic response to Shakespeare's prose and admire it. Yet we can also be moved by what Shakespeare's Henry says and how he says it. To imagine the Henry of a Shakespearean performance rousing the troops and to imagine this with excitement and admiration is to imagine his saying just the things Shakespeare wrote.

The point made above extends to prose style in the novel. Even the descriptions of an omniscient narrator can have stylistic features that determine what states of affairs are included in the world of a work. Two hypothetical novels can describe very similar events with minor variations in stylistic presentation. Let us assume that novel A contains the sentence "The dog came up to Spike and barked, so Spike knew it was time to feed her." Novel B contains the sentence "The dog importuned Spike for her supper." These sentences already demonstrate a difference between the states of affairs comprising the world of A and those comprising the world of B. For one thing, it is true that barking occurred in A, whereas it is neither true nor false in B. For another, barring further explanations, the state of affairs of Spike knowing it is time to feed the dog is included in A but may not be included in B. (Spike might be distracted, or just plain dense, in B. The single sentence does not give us enough information.) On the other hand, an importunate or unreasonably persistent dog occupies the B world, whereas this may be neither true nor false in the A world.

Another point about prose style is that what has been symbolically or metaphorically indicated is also contained in the world of the work. Further, the kind of metaphor or symbol used may itself contribute to the states of affairs in a work's world. If a text informs us that a television's reception is "schizophrenic," this would make it true in the fictional world that it was in some way unreliable or unpredictable. Cleopatra's telling Antony that "eternity was in our lips and eyes" makes something fictionally true about the way Cleopatra claims to view the intensity and significance of their relationship, and may make it fictionally true that she regards it as having been exalted and uncommon. The use of such metaphors will probably affect *how* we imagine a given state of affairs, a topic reserved for Chapter 7.

Similarly, the state of affairs of someone's missing a child might be included in the world of a work that describes the person clutching the child's toy tearfully but that refrains from any explicit references to sadness or despair. Not all cases of symbolism are quite as obvious, however. Consider the kind of symbolism that is frequently worked into Eugene O'Neill's stage directions and scene descriptions. The first act of *Mourning Becomes Electra* opens with a detailed description of the house, whose "white columns cast black bars of shadow on the gray wall behind them."[4] This description recurs, most notably, in the final act. The play closes with Lavinia's exit into the family home she has tried to escape.[5] Certainly, the reader of the play will imagine the house a prison, in the sense that the characters appear to be trapped in a life-sapping network of familial relationships from which escape is ultimately impossible. Just as certainly, the setting echoes this and was intended to do so. What concerns me is whether the initial symbolic indication of entrapment, the black bars of shadow, makes it fictional that the characters are trapped before the action has even started. I think it does, but I will suspend any further judgment on this for the moment, since the question of distinguishing what is fictionally true from what is true in the world of the reader's imagination will be addressed in later sections.

Thus far, I have restricted the fictional world to states of affairs explicitly indicated by what an author has written, a camera has shown, an actor has said and done. The states of affairs entailed by these do not involve any extensive further contribution. The state of affairs of Ripley's being pursued by an alien, for instance, entails the state of affairs of a woman's being pursued by a predator. The state of affairs of a bored student's inscribing a triangle on his desk with a penknife entails the state of affairs of someone's inscribing a mathematical figure. But do fictional worlds not include more than this? When I imagine Henry's speech, do I not also imagine something about his motives and intentions in so addressing his troops?

IMAGINING FICTIONS

Most of our imaginings go far beyond what is explicitly presented in a work. Indeed, they can include events that works do not mention or depict at all. Consider the following example:

> "You can't imagine," she sobbed, as the police handcuffed her and led her away from the blood-spattered apartment, "what it's like to live next door to the members of a tuba and kazoo ensemble who insist on practicing every night."

Those who have more of a background in things literary than I tell me that there was once a vogue for genuinely short stories, stories that were

---

4. Eugene O'Neill, *Mourning Becomes Electra*, in *Nine Plays by Eugene O'Neill* (New York: Modern Library, 1954), 687.

5. Ibid., 867.

only a few sentences long. The reader, by means of inference and imagination, was expected to fill in the blanks, to imagine the rest of the story on
the basis of those few sentences. Although these works were hardly
lauded as crowned masterpieces of literature and were seldom, if ever,
moving, they certainly fulfilled the aforementioned expectation. It is very
difficult *not* to embark on a course of imaginative supplementation almost
automatically when confronted with such a story.

I imagine a young woman pacing her bedroom, sleepless yet again. It is
a hot, humid summer night, the absence of air-conditioning mandating
that the windows be kept open. The not-so-dulcet strains of off-key tuba
and kazoo music waft in on an errant breeze. Crazed and exhausted, she
trembles. She can take it no longer. She has pleaded and complained to no
avail. Her sanity has finally shattered. Slowly, she reaches for her L. L. Bean
Swiss Army Adventurer Knife, complete with all five optional blades and
attachments, and . . .

Despite the heroine's claim in the one-sentence story, it is obvious that
we can imagine what her experience was like. By means of inductive
inferences and outright invention, I filled out the story, imagining a state of
affairs that culminated in the fictional event that gave my invention its
impetus. Others might envision a different scenario, but most would
include the state of affairs of the woman's being kept up at night and that
of her assault on members of the ensemble. That is, a lot of us would draw
the same inferences. Do these additional states of affairs belong to the
fictional world of the work? Can we say they are true in the fictional world,
regardless of who imagines that world? The example raises the question of
what distinctions should be drawn between what it is we just imagine and
what is true in the fictional world of the work. Where, exactly, should the
line be drawn?

Nicholas Wolterstorff and David Lewis have both proposed methods
whereby we can expand and supplement the fictional world and determine what is true within it beyond what has been explicitly indicated.
These are both based on a counterfactual approach of the sort advocated
by David Lewis, who introduces the idea of relative similarity between
worlds.[6] A simplified version of Lewis's treatment of counterfactuals runs
as follows: "A counterfactual of the form 'If it were that [p], then it would
be that [q]' is non-vacuously true iff some possible world where both [p]
and [q] are true differs less from our actual world, on balance, than does
any world where [p] is true but [q] is not true."[7] Marie-Laure Ryan refers to

---

6. David Lewis, *Counterfactuals* (Cambridge: Harvard University Press, 1973).
7. David Lewis, "Truth in Fiction," 42.

this as the "principle of minimal departure." Insofar as it relates to fictions, it enables us to consider fictional states of affairs against a backdrop of everything we know about the actual world, making only those adjustments necessitated by inconsistencies.[8] Lewis proposes that statements of truth in fiction be analyzed as counterfactuals in the following way: "A sentence of the form 'In the fiction f, [p]' is non-vacuously true iff some world where f is told as a known fact and [p] is true differs less from our actual world, on balance, than does any world where f is told as a known fact and [p] is not true."[9] This has more or less the import of the principle of alpha-extrapolation that Wolterstorff proposes.

On the basis of Wolterstorff's alpha-principle, we can include in the fictional world the states of affairs that would occur were those indicated in the work actually to occur.[10] The process becomes more complicated if there is an inconsistency among those states of affairs already indicated in the work. Setting that possibility aside for the moment, the alpha-principle is intended to let us include in the fictional world of my abbreviated story the state of affairs of a woman's having been arrested. This is not required by what is indicated in the story, for it is possible to have been handcuffed and led away by the police without having been arrested. Wolterstorff's own examples show that extrapolation does not involve entailment.

The principle of extrapolation presents certain difficulties, however, for it makes authorial intentions and the assumptions prevalent in the author's age entirely irrelevant. Even William K. Wimsatt and Monroe C. Beardsley, who question the relevance of such intentions in "The Intentional Fallacy," say that we can discover the meaning of a work not only by means of our knowledge of a language but through "all that makes a language and a culture."[11] By making authorial and historical assumptions irrelevant, we make the customs, values, science, and beliefs of another age irrelevant when we consider the fictional world of a work of that age.

Where no specific cause is mentioned in an eighteenth-century novel describing a lovable invalid who swills large, purportedly medicinal doses of laudanum for a nervous condition that would have been assumed by the author and his audience to involve some physical defect in the nervous system, we might begin to import drug addiction and withdrawal symp-

---

8. Marie-Laure Ryan, "Fiction, Non-Factuals, and the Principle of Minimal Departure," *Poetics* 9 (1980): 405–6.

9. Lewis, "Truth in Fiction," 42.

10. Wolterstorff, *Works and Worlds of Art*, 120.

11. Gregory Currie cites this passage in making a point similar to my own in *The Nature of Fiction*, 110. Wimsatt and Beardsley's paper appeared originally in the *Sewanee Review* 54 (1946): 468–88.

toms into the world of the work. Where an author ascribes a character's failing health to a weakness of constitution, we might ascribe it to the medical treatment (e.g., bleeding) said to provide the patient with relief, even though the author (along with the audience of his time) may have assumed that such treatments had significant health benefits.

David Lewis also considers cases in which such difficulties might arise. For instance, there is Arthur Conan Doyle's "The Adventure of the Speckled Band," in which Holmes announces that someone has been killed by a Russell's viper that has climbed a bell rope. Lewis discovered, upon reading an article by Carl Gans in the *Scientific American*, that the Russell's viper is not a constrictor and therefore could not have climbed a rope of any sort.[12] An application of Lewis's analysis or Wolterstorff's alpha-principle of extrapolation imports the state of affairs of Holmes having bungled his deductions into the world of the work. Yet would we really want to make this (fictionally) true of the infallible Holmes?

Accordingly, Wolterstorff has proposed that an alternative to the alpha-principle be employed in such cases. This is the beta-principle, on the basis of which are included the states of affairs we think the author assumed his intended audience would believe would occur, were the states of affairs indicated in the work to occur.[13] Adoption of the beta-principle would eliminate difficulties such as those described above, since we would extrapolate on the basis of what the author assumed his intended audience would believe. Thus, Holmes's infallibility is preserved, since most readers could acknowledge that Conan Doyle assumed his intended audience would believe a Russell's viper could climb a bell rope. The application of the beta-principle has other interesting consequences as well. For instance, on the basis of the beta-principle, Freudian complexes could be imported into the world of O'Neill's *Mourning Becomes Electra*, but not into the world of Shakespeare's *Hamlet*.

Lewis's alternative analysis differs from the one proposed by Wolterstorff in that it does not bring authorial assumptions into the picture: "A sentence of the form 'In the fiction f, [p]' is non-vacuously true iff, whenever w is one of the collective belief worlds of the community of origin of f, then some world where f is told as known fact and [p] is true differs less from the world w, on balance, than does any world where f is told as known fact and [p] is not true."[14] This enables us to deal with the same kinds of problems that Wolterstorff's beta-principle was formulated to

---

12. Lewis, "Truth in Fiction," 43.
13. Wolterstorff, *Works and Worlds of Art*, 123.
14. Lewis, "Truth in Fiction," 45.

resolve, with the exception of cases that involve mistaken authorial assumptions about the beliefs of readers or viewers. What sort of difference might this make?

Imagine that absolutely everyone except Conan Doyle knew about a Russell's viper not being able to climb a rope. Perhaps the viper and its less-than-agile disposition had been described in major newspaper stories (a Russell's viper was adopted by someone famous, it bit someone famous, it insinuated itself into the shoe of someone famous) while Conan Doyle was in complete seclusion writing "The Adventure of the Speckled Band." Are we to take it that, in the world of the work, Holmes made a mistake? Perhaps we can just assume that Conan Doyle made a mistake (given employment of the beta-principle) and leave Holmes's reputation untarnished. However, this still leaves unanswered the question of how we are to address fictional worlds that include impossible states of affairs.

It has been held that states of affairs featuring outright logical impossibilities like married bachelors or empirical impossibilities or implausibilities like Ripley's alien cannot ground extrapolation (though the latter can certainly be imagined). Neither authorial assumptions about people's beliefs nor our own assumptions about what can happen are at all likely to include any firm belief that married bachelors or hostile aliens could exist. That is, it is not clear we can have beliefs about what *would* occur, given the occurrence of a certain event, if we do not believe that event *could* occur.[15] But these states of affairs entail other, more general states of affairs on whose basis extrapolation is unproblematic. Fictional situations involving married bachelors entail fictional situations that involve men, whatever their marital status. Fictional situations involving Ripley's alien entail fictional situations that involve a fierce predator. When we consider extrapolation on the basis of these less problematic states of affairs, the difficulty is eliminated.

I previously stipulated that the belief that a given kind of event could occur was necessary for an emotional response to fiction. The above presents an additional motive for doing so. It might be thought that extrapolation would be difficult or perhaps even impossible without such a belief. We could make no contribution of our own to the world we imagine, we could not even react to it, without believing in the possibility of that *kind* of event (where "kind" derives its specificity from characteristics instantiated in fictional states of affairs or in states of affairs entailed by these).

---

15. This appears to be Wolterstorff's position in *Works and Worlds of Art*, 123.

But what of less easily resolvable inconsistencies among the fictional states of affairs themselves or among these and the states of affairs derived from them on the basis of imaginative inference and extrapolation? In the previous chapter, I held that the apprehension of inconsistencies could sometimes lead to imaginative disengagement. Let us consider a source of such potential paradoxes. Mark Twain provides us with one of the funniest and most incisive descriptions of this problem when he outlines the literary offenses of Fenimore Cooper.

A number of Twain's criticisms focus specifically on inconsistencies. He tells us, for instance, that the rules of literary art "require that when a personage talks like an illustrated, gilt-edged, tree-calf, hand-tooled, seven-dollar Friendship's Offering in the beginning of a paragraph, he shall not talk like a Negro minstrel at the end of it. But this rule is flung down and danced upon in the *Deerslayer* tale."[16] Here, the difficulty I wish to focus on is not primarily that of believing that no real person could exhibit such changes in diction (though this does involve the violation of an implicit commitment to realism Twain himself espoused). Rather, it lies in the fact that we may imagine persons with particular capacities and predispositions on the one hand, yet imagine these same people with entirely different capacities and predispositions on the other. If I have imaginatively inferred that a person has certain capacities and predispositions on the basis of the fictional state of affairs of the individual's talking like a seven-dollar Friendship's Offering, these inferences are likely to be inconsistent with those drawn on the basis of the fictional state of affairs of the person's talking like a minstrel. This does not signify any inevitable disengagement. I only mean to suggest that if a reader does make inferences of this kind in this particular way, he or she *may* experience some level of disengagement.

Such inconsistencies are the result of reader inferences and therefore cannot be directly attributed to the fictional world itself or held to afflict the imaginings of every reader. Consider the question of a character's self-reflective language when it is endowed with a complexity, richness, and sophistication that the character's linguistic capacities cannot reflect. Such texts need not give rise to imaginative resistance. A character's thoughts and mental states can be described or expressed in particular sentences, but it is not clear that these must be regarded merely as silent speech acts. The verbatim presentation of a character's thoughts could be

---

16. Mark Twain, "Fenimore Cooper's Literary Offenses," in Bernard DeVoto, ed., *The Portable Mark Twain* (New York: Viking, 1946), 543.

taken as a presentation of the character's attitudes and concerns rather than a vocabulary list or inner recitation. No apprehension of inconsistency need arise in such cases.

However, Twain's enumeration of Cooper's literary iniquities addresses cases that are far more problematic. He goes on to point out fictional states of affairs that may involve an outright contradiction. First, Cooper's story invites us to imagine a nail, which serves as a target visible to the hero from a distance of a hundred yards. Indeed, it is even suggested that the hero *sees* his bullet fly through the air and hit the target. Readers who have imagined that various truths of biology and optics obtain in the world of the work may already experience difficulty at this stage. Twain certainly did. But what Twain refers to as "Cooper miracles" do not end here, for we are asked to imagine that there are three bullets embedded processionally in the body of a stump behind the target nail head, and asked also to imagine that all the observers have ascertained and *know* this with absolute certainty, even though no one has dug any of the bullets out of the stump (the observers have not seen the bullets go in—only Pathfinder's eyes are good enough to do that).[17]

Most of the inferences one would draw on the basis of fictional events such as these would result in some contradiction or other. Unless one made imaginative inferences about X-ray vision or telepathy, something I think most Cooper fans would be disinclined to do, one would have to imagine a wholly unjustified belief (for there is little sensory or other evidence for the belief that there are three bullets embedded processionally in the stump) that constituted certain knowledge. I concede that many readers simply gloss over this passage, but I suggest that the imaginative involvement of, say, an epistemologist would probably be curtailed.

Imaginative disengagement might also occur in the case of fictions that violate an implicit or explicit commitment to realism. There are works in whose worlds it is true that, for instance, the laws of physics obtain, or that can be taken to assume the functioning of the laws of nature as they were believed to function at the time of the writing. A few such worlds can at the same time include states of affairs on the basis of which it can be inferred that those laws do not obtain. Opportunities for inconsistency arise in such cases and might curtail an imaginative experience.

The point is not that consumers of fiction cannot *imagine* what they do not believe could occur in the actual world. This has already been denied in Chapter 4's discussion of science fiction. Rather, I maintain that they

---

17. Twain, "Fenimore Cooper's Literary Offenses," 550–52.

cannot imagine what they believe to constitute outright logical impossibilities. Being confronted with these depends largely on the kinds of imaginative inferences one makes on the basis of fictional states of affairs. Imaginative disengagement from the work is not inevitable in such cases, of course. Readers or viewers could disregard certain of their imaginative inferences or could cease to attend to certain fictional states of affairs, focusing attention on less problematic ones. In considering possible reasons for imaginative disengagement, however, experiences of this sort should be kept in mind.

IMAGINATION AS INTERPRETATION

It is not wholly clear where extrapolation ends and other processes of imaginative supplementation begin. What are the boundaries of the fictional world? Wolterstorff acknowledges that a given work could probably have at least two different worlds associated with it: an alpha world and a beta world—perhaps a world that makes *The Turn of the Screw* a story about neurosis and hallucination and a world that makes it a story about the supernatural.[18] But it would seem that there could be more than one alpha world as well, based on different and conflicting alpha extrapolations.

Take the world of *Othello*. To simplify matters, let us consider the play as written, not as performed. I could conclude that were it the case that a man became convinced of his wife's guilt on the basis of such scanty evidence as Iago presents, then that man would be either a fool or someone who was so deranged with jealousy as to be mentally unbalanced. Alternatively, I might conclude that, were it the case that a man became convinced on the basis of such scanty evidence, then the one presenting that evidence must have insinuated himself into a virtually unassailable position of trust, must have had great charm and unusual powers of persuasion. The difference here is that, on the basis of the first extrapolation, Othello is as much the victim of his own jealous folly and credulity as he is of Iago. In the second world he is a jealous, insecure man whose

---

18. I am allying James's assumptions with the "supernatural" interpretation because he states that Peter Quint and Miss Jessie are goblins, devils, or imps in his preface to the novel and because of some of Robert Liddell's excellent arguments against adopting the Freudian interpretation: Robert Liddell, *Robert Liddell on the Novel* (Chicago: University of Chicago Press, 1969), 128–35.

otherwise controllable character flaws are intensified to fever pitch by Iago's expert manipulation. These seem to be incompatible states of affairs, yet both are based on extrapolations grounded in the same work.

Perhaps what is indicated about Iago and Othello in the work is insufficient for the consequent of either of the subjunctive conditionals. This raises questions, however, about the initial examples given of alpha extrapolation. Consider once again the tearful victim of the tuba and kazoo aficionados. Being handcuffed and led away by the police might not always signify arrest (e.g., the woman might have been handcuffed to prevent attempts to harm herself and led away because the scene was gruesome). Several extrapolations might prove equally consistent with what was indicated in the world of the work. I am disinclined to bring probability into the picture, although presumably we could try to determine which eventuality (or which product of extrapolation) differed less from what was typically true in the actual world. I am not sure, however, that this would solve the problem of *Othello*.

It might simply be the case that extrapolation could itself explain why different readers have different responses to and interpretations of the same work. They imagine different worlds. This is quite compatible with the claims of Peter Lamarque, which were discussed in Chapter 3. People may react to the same fictional state of affairs or character yet entertain different thoughts in imagination.

I encountered proof positive of just such a divergence when a close friend and I went to see the film *Robin Hood, Prince of Thieves*. A scene in the film depicts the final battle between Robin Hood and the wicked Sheriff of Nottingham. Maid Marian is present throughout this duel to the death and makes only two efforts to influence its outcome. Although Marian wants Robin to win, she is afraid of the Sheriff, whose assault on her person our hero has but recently interrupted. She at one point spills hot wax on the Sheriff and at another slams a table into him. She makes no other effort to intervene and spends the rest of the time quivering and giving the occasional warning. I came away from this film seriously annoyed with Marian. Any sensible woman, I felt, would have tried to bat the Sheriff over the head with one of the pieces of lumber lying conveniently about. What a wimp. My friend Rosemary, on the other hand, saw Marian as a traumatized victim of assault whose admirable courage in the face of adversity was amply demonstrated by the two assaults she did make on the Sheriff.

What accounts for this divergence in emotional responses is, I think, the fact that we imaginatively entertained entirely different states of affairs. I imagined a state of affairs in which a more or less competent fighter

(Marian is shown in armor, wielding a sword, early on in the film) who is perfectly capable of making a difference in the outcome of a conflict such as this refrains from any significant participation because of sheer weak-mindedness. Rosemary had been contemplating an agitated victim of assault (whose fighting expertise was minimal — she was not very good at wielding that sword because Robin disarmed her during the course of the early scene) who was incapable of making any significant difference in the outcome of the combat and whose intervention might actually have hindered rather than precipitated a desirable result.

We had both supplemented the fictional states of affairs depicted in the film with conflicting estimates of Marian's capacities to aid and abet in a fight. Neither of these assumptions was entirely inconsistent with the things that were true in the fictional world: the extent of Marian's competence as a fighter was never fully disclosed, nor was the degree to which that competence could be diminished by personal distress, so each of us filled in the gap differently. A thousand things about us probably led us to diverge in our acts of imaginative supplementation (e.g., my childhood fantasy of growing up to be Emma Peel), but these things are not at issue here. The kinds of extrapolations in which we engage depend to some extent on our existing sympathies and predilections, on our expectations, and on our normative judgments. I propose, therefore, that a distinction be drawn between the fictional world and the world we imagine.

Wolterstorff allies extrapolation with interpretation. Interpretation and extrapolation are something *we* do on the basis of the work. The fictional world, on the other hand, is said to be projected by the author by means of the work. Accordingly, when I speak of the fictional world, I will speak only of those states of affairs (and what they entail) that have been mentioned or metaphorically or symbolically indicated by the author, director, or actor. When I speak of the worlds we imagine, I will speak of fictional worlds conjoined with the states of affairs with which we have supplemented them on the basis of extrapolation, inference, and invention. It should also be stressed that such extrapolations and inferences may be virtually spontaneous rather than deliberate. Nevertheless, if what we imagine is inconsistent with the states of affairs in the fictional world (provided fictional states of affairs are consistent with each other), then it can be held that we have misinterpreted the work.

But does this not put all interpretations on a par, provided they are consistent with what is indicated in the work? I certainly hope not. For one thing, the truth and applicability of the counterfactuals used in extrapolation could be debated, as could the kind and quantity of evidence that warranted various inferences. The world we imagine is the fictional world as *we* envision it or understand it. Some things will be true in that world that will be neither true nor false in the fictional one. This does not preclude the possibility of misunderstanding or misconceiving the fictional world, nor does it prevent the possibility that there could be better or worse understandings and more or less convincing extrapolations. It does, however, account for the fact that people can interpret the same fiction in different ways and respond differently to it. The reason that I want to remove the products of extrapolation from the fictional world is that most readers do not draw exactly the same inferences, nor do they adhere to the same standards about what kind of evidence might warrant a given inference.

Louise Rosenblatt's inspired analogy between aesthetic reading and musical performance reinforces my motivation for drawing the preceding distinction. Just as there may be many performances of a Mozart concerto — some sentimental, some halting, some exalting — so there may be different readings of a text. Not every reader will be a virtuoso, but then "all the more reason . . . for the ordinary reader's refusing to abdicate his own role as a creator, or evoker" of an imaginary world, for no one else can evoke that world for that particular reader. Of course, there can be better and worse readings. The latter may involve speculative or biased imaginative inferences. There can be mistaken readings or interpretations when what the reader imagines is inconsistent with what is true in the fictional world. But Rosenblatt rightly stresses the significance to the individual of making such attempts: "drawing on the reservoir of his own past life and reading, he has lived through the experience himself, he has struggled to organize it, felt it on his own pulses. It is now part of the life experience with which he encounters the future."[19] One does not fall prey to relativism in denying that there can be only a single correct interpretation of each and every literary work. It is not the case that there is only one correct reading of a work any more than there could be only one correct rendition of a concerto. This does not alter the fact that there remain grounds on the basis of which both kinds of interpretations can be evaluated.

I have already indicated that I think there is an interactive relationship between the role of the imagination and the role of belief involved in some of those encounters with fictions that move us. Part of this interaction naturally involves beliefs we have about what could occur and about what would occur under one set of circumstances or another. The absence of a

---

19. Louise M. Rosenblatt, *The Reader, the Text, the Poem: The Transactional Theory of the Literary Work* (Carbondale: Southern Illinois University Press, 1978), 140–42.

belief that a state of affairs of the kind presented could occur (where "kind" is broadly construed) can result in our imaginative disengagement from the work. More important, however, beliefs of this sort can ground extrapolations and inferences that supplement the states of affairs indicated in the work and contribute to the world we imagine.

Our evaluative beliefs also inform what it is we imagine, for they may focus our attention on one state of affairs rather than another or lead us to imagine the perspective of one character rather than another, inclining us to extrapolate or draw inferences on the basis of one aspect of the fictional world rather than another. Let us return once more to Thackeray's *Vanity Fair* and assume that among the beliefs in my doxastic repertoire are several that place a very high value on intelligence, ingenuity, and artistic ability, and others that place a correspondingly low value on passivity, dependence, and incompetence. When I read *Vanity Fair*, what I imagine is influenced by these beliefs. For one thing, in part because of my admiration of Becky Sharp's intelligence and talent, I find myself focusing on aspects of her life and circumstances that might serve to mitigate her culpability for certain acts. I might concentrate on her youth in unpleasantly straitened circumstances, her penniless situation. Of course, I extrapolate on the basis of, for example, what character deficiencies might inevitably result were someone to suffer such a deprived childhood. I leave readers to draw their own conclusions about the less generous inferences I will be inclined to make about Amelia.

The point here is that what it is I imagine, the kind of world I imagine, depends to some extent on the evaluative beliefs I possess, as well as my belief in the truth of the subjunctive conditionals underlying my extrapolations and beliefs about what kinds of events can occur. This again emphasizes the difference between fictional and imaginary worlds, for the imaginary world of a work is funded by the experience, concerns, and convictions of the one who imagines it.

IMAGINATIVE ENGAGEMENT

I have written a good deal about the distinction between the imaginative entertainment of a proposition (imagining *that* something is the case) and imagining states of affairs or entertaining the thought of a given state of affairs in imagination. It is the latter that has been associated with emotional response to fiction. I have already voiced the complaint that this second kind of imagining has fallen prey to descriptions and explications so poetic and metaphorical in their terminology that a student of the subject can be left with the impression that "imagining" in the second sense amounts to little more than extraordinarily vivid visualization. Indeed, some impassioned advocates make imaginative engagement sound suspiciously like a species of self-induced hallucination. To account for the difference between simply taking something as true in a fiction and getting completely wrapped up in the fictional states of affairs, even far more precise philosophers speak of "vividness" and "envisioning," terms which could still suggest picture thinking and purely phenomenological content.[20] Nothing could be further from the truth.

Francis Sparshott has spoken eloquently of the distinction between a sense of "imagination" identified with "conjuring up simulacra" and "imaginativeness, the possibility of conceiving or conjuring up alternative realities." He continues by speaking of his response to fiction: "When I read a novel, I enter the world of the novel, which I recreate from the author's cues. . . . Whether he and I imagine the same world has nothing to do with whether or not we have any mental images at all. . . . Imagining in this sense is simply envisaging alternative realities."[21] Sparshott refers specifically to Mary Warnock's idea of envisagement, which she describes as "a power . . . which enables us to see the world, whether present or absent, as significant. . . . This power is not only intellectual. Its impetus comes as much from emotions as from reason."[22]

Warnock's point suggests the further distinction made by Richard Moran, a distinction between the hypothetical and dramatic imagination.[23] The dramatic imagination requires a point of view or perspective on the situation that involves more than entertaining a proposition. Someone can coolly entertain the proposition that Ripley is in danger, acknowledge that it is true in the fictional world, with no imaginative involvement. In contrast, imagining Ripley's situation (aside from entertaining that proposition) amounts to taking thoughts of that situation *seriously*. This involves a whole complex of mental states and events, a pattern of thoughts, desires, reflections, suppositions, evaluations, responses, and frequently

---

20. Richard Moran complains of this in "The Expression of Feeling in Imagination," *Philosophical Review* 103 (1994): 86–90. Bijoy Boruah uses the term "envisagement" in *Fiction and Emotion* (Oxford: Clarendon Press, 1988) but allies envisagement with the empathetic imagination on pages 110–17.

21. Francis Sparshott, *The Theory of the Arts* (Princeton: Princeton University Press, 1982), 141.

22. Mary Warnock, *Imagination* (Berkeley: University of California Press, 1976), 196.

23. Moran, "The Expression of Feeling in Imagination," 104–6.

feelings and emotions.[24] According to Louise Rosenblatt, the process involves a "continuing flow of responses, syntheses, readjustment and assimilation." Every sentence in a text (and, I wish to add, every depiction in a film):

> will signal certain possibilities and exclude others, thus limiting the arc of expectations. What the reader has elicited from the text up to any point generates a receptivity to certain kinds of ideas, overtones, or attitudes. Perhaps one can think of this as an alerting of certain areas of memory, a stirring up of certain reservoirs of experience, knowledge, and feeling. As the reading proceeds, attention will be fixed on the reverberations or implications that result from fulfillment or frustration of those expectations.[25]

We extrapolate and infer to draw conclusions about Ripley's mental states, we have expectations, form spontaneous hypotheses about where the alien may be lurking, wonder what Ripley will do once she fails to override the ship's emergency destruct system, think about what she *should* do, want her to escape, suspect that she may not be able to escape, listen to the countdown to detonation, want her to hurry, think she's a goner, notice the shallowness of her breathing, remember what that feels like, flinch with her at a sudden explosion of steam, notice it's obscuring the passage, realize it might conceal the alien from view until it's too late, wonder if the shuttle has been damaged, want it to be over with, figure Ripley wants it to be over with, think Ripley's incredibly brave, wonder how she can be so determined when she's so scared, decide she's a lot braver than we'd be, want her to remember to pick up the cat on the way to the shuttle, will her not to forget the cat, realize she's the best person in the universe because she remembered the cat, suddenly wonder if the cat is incubating a midget alien, expect an alien to jump out of the cat . . .

Imagining Ripley is an active, constructive thing. We imagine Ripley and her situation responsively, inquiringly, expectantly, curiously, hopefully, judgmentally, sympathetically, fearfully. As our imaginative attention is focused in different ways, the states of affairs we imagine change, acquire depth, increase. Imagination can be, in a fundamental way, productive.

It is not that we imagine our own responses or evaluations as an account

---

24. Susan Feagin speaks of such patterns of thinking and imagining when describing empathetic responses to fiction in "Imagining Emotions and Appreciating Fiction," *Canadian Journal of Philosophy* 18 (1988): 485–500.

25. Rosenblatt, *The Reader, the Text, the Poem*, 58, 54.

like Walton's might suggest. Rather, our responses and evaluations can change our expectations and reactions. If, for instance, I have construed Ripley as courageous and resourceful and admire her because I value such qualities—that is, if I entertain the thought of a brave and resourceful woman admiringly, then this will affect my expectations with regard to her behavior and probable success, will affect any extrapolations I make concerning her mental states and motives, and will affect my reactions to her future behavior and the constructions I place on it. We construct the world we imagine by imagining it in certain ways. Our emotional and other responses contribute to the world we imagine not by being imaginary in themselves but by developing the story we began with and making it our own.

IMAGINING THE REAL

I also think that imagination frequently plays a role in our responses to what we take to be actual events. I have made it clear that the role of the imagination in our emotional experience of fictions amounts to more than that of stand-in for an existentially committed belief. In this chapter I have tried to describe at least a part of what I think that role might be. But there is no reason to think that we imagine states of affairs and proceed to imaginatively supplement them only in our encounters with fictions. Indeed, I think that we extrapolate and draw inferences to fill in the blanks in our knowledge of actual events just as we do to supplement what is indicated in a fictional work. It could be that certain philosophers only become interested in the role of the imagination in the context of our encounters with fiction because it is taken to provide an *alternative* to our awareness of reality or an alternative to believing. The latter is somehow always presumed to be more direct and more immediate. But, in fact, many of the things we believe about the world at large are things we believe on the basis of second-hand reports that invite just as much imaginative supplementation as do fictional descriptions.

Consider the kinds of brief, odd, newspaper stories that one sees practically every morning at the breakfast table: "Teed-off Golfers Blocked Her Game, Woman Testifies." The headline captured my interest, and I began to read the AP wire story. "A female golfer testified Monday she feared for her life when she was bullied and cursed by a group of men who tried to block her from playing during male-only hours at an exclusive Long Island

country club last year."[26] How bizarre. What were "male-only hours"? I
continued to read and found that the woman, a member of the club, had
filed harassment charges against one of the members. This individual
acknowledged telling her she could not play but denied all other allegations. These included the claim that twenty men had surrounded her with
their golf carts to prevent her from playing, that obscenities were shouted
at her, that a golf ball was hurled at her. The story was short, and few other
details were offered.

My extrapolations began almost immediately. Since the testimony of the
defendant and the woman could not both be true, I (not surprisingly)
chose to extrapolate on the basis of the woman's testimony. I imagined her
being surrounded by twenty golf carts filled with irate male golfers and
potentially lethal clubs. She must have been initially stunned, I thought.
Nobody expects something that strange and creepy to happen. When they
started yelling, she must have been scared and angry at once. I knew what
that felt like. I remembered the many occasions during the course of
which I had felt the frustrated and frustrating desire for a black belt in
karate. What were those guys thinking of? What was their problem? Jerks!
I hoped they'd throw the book at the defendant.

The obvious difference between my response to the newspaper article
and my response to a fiction is that I believe events described in the article
occurred: that a woman tried to play golf at a country club that had rules
barring women from playing at certain times, that several men attempted
to prevent her playing, that at least one of these addressed her directly and
acrimoniously, that she was afraid. Aside from this, however, I also imagine
the incident (whether my imaginings are accurate or not is irrelevant to the
present point) and infer various things on the basis of what is described. I
extrapolate, as Wolterstorff says we do in the case of fictions. My attention
is focused mainly on the scene as I imagine or envision it, as Novitz says is
the case in our experiences of fictions. As Levinson thinks we do when we
are moved by fictions, I have "tapped into and reactivated" emotions I have
previously experienced, because the news story "resonates" with those
emotional experiences.[27] Just as McCormick thinks we can make a character's experience virtually our own,[28] I have at least to some extent made

---

26. This article appeared in the *Syracuse Post Standard* between 1989 and 1992. I
clipped the story, for which I do not have a precise date.

27. Jerrold Levinson, "The Place of Real Emotion in Response to Fiction," *Journal of
Aesthetics and Art Criticism* 49 (1990): 79.

28. Peter McCormick, *Fictions, Philosophies, and the Problems of Poetics* (Ithaca:
Cornell University Press, 1988), 142–45.

the experience of the woman described in the newspaper (i.e., her experience as I imagine it) virtually my own, insofar as I am angry on her behalf.

The difference between our emotional responses to fictional and actual events is not necessarily to be found in the role of the imagination or the intensity of our feelings. The difference lies in our existential commitment to the state of affairs being contemplated and sometimes in the behavioral impulses and desires consequent on such a belief. There may be a difference in the duration of each type of emotional response. Perhaps there will also be a diminished response to *how* the state of affairs is described or depicted when we believe it is actual. However, I am wary of pushing this too far. For instance, it seems perfectly possible to be harrowed by a speech about harrowing events in the inner city given by a politician who is trying to oust the incumbent, and at the same time possible to derive a certain satisfaction from the way the speech is constructed and delivered. Similarly, we can enjoy reading an eloquent biographical account of a sad life, even if we do feel pity for its subject. There is also some difficulty in distinguishing responses to the mode of presentation from responses experienced because of content. My contention that the two are interdependent will be addressed in Chapter 7.

I have hitherto been paralleling fictional events with those actual events that do not directly affect our lives and are unlikely to do so. Of course, we will feel more intensely about something that might directly affect us (or people we know) than we will about a fictional event. But we also feel less strongly about actual events that cannot affect us directly. I have no intention of claiming that our emotional responses to fictions do not vary in intensity from our responses to actual events that do not affect us. I only wish to indicate that I think a blanket assessment of the former as less intense than the latter would probably be inaccurate.

What about responses to people rather than events? Michael Weston has maintained that we can be "moved by the mere statement of facts, but not by the mere statement of what occurs to fictional characters," that we cannot respond to characters as agents. He indicates that we can be moved by being told that a friend's son has died "in a way that renders irrelevant the detail of events leading up to his death," but not moved by the statement "Mercutio is dead." To be moved by the second statement, one must have been attending to the sense of the play.[29] Actual people and their

---

29. Michael Weston, "How Can We Be Moved by the Fate of Anna Karenina? (II)," *Proceedings of the Aristotelian Society* 49, suppl. 6 (1975): 85.

situations are said to be separable in a way that characters and the fictional events involving them are not.

However, I do not think that Weston has offered a fair comparison. Surely we are moved by the mere statement of fact at least in part as the result of our familiarity with the person who died and his family. We know how that family will suffer; we can imagine at least to some extent what their experience must be like. The objects of our pity and distress are our friend and the event of his son's death, but the origin of that pity and distress encompasses the various beliefs we have about our friend and his son, and what it is we imagine or believe our friend is experiencing. It is within the context of our awareness of these events and experiences that we pity our friend and are distressed by his son's death, just as it is within the context of our awareness of the fictional events and experiences in the world of *Romeo and Juliet* that we are distressed by Mercutio's death.

That the mere statement of fact about the actual death is undetailed is beside the point, for we are *already* in possession of details about our friend and his son. Consider the alternative example of glancing at the obituary page in the newspaper and learning that someone whom one has never met and whose absence will not affect one's life has died. Acquiring such knowledge is far less likely to arouse our distress.

Perhaps Weston means to point out the fact that even though I have read *Romeo and Juliet* and seen several performances of the play, I am not going to be distressed by an announcement of Mercutio's death unless that announcement occurs in the context of my reading the play or attending a performance of it. Yet I *will* be distressed at the announcement of the death of my friend's son, he might maintain, and that distress will not depend on my attending to some long and detailed story about that death. My answer to this is the same as the answer I have already given. We are already in possession of a "story" about our friend and his son, and we are in the midst of that story just on account of its constituting a part of our lives. We know all kinds of things about them and can imagine even more. It is what we believe and imagine that is central to our distress in that case, while it is only what we imagine that is central to our distress at Mercutio's death and our pity for him as he dies (though our pity is informed by our evaluative beliefs in both cases). Our inability to interact with dramatic personae need not preclude our responding to characters as agents any more than our not being acquainted with someone (and it being impossible that we ever will be) need stop us from responding to him as an agent. We can, for instance, respond to historical figures as agents, despite the fact that we cannot interact with them.

My motive for bringing Weston's claims into the picture at this point has to do with his delineation of a sharp distinction between our emotional responses to actual and fictional events. Naturally, I think there is a sharp distinction, but I think that it is to be found among our existentially committed beliefs rather than in our emotions. The obvious distinction between a real and a fictional object of emotion need not preclude our responding to characters as agents. We can emotionally entertain thoughts of people we imagine as well as people in whose existence we believe.

CONCLUSION

I have attempted to show how it is that we entertain the states of affairs projected by means of a fictional work and how we may imaginatively supplement those states of affairs. This process of imaginative engagement is both directed and creative, for it is a creative elaboration of the fictional funded by the beliefs and experiences of the participant. It is not a passive experience or a mere receiving of information but an active imaginative process whose arena and direction are provided by the work. One of the names for such a process can be "interpretation." The workings of the imagination can provide an explanation of divergences among the ways in which a work can be understood, and can do so without removing groundwork for the assessment and comparison of variant understandings and interpretations.

I have also claimed that the role of the imagination in our response to actual events can in many respects resemble the role it plays in our responses to fictional ones. Empathetic responses in particular can demonstrate this resemblance and can further demonstrate similarities between the way we respond to characters and to agents in the world. Empathy is an imaginative activity I have discussed in preceding chapters. Often highlighted in discussions of our emotional response to fiction, empathy has also become a frequent topic of discussion in ethics. The next chapter will focus on this phenomenon and show that these two areas of investigation may not be as divergent as at first they may appear.

6

Feeling with Fiction:
Empathy and Imagination

This chapter will explore the phenomenon of empathetic emotion. Empathy in both fictional and nonfictional contexts involves the adoption of new perspectives or different points of vantage. To empathize can be, as Mark Johnson puts it, to inhabit the worlds of others.[1] In this sense, empathetic emotion is participatory; it involves a mutuality of response. As with the approach taken toward emotion in Chapter 1, the nature of and conditions for empathy in nonfictional contexts will be initially explored. These investigations involve questions about the difference between empathetic and nonempathetic emotions. An attempt will be made to discover conditions necessary for experiencing an emotion empathetically. It will be suggested that empathetic emotions felt on behalf of actual persons may resemble emotional responses to the fictitious in significant respects. Empathy with fictional characters will then be considered in light of its similarity to empathy with real people. While it will be argued that empathy cannot constitute a necessary condition for emotional response to fictional entities or events, the very frequency of our empathy with characters can be taken to attest once more to the moral significance that fictions can have for us.

---

1. Mark Johnson, *Moral Imagination: Implications of Cognitive Science for Ethics* (Chicago: University of Chicago Press, 1993), 200.

EMOTION AND EMPATHY

Since empathy is said to involve the adoption of another's perspective or point of vantage on the world, an empathetic emotion may be taken to co-opt those facets of other people's experiences that dictate their emotional apprehension of their situation. Thus, Susan Feagin suggests that empathetic emotions depend in a fundamental way on our beliefs about the thoughts, beliefs, desires, and impulses of other people.[2] An empathetic emotional response is therefore linked to our contemplation of the features of another's experience, features that can be held to constitute or comprise a part of that individual's own emotion.

This indicates that empathetic emotion, at its inception, involves a series of inferences and extrapolations about the mental states of others, about the nature and quality of their internal experience. Empathetic responses require neither personal acquaintance nor familiarity, insofar as our inferences about the mental states of others do not always require these. We can make inferences about the mental states of strangers on the basis of how we believe most people would respond to the situation in which they are placed or on the basis of what mental states we believe are suggested by the behavior they exhibit. Such generalizations often find their way into our doxastic repertoire by means of analogies involving our suppositions about the mental states we ourselves would experience if we were to find ourselves in certain situations or to exhibit certain behaviors. That is, assumptions about the beliefs, thoughts, and desires of others may be based on a set of assumptions about oneself and what one's own experience would be, could be, or has been.

Assumptions about the mental states of others may be both warranted and unwarranted in both actual and fictional contexts. A response of nervousness on behalf, as it were, of a friend who presents a paper is unwarranted (even if we would be nervous in those circumstances ourselves) when the friend is one of those individuals who exudes confidence with every gesture, who has never exhibited any characteristic sign of nervousness, and who boldly announces her conviction of her paper's incisiveness and brilliance. Thus, an apparently empathetic emotional response can be based on unwarranted assumptions about someone's mental states, assumptions that are unsupported by all behavioral cues. Such a response is not genuinely empathetic and may even be irrational. A

---

2. Susan L. Feagin, "Imagining Emotions and Appreciating Fiction," *Canadian Journal of Philosophy* 18 (1988): 485–500.

similar criterion can be applied to fiction. Feeling affection for Sergeant Hartman on the beleaguered recruit's behalf involves imaginative assumptions about the recruit's mental states that are inconsistent with what is true in the fictional world of *Full Metal Jacket*.

Seemingly empathetic responses to the situations of real people can be contrasted with empathetic responses to the situations of fictional characters on a different score. The assumptions I make about the mental states of an actual person may be entirely justified, yet may still be false. The individual about whom I make these assumptions may be prone to idiosyncratic behaviors or may intend to deceive me. The situation or that person's reactions may be ambiguous in a number of respects that are not immediately apparent to me. Whatever the reason, as critics of arguments for the existence of other minds point out, the justifiability of my assumptions does not guarantee their truth. My response may seem empathetic to me, may be based on justified beliefs, but may nevertheless fail to be an instance of empathy when my beliefs are false. In the case of fictions, on the other hand, consistency with the states of affairs that obtain in the world of the work is all we have to go on. That is, if what we imagine concerning the mental states of a character is not inconsistent with what is true in the fictional world, there is no further level of corroboration to which our response is subject.

Keeping such distinctions in mind, let us begin by considering empathy for real people. What we believe about the beliefs, thoughts, and experiences of other individuals is said by Susan Feagin to constitute a necessary condition for empathetic emotion. This immediately suggests a distinction between empathetic and nonempathetic emotion, for the former is allied with second-order belief, while the latter is not. The difference between fear *for* another and empathetic fear *with* another could thus be explained by reviewing the kinds of beliefs associated with each response. Fear for another would involve some belief about that person being in danger, a focus of attention on aspects of the individual's situation one believed to be dangerous. One can fear for people even if they themselves apprehend no danger, and one can fear for them even if one has no beliefs about their beliefs. In contrast, empathetic fear would involve beliefs about other people's beliefs and thoughts. It would involve the contemplation of their situation as dangerous just because it was believed that they believed it dangerous.

The distinction between empathy and sympathy should be addressed, and it is a problematic one. The use of the terms themselves has varied over time and has frequently been ambiguous. Consider, for instance, that Humean "sympathy" has many characteristics in common with the conception of empathy advocated here. David Hume maintains that sympathy is not an immediate impression (as a feeling or emotion might be characterized). Instead, it is thought to account for both our capacity to vicariously experience the feelings of others and our concern for society at large: "When I see the *effects* of a passion in the voice and gesture of any person, my mind immediately passes from these effects to their causes, and forms such a lively idea of the passion as is presently converted into the passion itself. . . . No passion of another discovers itself immediately to the mind. We are only sensible of its causes and effects. From *these* we infer the passion and consequently *these* give rise to our sympathy."[3]

It is our awareness of another's behavior (the *effect* of an emotion) coupled with an awareness of an emotion's causes that leads us to feel the same emotion as that felt by the individual with whom we sympathize. A lot depends on how we choose to define "cause" in this context. Elsewhere in the *Treatise*, Hume indicates that the cause of an indirect emotion is an idea. So, for instance, an emotion like pride is said to be caused by an idea of a valuable quality in an object affiliated with oneself.[4] If it is permissible to read "idea" as "thought" or "belief," then Hume could be held to maintain that the vicarious experience of emotion rested on entertaining the thought of another's thoughts, beliefs, or ideas. That interpretation is very much in line with the conception of empathy that has been proposed.

The passage could be interpreted differently, of course. A broader interpretation might characterize the sympathizer's *sensible* awareness of the cause of another's emotion as a general awareness of that individual's situation or circumstances. On this account, Hume's sympathy no longer corresponds to empathy as my initial interpretation of the passage does, for one's emotion no longer depends on considering the beliefs or thoughts of another individual. For instance, imagine that my friend has won a major award. She repeatedly voices her delight and throws a party to celebrate. I know she is happy, since I am a witness to many behavioral manifestations of happiness. I will probably be happy that such a deserving person has succeeded. But note that my happiness can be based on my *own* evaluation (that my friend's success and her happiness are wonderful, are causes for celebration, are in accordance with her deserts, and so forth) rather than on any evaluation that I believe my friend has made. I would not consider this a case of empathy.

---

3. David Hume, *Treatise of Human Nature* 3.3.1 (Buffalo: Prometheus, 1992), 576.

4. Hume, *Treatise of Human Nature* 2.1.2, 277–80.

Douglas Chismar indicates that to empathize is to "respond to another's perceived emotional state by experiencing feelings of a similar sort," and he associates empathy with the vicarious experience of emotion, with participation in the perceived psychological stresses on another. Chismar identifies sympathy as a particular kind of empathetic response—one accompanied by a positive or supportive attitude toward the other person.[5] This accords both with the concepts of fellow feeling and affinity with which sympathy is typically associated and with some of our usage (e.g., "sympathizer" is usually taken to convey a supportiveness that "empathizer" does not). I agree that the term has such connotations but do not regard sympathy as a form of empathy, for I believe that an individual can be held to sympathize with another without considering any evaluations but his own.

The term "sympathy" appears to give rise to as much dispute among philosophers as does "empathy." For instance, it is frequently considered a synonym for "pity" or "compassion." Some philosophers take it to refer to a particular emotion, rather than to a faculty, capacity, or way of experiencing an emotion.[6] Some regard sympathy as the capacity to be concerned for the well-being of others. Some go so far as to insist that sympathetic and empathetic emotions have different content (I would say, are based on different thoughts or beliefs) and so can be regarded as distinct.[7] The preceding could be tied to the kind of distinction made between the broad and narrow construals of Humean sympathy: sympathy, as distinct from empathy, could involve entertaining the thought of another's situation and feelings exclusively from one's *own* perspective (from the standpoint of one's own evaluations) rather than that of the other person (from the standpoint of another's evaluations). The cognitive constituent of the sympathetic emotion could be one's *own* evaluative belief about another's situation or experience.

In distinguishing empathy from sympathy, Susan Feagin indicates that "whereas empathy requires responding as if I were someone else who had certain sorts of beliefs, sympathy does not necessarily require this. . . .

---

5. Douglas Chismar, "Empathy and Sympathy: The Important Difference," *Journal of Value Inquiry* 22 (1988): 257–58.

6. For instance, Arne Johan Vetlesen in *Perception, Empathy, and Judgment: An Inquiry into the Preconditions of Moral Performance* (University Park: Pennsylvania State University Press, 1994), 2.

7. Although her central distinction rests on whether a given response can be considered "primordial," Edith Stein distinguishes between sympathy and empathy on the basis of content in *On the Problem of Empathy*, 3d rev. ed. (Washington, D.C.: ICS Publications, 1989), 14–15.

The basis for my sympathetic response is not so much how the other person responds . . . but rather my judgment about how the situation is or would be likely to affect him or her."[8] It seems to be implied that to respond empathetically, one must regard a situation as another regards it, apprehend the same aspects of it as salient, entertain the thought of these aspects of the situation in the same way. Roughly, then, empathy would appear to involve a mutuality of construal or evaluation.

Yet this cannot be the case on the adoption of Feagin's account, for she clearly states that the beliefs or evaluations of the empathizer and the one with whom she empathizes must differ. For Feagin, empathetic response in nonfictional contexts involves forming second-order beliefs.[9] My empathetic fear for someone depends on my believing that he believes himself endangered. Yet the fear of the person with whom I empathize is in part constituted by a construal that can be identified with *his* belief that he is endangered. Since we have different beliefs, these cases involve different construals.

A further difficulty is posed by casting second-order beliefs as construals or the cognitive constituents of emotions. What object is it, for instance, that is construed or evaluated as dangerous? The person with whom I empathize may evaluate his circumstances or situation in this way. But I, in empathizing with him, cannot be said to do so just because of my second-order beliefs. My belief is not about his circumstances but about his beliefs. I need not and probably will not regard his beliefs as posing any danger to him.[10] These questions about second-order beliefs will be taken up in the next section.

EMPATHETIC EMOTION AND SECOND-ORDER BELIEF

The puzzle of second-order belief is further complicated when we consider cases of empathizing involving emotions that more obviously necessitate some form of self-regard. Shame or humiliation normally take *personal* experiences of wrongdoing, failure, or incompetence as objects. The cognitive constituent of pride is some thought or belief about one's

---

8. Feagin, "Imagining Emotions and Appreciating Fiction," 490.

9. Ibid., 494.

10. Of course, beliefs can be thought dangerous. However, since we are concerned with a case of empathy, such considerations are irrelevant unless one empathizes with someone who fears his own beliefs.

own achievements or affiliations. Can a belief or thought about someone else's mental states provide us with an adequate cognitive consort for empathetic pride or empathetic humiliation? Let us consider a further contrast, this time between empathy and sympathetic pity, in order to pursue this question.

The reactions of spectators to sporting events are very frequently emotional and sometimes empathetic. We will weigh the reactions of observers of the final round of the Olympic men's figure skating competition. First, both empathetic and sympathetic observers will almost inevitably make certain assumptions about the mental states of the competitors: that they want to win, that losing or making a serious mistake would distress them, that the quality of their performance is terribly important to them, that they are aware of being judged. These assumptions are virtually automatic and not particularly specific. The general circumstance of these individuals' participation in an Olympic competition could be held to justify many of the beliefs above.

A contender for the gold medal now skates out onto the ice. He begins his routine, and all goes smoothly at first. However, the first jump is botched. The skater descends too soon, in midrevolution, and wobbles precariously. As the skater wavers, empathetic observers may lean over in their seats, as if to help him regain his balance. Indeed, Robert Gordon indicates that "there is solid experimental evidence . . . that in observing others we engage in subliminal muscular activity (measurable by electromyography) that mimics their facial expressions and overt bodily motions. Feedback from such motor mimicry is thought by some psychologists to be an important factor in the recognition of emotions in others."[11] A worse fate befalls the skater. Empathizers wince as he falls sprawling on the ice, even though he is obviously not physically injured.

Sympathetic spectators will, of course, feel sorry for the skater. Just as empathetic observers do, sympathizers will make further assumptions about the skater's mental states: his lowered self-esteem, his probable belief that he has failed to exhibit his expertise adequately and that this failure has countless witnesses, his probable belief in the disapproval of judges and the contempt of observers. The sympathizer can make these assumptions about the skater's mental states the focus of his attention. To have such beliefs and experiences must be painful and unpleasant, the sympathizer believes. That is, he construes the possession of such beliefs

---

11. Robert Gordon, *The Structure of Emotions: Investigations in Cognitive Psychology* (Cambridge: Cambridge University Press, 1987), 153.

as painful and pities the skater on account of his pain. The sympathizer entertains the thought of the skater's unpleasant mental experiences compassionately. It is the belief that the skater suffers that is integral to the sympathizer's emotion. Poor guy. He must feel awful.

The empathizer entertains similar beliefs about the skater's beliefs and thoughts, the constituents of the skater's emotion. She need not take these to provide an evidential basis for the construal of the skater's plight as a painful one, however, for her empathy need involve no pity for the skater. An empathetic response may well involve a kind of excruciating embarrassment or humiliation on behalf of the skater, an emotion unlike the pity one can feel on account of another's pain. Rather than being regarded as evidence of a pitiable pain, assumptions about what the skater believes somehow provide a vantage point from which the skater's situation can be considered by the empathizer. Yet how can such a set of assumptions provide that perspective?

This example is intended to highlight the difficulty in maintaining that second-order beliefs are the central constituents of empathetic emotional response. First, though it is possible for beliefs about another's beliefs to be the focal cognitive constituents of an emotional response, this seems to occur in precisely those cases where an emotional response is not an empathetic one. That is, we can construe the possession of certain beliefs as indicative of bias or prejudice and entertain the thought of the beliefs (or the thought of their possession by someone) angrily or contemptuously. We can construe the possession of certain beliefs as indicative of self-destructiveness and entertain the thought of their being possessed by someone with worry or fear. However, none of these responses is empathetic. In no case is the perspective of the possessor of the beliefs adopted.

Moreover, the example of empathetic shame or embarrassment presents difficulties that examples focusing on emotions like fear may not make readily apparent. I can fear for myself, for others, or with others. It is easy to conflate the different types of fear in a way that makes no significant distinction between the last two cases. In the case of embarrassment or humiliation, however, it is more obvious that the emotions can only concern the actions and properties of their possessor. That is, the cognitive constituent of the skater's embarrassment or humiliation would be a consciousness of error, a belief that he had made a mistake before an abundance of (probably contemptuous) witnesses. Typically, then, humiliation or embarrassment can be associated with some estimate of one's own actions as erroneous, defective, or deserving of contempt. How, then, could a belief that someone has a certain belief represent a construal that is to be identified with empathetic embarrassment? How could the object of such a construal be a belief held by someone else? The empathizer surely does not construe the skater's *beliefs* as errors or failures, let alone as errors or failures of her own.

The proposal that second-order beliefs can constitute the cognitive elements of emotions has already arisen in other contexts. For instance, Alex Neill has proposed that our emotional responses to fiction can have beliefs about what is fictionally the case as constituent cognitions.[12] Now, it is clear that we do have such second-order beliefs, and it is also clear that they are instrumentally related both to our empathetic responses (in the case of beliefs about what is believed by another) and our emotional responses to fiction (in the case of beliefs about what is fictional). My difficulty lies in considering such second-order beliefs as construals or as thoughts we entertain emotionally. Consider my belief that it is fictional that a woman named Desdemona is treated brutally. This belief is not about either a woman or brutality but only about what is fictional. I have no intention of denying a role in emotional response to such beliefs, for a recognition of what is fictionally the case seems necessary for an imaginative engagement with the work. Perhaps to contemplate a fictional state of affairs is to form beliefs about what is fictionally the case, and that may lead to imagining that something is the case. Similarly, I think that having beliefs about the beliefs of others is necessary for empathizing with them.

I do, however, want to raise questions about how a belief that something is fictional or a belief that something is believed can be said to take the role of the kind of evaluative belief or construal typically associated with emotion, when neither of these second-order beliefs is a normative or evaluative judgment about the possession of properties having a logical or analytic connection to some emotion. Beliefs associated with empathy could be taken to ascribe the property of holding certain beliefs to certain subjects, and beliefs that something is fictionally the case could be taken to ascribe either the property of fictionality to certain states of affairs or the property of having a certain content to fictional works. None of these properties, however, have the remotest resemblance to those ascribed to objects in the course of emotional construals or evaluations.

Nor does it help to revise one's approach and claim that an empathizer humiliatedly entertains the thought that the skater believes himself to have failed and earned the contempt of others, for the empathizer does not believe of either the skater or the skater's beliefs that they are instances of

---

12. Alex Neill, "Fiction and the Emotions," *American Philosophical Quarterly* 30 (1993): 1–13.

a failure or error of her own. Similarly, to entertain the thought that, in a fiction, it is true that Desdemona is brutalized does not seem to involve entertaining that thought pityingly. Neither fictionality nor the property of having certain content (e.g., of being *about* brutal treatment) are believed to involve pain or suffering in themselves.

A way out of this quandary might involve a claim that we are considering the wrong thoughts or beliefs altogether. The cognitive constituent of empathetic embarrassment or humiliation could be the belief that the possession of beliefs about having one's errors exposed to the world is embarrassing. Or, more specifically, it could be held, not that the empathizer simply believes that the skater believes he has failed, but rather that the empathizer believes that the skater's conviction of failure is a humiliating or shaming one to have. Likewise, we could consider the belief that the state of affairs a fiction depicts or describes is a distressing one. But, again, there is a problem. The properties associated with emotional response are lacking. Why should one entertain the thought of the embarrassment contingent on the possession of certain beliefs *with* embarrassment? Why should one regard the thought of the "distressingness" contingent on a fiction's description of a certain state of affairs *with* distress? Perhaps one could, but only if one found the embarrassment of another embarrassing to oneself (if this individual's embarrassment constituted a failure of one's own or of one's affiliates), or only if one found another's distress on account of reading or viewing the fiction distressing in itself (if, for instance, one's child were terribly distressed by a horror story).

The solution here is not to reject the claims of either Feagin or Neill, for it is perfectly true that we have the second-order beliefs that they say we do, and it is also true that these beliefs are crucial to an explanation of our emotional response. I will maintain, however, that these beliefs are not the thoughts we emotionally entertain but preliminary conditions for our having such thoughts. Thus, the beliefs in question are not emotional construals and not the primary cognitive constituents of the emotions in question. Emotional responses can involve more than one cognition, of course, so my restriction applies only to the kind of cognition that has been held central to emotional response in this book.

My claims about the primary cognitive constituents of emotional responses to fiction have already been canvassed at length, and I think that a similar approach can be taken to empathetic emotion. If empathetic emotion requires the empathizer to respond as if she were someone else, as Susan Feagin indicates, then what the empathizer assumes that the skater believes and thinks is not the focus of her attention but its necessary guide.

What the empathetic observer attends to is determined by what she believes the skater believes and what she believes the skater attends to. So, for instance, the empathizer believes that the skater believes he has culpably erred while under the observation of critical or contemptuous witnesses. The empathizer does not share all of the skater's beliefs, of course. She is a witness of his fall, and she is not at all contemptuous. But she does have beliefs about how the world can seem from the skater's point of vantage: disapproving, judgmental, contemptuous. She also believes that to err in a personally and financially important demonstration of one's expertise before numerous witnesses is to diminish one's self-respect and the respect of others for oneself.

The content of the latter belief is derived from the empathetic observer's second-order beliefs — from her beliefs about the beliefs of the skater and her beliefs about what she herself and others would believe in similar circumstances. These beliefs could lead the empathizer to entertain the thought of possible disapproval on the part of the judges or possible contempt on the part of spectators. That is, the empathizer could focus her attention on beliefs embodying a perspective similar to that of the skater.

Thus far, the cognitive elements of the empathizer's emotion can still be described as beliefs. The effort has been to highlight those construals the empathetic observer can share with the skater, without venturing beyond what the observer believes to be the case. Because of this constraint, such an approach is unsatisfying. It does not explain, for instance, why it is empathetic embarrassment rather than pity that the observer feels. The empathizer, after all, does not believe that the contempt of the spectators is directed at herself; nor is she ashamed of or embarrassed about the *skater's* failure, since he and it are not her responsibility.

I think that we do hold beliefs such as those I have mentioned when we empathize, but I also think that they cannot by themselves demonstrate what it is that leads to vicariously experiencing the emotion of another. The sympathizer could have all of the beliefs that I have mentioned (about the disapproval and contempt of judges and spectators, about reduced self-esteem) and simply regard them as demonstrations of the pitiable awfulness of the skater's experience. What I am after is some further condition that will allow us to identify a distinction between sympathy and empathy. As the case stands, I am irresistibly reminded of a *Far Side* cartoon, in which a scientist's rendering of complex formulae on a blackboard is interrupted just before the final equals sign by the phrase "and then a miracle happens." Talk of the empathizer's beliefs alone, while the beliefs described are clearly involved in focusing her attention, does not permit us to discriminate between empathetic and sympathetic reactions.

EMPATHETIC IMAGINATION

What is lacking in the preceding treatment of empathy is some acknowledgment of the thoughts an empathizer entertains in imagination. It is the imagination that may explain the puzzle posed by the claim that we can feel an emotion on another's behalf when that emotion takes as objects only the personal experiences, actions, or attributes of the one who feels it. For instance, in speaking of empathy, Robert Gordon refers to "as if" emotions: emotions experienced in a simulational context.[13] In a presidential address to the American Philosophical Association, Alvin Goldman follows Gordon in proposing a simulation heuristic that can afford insight into the workings of empathy, and his model is largely based on the powers of the imagination.[14] If empathy involves picturing the skater's situation from his point of view, then it must involve imagining his point of view. Even imagining doing what the skater does must involve imagining his thoughts and beliefs. Adam Morton speaks of imagining actions and indicates that imagining an action from the perspective of a participant involves "thinking as if from the inside. . . . One cannot imagine actions without imagining thoughts also . . . to the extent that one represents the *complete* production of the action, one represents the agent's perception and thought."[15]

In the case of an emotion like humiliation, given its cognitive consorts, there are relatively few things we can believe *with* the skater, for there are few relevant beliefs we share with him. It therefore seems that the empathizer, in addition to believing that the skater has certain beliefs, imagines having those beliefs (and desires, thoughts, and impulses). She imagines believing that she has just loused up her chances for a major award, that she has failed in a demonstration of her expertise before the very witnesses who count most, that she is regarded with contempt or disapproval, that she has culpably erred. This is as close as I can get to a partial description of what it might be like to imagine being the skater in that particular situation.

The empathizer need not imagine what it would be like to be male,[16] or

---

13. Gordon, *The Structure of Emotions*, 152–53.

14. Alvin I. Goldman, *Proceedings of the American Philosophical Association* 66, no. 3 (1992): 21–24.

15. Adam Morton, *Frames of Mind: Constraints on the Common-Sense Conception of the Mental* (Oxford: Clarendon Press, 1980), 57.

16. The question of what imagining something like this could involve is addressed in the final section of this chapter.

to be someone who endorses certain products, for these are irrelevant to the emotion with which she empathizes. Her imaginative engagement is based on her assumptions about the skater's beliefs and attitudes concerning his fall. These assumptions lead her to focus serious attention on certain thoughts entertained in imagination, for instance, the thought of failure before contemptuous or disapproving spectators or judges. Because she believes that such failures and such disapproval warrant a decrease in one's estimate of one's own capacities or signify some variety of culpability, she entertains these thoughts with humiliation, shame, or embarrassment. The empathizer construes the beliefs she imagines having as beliefs whose possession warrants a diminution of self-esteem. She may, in these circumstances, feel empathetic embarrassment or humiliation with the skater.

To empathize is therefore to imagine having certain beliefs, desires, and impulses — just the beliefs, desires, and impulses one believes the individual with whom one empathizes to possess. In addition, the empathizer believes that the possession of beliefs of the kind she imagines having signifies the possession of some further property characteristically associated with the empathetic emotion in question. Thus, to employ a much simpler example, empathetic fear for someone being pursued by a maddened lion would involve imagining the possession of certain beliefs (e.g., the belief that one was just about to become a lion's dinner) and believing that the possession of beliefs of this kind usually signified being endangered (or the belief that one would be endangered, were one to be placed in that kind of situation).

Empathetic emotion does not, thankfully, meet the possible conditions for ascribing irrationality to emotion that were outlined in Chapter 1. Although the empathizer imagines having beliefs she does not believe herself to possess, and although her embarrassment can be thought to involve an imagined consciousness of having erred or exposed herself to censure or an awareness of the disapproval of others, these factors are not sufficient for labeling an empathetic embarrassment irrational. The empathetic observer does not, for instance, perform deliberate actions that are consonant with her construal rather than her belief, as was the case when Smith struck and shouted at his computer, nor does she experience any inclination to perform them. She is not inclined to avoid the eyes of spectators, slink from the arena, or announce her chagrin. Those of her physical reactions that could be termed empathetic — the wince at the skater's fall, for instance — are involuntary. She has no unjustified beliefs and no unwarranted suspicions about herself and her situation.

With the exception of the self-regarding attitude that can be explicitly identified with her empathetic embarrassment, the empathizer's attitudes toward herself and her own actions and experiences do not change. She suffers no abiding loss of self-esteem; she does not upbraid herself; she suffers from no resultant depression or self-hatred on account of having empathized. That is, she does not project what she imagines into the context of her *own* life. The empathizer imagines the self-recriminatory attitudes she would have, were she to have certain beliefs about her own experience, by imagining that she has those beliefs. Her imagining she instantiates a set of characteristics (e.g., the characteristic of having the belief that one has fallen) is sufficient for her imagining that she believes she has erred.

In Chapter 1, I suggested that irrationality could be ascribed to construals that took real objects and were inconsistent with belief only when there was some indication that behaviors and behavioral dispositions and inclinations (as well as broader attitudes) were under the influence of what was imagined rather than what was believed. In other words, we may suspect someone of irrationality when what they imagine is projected into the context of their own lives. Thus, for instance, a case of irrational pride would have to involve more than imagining one had capacities (or could claim achievements) one did not believe oneself to possess. The entertainment of such thoughts in imagination could be involved in perfectly innocuous fantasies. To be called irrational, such a state would also have to lead to unjustified beliefs, or behaviors, or behavioral inclinations consonant with what was imagined and at odds with what was believed, perhaps to emotional attitudes of contempt for the capacities of others that were dictated by what was imagined rather than what was believed. Empathetic emotion as it has been described here exhibits none of these characteristics.

The response of our empathizer could, of course, also be termed irrational if beliefs about the mental states of the skater were unwarranted or unjustified. If she assumed, for instance, that the skater considered his fall an achievement, any pride she felt could not be empathetic and would seem irrational. Likewise, if the more general evaluative beliefs involved in her response were obviously unwarranted, we could draw similar conclusions about her emotional response. The response of the empathetic observer could also be termed irrational if she empathized with an irrational response.

Two possibilities emerge when we consider such irrationality. Perhaps the empathizer believes that the belief most closely associated with the emotion with which she empathizes is entirely unjustified.[17] While it may be a simple matter to entertain the proposition that one has unjustified beliefs, it appears to me to be far more difficult to imagine believing something stupidly or unwarrantedly. Had the skater fallen a dozen times and then displayed behavioral signs of outrage at receiving low marks, a potential empathizer would still have beliefs about his beliefs: that he believed himself unjustly treated, for instance. However, the observer could consider that belief unjustified. I am not sure that she could empathize without exercising great selectivity in which beliefs she imagined, and I am not sure that empathizing with an emotion one considers irrational is not irrational in itself.

On the other hand, if the empathizer mistakenly did not believe the beliefs of the skater unjustified (assume the empathizer is the skater's doting parent) the empathetic response seems irrational for the same reason that the response empathized with is irrational. As the case stands, however, the empathetic embarrassment described in the original example involves no unjustified beliefs on the part of the empathizer or the skater. Indeed, it would be more than distressing if one of the chief sources of our understanding of others were to be considered irrational.

A further aspect of empathetic emotion should be considered. The process of empathizing as I have described it must clearly also involve imagining the construals of the individual with whom one empathizes, since it involves imagining one has that individual's beliefs. Thus, a number of beliefs the empathizer imagines having can be identified as cognitive constituents of the emotion felt by the one with whom he or she empathizes. In imagining the beliefs we believe others to possess, we may well imagine their emotions on the basis of fairly obvious inferences (e.g., anyone who believed he or she was being pursued by a lion would be terrified). To imagine believing what we believe these people do could be to imagine making certain construals. However, I do not think this means that our empathetic response amounts to nothing more than a case in which we imagine our own emotions. That would seem to suggest that we entertain the thought of having an emotion emotionally. While the thought of one's fear can sometimes be frightening (because such fear could be bad for one's heart or could lead one to make bad decisions) and

---

17. The truth or falsity of the belief is irrelevant in this case, except insofar as the truth of the second-order beliefs of the empathizer determines whether the emotion she feels is genuinely empathetic. However, one may empathize with a fear one knows to be groundless without irrationality, if the individual with whom one empathizes justifiably believes himself threatened.

the thought of one's irritation irritating (perhaps if one feels one's behavior is altogether too curmudgeonly), emotions themselves seem most unsuitable as objects for empathetic emotion.

If I feel empathy for Sam, who is pursued by lions, I imagine he believes he will probably be caught, and I imagine he is afraid. Further, I imagine believing I am about to be caught by lions. The belief I imagine is the kind of belief associated with a construal, for it amounts to imagining I believe that I am in the kind of situation I really do believe is dangerous. But the cognitive constituent of my empathetic response is not the thought of my own fear. It is the thought of the precipitous approach of hungry lions that is entertained fearfully. My attention is focused not on Sam's belief but on the content of that belief. When I imagine having the belief, I imaginatively put myself in the same relation as Sam does to the object of Sam's emotion. The thought he entertains fearfully is about the lions' approach, and this is the same thought that I fearfully entertain. More to the point, imagined or imaginative construals can be considered perfectly legitimate cognitive constituents of emotion. That the cognitive constituent of an emotion is a thought entertained in imagination need not be held to render the emotion itself unreal, as has been argued in Chapter 2, since there is no compelling reason for maintaining that the construals associated with genuine emotion must take the form of existentially committed beliefs.

For instance, the cognitive constituent of my fear for Ripley is a thought entertained in imagination: the thought that Ripley's situation is perilous, the thought of a perilous situation. Similarly, my empathetic fear involves entertaining the thought of a perilous situation in imagination, as well as the thought that this situation is perilous. Both responses are grounded in beliefs about what conditions are sufficient for the ascription of danger to a situation. Both involve imagining a state of affairs of a kind that is dangerous. Thus, the imaginative evaluations, as well as the (doxastic) grounds for each evaluation, are the same. The difference lies only in the third- and first-person perspective. That distinction could not, in and of itself, ground any claim that the second reaction was imaginary while the first was not.

To imagine believing one is endangered is not necessarily to experience fear, of course. I can imagine that I am threatened by ravening lions, evil space aliens, or tenure committees, without experiencing any symptoms of fear in the course of the imaginative contemplation of such dire and horrible threats to my well-being. Construals are necessary rather than sufficient for emotion, and a good deal depends on the nature of my imaginative engagement, on whether my imagining involves something more than the entertainment of a proposition.

The purpose in pursuing an account of empathy to this stage has not been to develop a set of necessary and sufficient conditions for empathetic response. Rather, it has been to develop a set of necessary conditions specific enough to permit a distinction between empathetic and nonempathetic emotion. Conditions sufficient for empathetic emotion would probably include stipulations similar to those involved in like conditions for other emotions: stipulations about what it was to focus the attention seriously and concernedly (or with disinterested interest, in the case of humor). The degree of that seriousness, concern, or interest and the degree of that attentiveness could be characterized as instrumental.

Thus, to seriously focus the whole of one's attention on the thought of another's suffering can be to regard it pityingly. To seriously and concernedly focus attention on the thought of culpable personal failure and the consequent contempt of others can, in empathy with the skater, amount to entertaining that thought with empathetic humiliation. Whether these thoughts are entertained emotionally depends in part on how seriously they are entertained and on how exclusively one's attention is focused, that is, on the quality and nature of the imaginative engagement.

Having established some idea of necessary conditions for empathetic emotional response, a further step is to consider the nature of such response in fictional contexts. The next section treats our empathy with characters as a special case of empathy in which what we imagine is dictated not by what we believe about the beliefs of others but by what we imagine the beliefs, desires, and thoughts of characters to be. The section opens with a discussion of what one might imagine of the beliefs, thoughts, and desires of Shakespeare's Cleopatra.

FEELING WITH THE FICTIONAL

"He words, me, girls; he words me that I should not be noble to myself."[18] She does not believe the words of Caesar, has nothing but contempt for conquests that are not one's own but those of chance: " 'Tis paltry to be Caesar; not being fortune, he's but fortune's knave." Her thoughts are not the prisons he intends for her; she knows that well, and Dolabella gives it confirmation. Caesar's own professed regard will soon confine her in an

---

18. This quotation and all other quotations in this passage are from William Shakespeare's *Antony and Cleopatra* V.ii, *The Riverside Shakespeare* (Boston: Houghton Mifflin Co., 1974).

antic sideshow of his victories, will play her for her worth to him and far beneath her own. She knows the playbill well enough. She is booked and advertised a thing of savage and barbarian appetite. And wonderfully barbarous it is to look at wholly human traits, at love and pleasure, celebration, as horrors much to be deplored, as things for exhibition rather than as ways to live. She can sense his gloating, see him point and give a catalog of crimes against the reasonable or civilized that makes of what he cannot understand and fears to feel a risible and errant curiosity. Easier by far to make denials in the face of what one cannot have, to conquer by pretending there was nothing worth the having and nothing there to threaten or to understand. Being Caesar civilized, he takes his human side and puts it at a distance: not mine, but hers! Or, mine indeed, but finally conquered, passions ruled and victory established over all not consonant with wisdoms of convention. If that's his victory—a conquest over things that threaten more and less than Rome—then it can still be overturned. Already he has made mistakes, as Egypt, crushed beneath the weight of Roman reasons, is reasoned with and comforted as if her trust were for the taking. He needs to think she is no queen, she can be ruled. He makes himself forget what she can still control and what she is. To be fooled, one must fool oneself. So Caesar is dismissed, and scorned, with some delighted expectation of his full chagrin. I do not think she is afraid. She means too much to win, assume a final regency that no one can dispute. Thus, she assumes the crown that licenses all such prerogatives. She is triumphant in anticipation, rushes toward the exercise of will that proves it sovereign. So, finally, she is queen, and maybe more: "I am fire and air; my other elements I give to baser life."

To say that I know Cleopatra wins at last because I *felt* her win (and mock Caesar in the winning) demands at least a little explanation. Cleopatra is, at the end of Shakespeare's play, tragic, indomitable, and magnificent. But she is also, and this is central to the use of my example, triumphant. Triumph is usually felt on account of a victory of one's own. On occasion, however, one can feel triumph on another's behalf. In this case, one can feel triumph *with* Cleopatra.

My experience of *Antony and Cleopatra* is characterized by a pattern of mental activity that involves extrapolation, inference, and supplementation of states of affairs as they are presented or described in the work. I imagine not just Cleopatra and her experiences but her thoughts, beliefs, and motivations, her feelings and reactions. My patterns of attention render facets of Cleopatra's experience more salient than others and also provide a ground for extrapolation, which provides further grounds for inferences, assumptions, and responses. Cleopatra's world expands or deepens as I imagine it and in the manner of my imagining.

Empathizing with a character involves imagining the beliefs, suspicions, impulses, perceptions, sensations, and reactions of that character. Susan Feagin states that such a pattern of imagining simulates or resembles the pattern of thinking or imagining one might engage in when experiencing an emotional response to a real situation.[19] Bijoy Boruah makes the empathetic imagination central to his theory of our response to fiction, identifying it with the imaginative adoption of the psychological perspective of a character.[20]

There is, moreover, a difference between a sympathetic assessment of a character's situation as tragic and an empathetic entering into a character's despair. There is a difference between an admiration of Cleopatra's resolve and courage, coupled with an awareness that she has cheated Caesar of his prize, and an empathetic sharing of her triumph, just as there is between sympathy for and empathy with actual persons. A response of sympathy or admiration entails a construal from my own point of vantage, a certain pattern of attention to states of affairs that involve the character. An empathetic response involves a different pattern of attention, informed by our imaginative adoption of the character's beliefs, desires, and sympathies. Here, the construal is made on behalf of the character or with the character. The point is to imagine the character's situation as it seems to the character, to attend imaginatively to those aspects of it that the character's beliefs and desires render salient. To put it another way, we imagine a fictional state of affairs with empathetic triumph when our focus of attention is not exclusively determined by our own evaluation of what can constitute victory, but when it is determined by what we imagine can constitute a victory for Cleopatra.

As the passage at the beginning of this section illustrates, the initial condition for empathetic response to characters involves imagining the mental states of characters rather than forming beliefs about the thoughts and responses of real people. These imaginative assumptions are made in much the same way as assumptions about actual persons. In fictional contexts, we extrapolate: we consider what would occur, what beliefs and thoughts someone would have, if that person were to say and do the things depicted or described in the fiction, or if that person were situated as a character is situated. Extrapolation, even in fictional contexts, therefore

---

19. Feagin, "Imagining Emotions and Appreciating Fiction," 494.
20. Bijoy H. Boruah, *Fiction and Emotion* (Oxford: Clarendon Press, 1988), 110–17.

involves beliefs as well as imagination. If I imaginatively entertain the thought of Cleopatra's believing that Caesar wishes to humiliate her, I do so in part because of what I believe. I believe, for instance, that if someone were actually to behave as Cleopatra does (utter the warnings she utters, for instance), this would be indicative of the person's conviction that another individual was bent on her humiliation. As was indicated in Chapter 5, extrapolation is based on what we believe would occur, were states of affairs depicted or described in the fiction to occur. A series of extrapolations about what mental states would be experienced were certain behaviors to be exhibited (or were a person placed in certain circumstances) can signify the fulfillment of initial conditions for empathetic response to fiction.

As in real-life contexts, some of our extrapolations about the mental states of characters will be based on generalizations we make or have made about people's probable experience of or reaction to different sets of circumstances. In turn, such generalizations are themselves frequently supported by beliefs about our own responses to certain situations and the characteristic sources of our own behaviors. Thus, at a certain level, any empathetic emotion can bear some relation to what one believes of oneself and one's own beliefs, thoughts, and desires.

On a parallel with empathetic response to actual persons, empathy with characters also involves imagining one has certain beliefs and thoughts: the beliefs and thoughts one imagines are possessed by the character. The empathetic triumph that I feel at the end of Shakespeare's *Antony and Cleopatra* is partly the result of imagining that I have certain beliefs: that suicide is the only alternative to a life of intolerable humiliation, that such a step is unforeseen by one's enemies, that it is a way of taking a great part of their victory from them and frustrating their plans, that, ultimately, it is a way of winning. To imagine these beliefs is to construe Cleopatra's suicide as a victory rather than a tragic escape. It is to imagine Cleopatra triumphant. To imagine *having* such beliefs can be to make that victory one's own, to feel empathetic triumph.

As has already been indicated, to imagine having certain beliefs can be to imagine making certain evaluations, for beliefs can be regarded as the cognitive constituents of emotion. To imagine having a belief can be to imagine making a construal. The belief that something one does constitutes a conquest of opposition can involve construing oneself as victorious. Such a construal is associated with the feeling of triumph. The thought of doing something that assures one of the conquest of opposition can be entertained triumphantly. It is not the case that we can only feel an illusory triumph in such circumstances. I have argued that the absence of existential commitment in the construal does not justify the classification of the associated affective reaction as nonemotional, for the cognitive constituent of an emotion need not be an existentially committed belief.

Whether the thought of conquering opposition is entertained triumphantly depends in part on whether one believes that conquests of the kind one contemplates can amount to victories, and in part on the seriousness and attention with which the thought is entertained. To imagine having the beliefs one imagines the character has is a necessary condition for empathy with characters, not a sufficient condition.

EMPATHY AND NECESSITY

It has been implied by some philosophers that empathy with characters, the adoption of their perspectives, is a necessary condition for any emotional response to fictional events and entities. I do not think this can be true. While I believe that empathetic responses to fiction are frequent, I also think that it is quite possible to be moved in the course of imagining fictional events and persons without experiencing empathetic emotion.

We can, as Bijoy Boruah suggests, adopt the psychological perspective of Desdemona, a perspective "from which the world appears to her as horrendously inauspicious."[21] The nature of the theatergoer's attention is said to be determined by adopting that point of vantage, as is his emotional response. In terms of the account put forward in this chapter, that would amount to imagining we have the beliefs we imagine Desdemona has, and feeling distress with Desdemona. But empathetic fear for Desdemona can only occur when, fictionally, Desdemona's awareness of the true nature of her situation leads her to fear for herself. Fear is only empathetic when it is shared — when it is inherent in the perspective of the one with whom one empathizes. Yet surely we fear for Desdemona prior to her awareness of Othello's dire suspicions. Surely we can anticipate a perfectly deafening explosion on Othello's part and fear for Desdemona *before* she fears for herself. This cannot be empathetic fear, but it is an emotional reaction nonetheless.

We can clearly be moved by a character's plight without empathizing with that character. Consider another example, that of George Orwell's *1984*. We are moved by imaginatively considering Winston Smith's plight,

---

21. Ibid., 111–12.

certainly. But some of us are also moved, perhaps more moved, by imaginatively considering the hopelessness of the situation of everyone in
Oceania, or the ultimate conversion and capitulation of Winston Smith. To
be horrified or distressed by imagining Smith's ultimate acceptance of the
system and the world he formerly abhorred is not to be moved by considering what it is like to be in Smith's circumstances. We are horrified
or distressed precisely because his circumstances (previously hated by
Smith) have not changed, but Smith's attitude toward those circumstances
has. So the final distress we feel is not brought about because we can see
Oceania through Smith's eyes. Nothing has changed in the external world
Smith experiences; his *beliefs* about it have changed. To imagine having
Smith's beliefs would amount to imagining a world one construed as
acceptable. Our distress is not due to our capacity to imagine what it is like
to be Smith, for I do not think it is possible for most of us to imagine in any
accurate and complete way what it would be like to be brainwashed. We
feel distress precisely because we see or imagine Smith from the *outside*.
We see that, in his struggle to change and resist a totalitarian society, that
society has not itself changed—it has simply changed and incorporated
Smith. That is not something we can see from Smith's perspective. To be
incorporated is to cease to be, or at least to cease to be the same.

In line with the last point, there is a further and more definite example
applicable to the case. Consider a film (or story, or play, or perhaps even a
picture) in which a nameless character (with no friends or relatives we
know of on the basis of information given in the work) is shot from behind
and killed instantly. The victim has not seen his killer approach, has not felt
fear, does not—as far as we can tell—have time to feel pain. Such scenes
have occurred in many films, books, and plays, and they can sometimes
elicit an emotional response. But surely it cannot be the case that they are
moving because we have entered in some way into the character's perspective. We cannot feel dislike for the attacker because we have somehow imaginatively entered into the victim's perspective, for the victim is
unaware of the attacker. We certainly cannot resent what has been done to
the victim or pity him just *because* we have imaginatively entered into his
perspective. In a manner of speaking he has no perspective: he is dead. We
can, of course, think that it would be dreadful to be killed unawares and for
no reason. But to think or imagine this is precisely *not* to enter into the
character's perspective. To enter into that perspective is to imagine what
it would be like to have an unsuspicious view of the world, a lack of
awareness of any danger. The character's experience and circumstances
have only two components: going about one's business and having one's
everyday experiences, unsuspicious of any threat, followed immediately

by death. So it is by imaginatively viewing the character and his circumstances from the outside, not from the inside, that we are moved.

Our distress at Winston Smith's ultimate plight and at the plight of the aforementioned victim *cannot* be empathetic, because they did not feel (and we cannot reasonably imagine their feeling) any distress. The beliefs, desires, perceptions, and awareness of both would never focus attention on distressing aspects of their situations, since neither is described or depicted as being aware of anything about which to be distressed.

Indeed, I believe that we can respond emotionally to fictions without entering the perspective of any character whatsoever. Imagine a film or story in which something beautiful—a painting stored in an attic, for instance—is unwittingly destroyed. No character knows that this painting is concealed in the attic of a building razed to the ground to make way for a housing development. Its destruction is never discovered, for no character in the fiction is even aware of its existence. I think that it is possible to find the (fictional) event of the painting's destruction moving. The author of the fiction may have intended to convey that beauty or the work of genius can be lost forever without anyone even noticing, without a whimper. We can be saddened by imagining the destruction of such a work of art, by believing that the destruction of works of genius is unfortunate and sad, without even momentarily entering into the perspective of any of the characters. That is, we can have an emotional response to a fictional state of affairs without empathy. I therefore conclude that emotional responses to fiction are not necessarily empathetic.

THE EMPATHETIC AND THE NORMATIVE

As was indicated in Chapter 4, our own evaluative beliefs and normative judgments may limit the extent of our imaginative response to fiction. This may apply to cases of empathetic response as well. However, that is not to say that beliefs, desires, and impulses one does not already possess cannot be imagined, and it is not to say that we cannot imagine having them. Our imaginative ability to grasp and contemplate human situations is not so rigidly circumscribed.

Consider Euripides' Medea, a character many of whose values and normative judgments it seems impossible to share. There are still moments at which one can empathize with Medea, particularly those during which Jason patronizes Medea, pompously defending his own actions and motives. He maintains, for instance, that he owes Medea no gratitude, for it was not she but "love's inescapable power that compelled" her to keep Jason safe.[22] I imagine that Medea believes Jason both a hypocrite and an ungrateful wretch, believes that she has been used and is being discarded once her usefulness is finished, believes that she is suffering an intolerable insult and humiliation. Indeed, at the end of the play she tells Jason that it is ultimately his insolence that destroyed their children,[23] a claim that intriguingly echoes Jason's assertion that he need not be grateful nor she responsible for actions compelled by love.

Be that as it may, I do imagine Medea's beliefs, her desire for vengeance, her rage at Jason. My evaluative beliefs enter into these imaginings even though I do not believe that the kind of vengeance Medea exacts is justified and even though I hold no retributory theory of justice. My beliefs about the wrongness of using people, about the nature of ingratitude, about the pain of rejection, about people who do not give credit where it is due, all ground my extrapolations about Medea's mental states, as do Medea's own professions. There are moments during the course of the play, even though its conclusion is unlikely to be one of them, during which many could empathize with Medea's anger toward Jason. To imagine believing that one has been used, and to entertain the thought of being used angrily, would not place any undue strain on the normative repertoire of the average spectator.

The Medea offers another example of the possibility for empathy that can be illustrated by reference to a somewhat ambiguous passage. This passage has prompted different and incompatible interpretations of Medea's beliefs and motivations.[24] It could thus be associated with different imaginative assumptions about those beliefs. At one point in the drama, Medea indicates that if she does not kill her own children, she suffers them "to be slain by another hand less kindly to them. Force every way will have it they must die."[25] But what of taking them to Athens with her? (There was room for their bodies in Medea's chariot, certainly.) Athens is referred to in an earlier passage, but what Medea believes remains somewhat obscure. She says to herself, "If they live with you in Athens they will cheer you. No! By hell's avenging furies, it shall not be — this shall never be that I should suffer my children to be the prey of

22. Euripides, *The Medea*, trans. Rex Warner, in David Grene and Richard Lattimore, eds., *Euripides I* of *The Complete Greek Tragedies* (Chicago: University of Chicago Press, 1972), lines 529–31, p. 76.

23. Ibid., lines 1364–66, p. 105.

24. The ambiguities cited here appear in three translations other than the one I use.

25. Euripides, *The Medea*, lines 1239–40, p. 101.

my enemies' insolence."[26] What exactly is the import of this passage? Does she foresee her children becoming the prey of her enemies in Athens? Will they be victimized in exile, perhaps due to the loss of social status that exile implies? Is her killing them the only alternative to their ill-usage?

There can be at least two interpretations of the passages, hence two ways of imagining Medea's motivations and beliefs. First, one could imagine that Medea believes that the only alternative to the killing of her children is their being brutalized, because she foresees a sad fate for them in exile, or because she herself has cursed them and expects the curse to bear fruit, or because she thinks that there are strong possibilities of her capture, and of the children's punishment in retribution for the deaths of Creon and his daughter. Her motivations still involve revenge on Jason, of course, but being the agent of Jason's misery is no longer paramount. It is conceivable that a person who imagined such beliefs and motivations might also imagine having to choose between death and a life of pain and ignominy for one's children and thus might feel an empathetic distress on behalf of Medea.

However, many find an alternative interpretation of the fictional states of affairs more convincing, perhaps because they find it difficult to imagine that Medea believes there is absolutely no alternative to killing her children. In this case one imagines Medea's vengefulness, her belief that this is the only way to exact full retribution. I have read commentaries that stress each reading, though the latter predominates and is itself supported by other passages. The second reading also involves beliefs and desires that it is more difficult to imagine having. In the former case, one's evaluative beliefs might not be at odds with the construal one imagines. For instance, one might believe that a swift death was preferable to a horrible and lingering one, and focus attention on only the former estimates of Medea's beliefs and concerns. On the other hand, to imagine believing that the killing of one's children was a justifiable (if horrible) act of retribution on their other parent, to entertain the thought of performing such an act with some degree of acceptance (to entertain it self-righteously, for example, or at least with resignation) would have to involve some judgment of one's own that acts of this kind *could* be justified.

Clearly, then, what one imagines of Medea's motives and beliefs, taken together with what one believes concerning the kind of act, event, or condition the beliefs one imagines are about, determines whether one can imagine having those beliefs and determines whether one can empathize

---

26. Ibid., lines 1058–61, p. 95.

with Medea. This does not mean that we cannot imagine believing what we do not in fact believe. It should simply be noted that we may experience difficulty in making imaginative construals that are wholly unsupported by or at odds with those of our normative judgments that we have not come to doubt. To imagine believing that one's action is justified or permissible can be to entertain the thought of that action with approval or acceptance and would seem to require believing that acts of this kind are permissible or acceptable at least in certain circumstances, believing that the act instantiates qualities that confer acceptability.

The upshot of the preceding is that empathy for a character can sometimes depend on considering *in isolation* some of the beliefs one imagines the character to have. The focus of attention, when consonant with broad evaluations and normative judgments, can result in an empathetic emotional response. Thus, it is quite possible that even paragons of probity and virtue can imagine having some of the beliefs and desires of the blackest fictional villain, if that villain's doxastic repertoire is imagined selectively enough or if the attention is focused selectively enough. Consider a typical chase scene, in which the villain, whether Mr. Hyde or a fugitive vampire, is vastly outnumbered and pursued relentlessly by do-gooders equipped with flaming torches. It is not so unusual to feel an empathetic twinge of fear on behalf of the evil-doer, if one imagines having the belief that one is being hounded to one's death by hostile adversaries. Empathy with characters, while one's focus of attention derives in part from one's evaluative beliefs, is not necessarily circumscribed either by any overall ethical assessment of a character or by some assumption of overall commonality between our own normative judgments and those of a character. Empathy rests not on these factors but on our ability to imagine having the beliefs and experiences of another and thus on our ability to imaginatively inhabit the situations of others.

Mark Johnson allies the empathetic imagination with imaginative participation in another's experience and describes it as "perhaps the most important imaginative exploration we can perform. It is not sufficient merely to manipulate a cool, detached, 'objective' reason toward the situation of others. We must, instead, go out toward people to inhabit their worlds, not just by rational calculations, but also in imagination, feeling, and expression."[27]

Insofar as fiction can work on and through our conceptions of the possible and the significant in life, insofar as it can inform our conceptions

---

27. Johnson, *Moral Imagination*, 200.

of how life could or should be lived, its connection with the empathetic is twofold. First, it should be noted that empathetic emotion in entirely nonfictional contexts takes on the structure of emotional response to fiction. Both involve an exploration of imagined worlds, one circumscribed by what is believed fictional, the other by what is believed to be experienced by another.

Second, empathy can provide new insights into the experience and motivation of others, and can thus lead us to a new awareness of or alteration in our existing normative judgments. The empathetic imagination is not considered morally significant merely because it can provide fodder for ethical debates about exculpatory motivations. The imaginative entertainment of beliefs, desires, and impulses that is necessary for empathy can provide insights into denial, self-deception, rationalization, self-destructiveness, and conflicts among desires. For instance, an imaginative investigation of the mental states of Euripides' Medea can expose the tendency to ascribe responsibility for one's actions to agencies (whether they are gods or neuroses, emotions or evil humors, nature or nurture) whose compulsion is claimed to be irresistible, and this is certainly relevant to ethical discourse.

Empathy can also provide insights into responses to certain kinds of treatment or experience. Different complexes of beliefs, desires, impulses, and reactions can constitute responses to the behavior of others, to one environment rather than another, to one mode of living rather than another. Clearly, this kind of empathizing, whether with a character or a person, can involve imagining what it may be like to be on the receiving end of certain kinds of treatment, or imagining what it may be like to live in a certain way. Empathetic responses to literature can often provide the clearest route to a work's ethical perspective on the human condition or on human nature, for empathy involves imaginatively entering into a perspective other than one's own.

Investigations of empathy have a clear application to human relationships and interactions. The imaginative adoption of alternative perspectives can involve extrapolations whose application transcends the fictional. Imagining how people *would* or *could* react to something can be involved in our own practical predictions, for example, when we imagine how someone could or would react to an action of ours, a criticism, or a change in environment, *before* they experience it. That is, we imagine what their beliefs, desires, and impulses would or could be, were they to have that experience. Indeed, we may even imagine *having* such beliefs. This suggests that the individuating features (the beliefs, desires, and impulses of the one with whom one empathizes) of an empathetic response are sometimes central to an assessment of the ethical import and impact of decisions, actions, and policies.

In the recent philosophical literature, the relevance of empathy to moral theory has been repeatedly stressed. Alvin Goldman characterizes empathy as a capacity that "seems to be a prime mechanism that disposes us to altruistic behavior."[28] Empathy has been thought integral to that which binds individuals to one another and drives them toward realizable social goals.[29] It has been offered as a justification for moral judgments, a justification held to prove more efficacious than those more commonly accepted.[30] An incapacity to empathize, conceived as a cognitive deficit, has even been put forward as an explanation of psychopathy as allied to certain kinds of criminal behavior.[31]

I cannot help but speculate that Hume may have had much of this in mind when he proposed that sympathy (which, on the narrower interpretation that was proposed, could be identified with empathy) "produces our sentiment of morals."[32] Furthermore, recent investigations in ethics might be enlisted in Hume's defense. We could, for instance, ally a failure to possess a "natural" moral impulse not with a failed generalization but with an *un*natural neurophysiological deficit. My suppositions depend largely on drawing connections between Hume's treatment of the indirect passions and his treatment of sympathy and benevolence elsewhere in the *Treatise*. Whether such a step is deemed acceptable or not, much of the preceding suggests that Hume remains in many respects a precursor of current investigations in moral theory.

One further area of both ethics and epistemology to which an account of empathy could contribute involves the question of what, precisely, it might take to know what the experience of a given group (e.g., a minority) is like. The question is usually treated as political, because it arises most frequently in political contexts. It has been argued that only those who know what it is like to have the experiences common to a given group should participate in the formulation of policies affecting the interests of that group. The pertinence of empathy to such arguments clearly concerns the knowledge claim rather than the political claim. Can one know

---

28. Goldman, "Empathy, Mind, and Morals," 35.

29. John M. Abbarno, "Empathy as Objective Moral Value," in Lee, ed., *Inquiries into Values* (Lewiston: Mellen Press), 161.

30. Joel K. Kupperman, "Ethics for Extraterrestrials," *American Philosophical Quarterly* 28 (1991): 311-20.

31. John Deigh, "Empathy and Universalizability," *Ethics* 105 (1995): 743-63.

32. Hume, *Treatise of Human Nature* 3.3.1.

what certain experiences are like, for instance, the experiences unique to a particular race, ethnic group, or gender, when one is not a member of the group that has them? Some hold that such knowledge claims should properly be analyzed not as claims concerning knowledge by acquaintance but as claims involving a limited set of sufficient cases of factual knowledge.[33]

The factual claims under consideration would, naturally, pertain to the kinds of experiences had and attitudes encountered by members of the relevant group. While such an approach is certainly not logically flawed, there remain many questions about the sheer number of factual claims that could be held sufficient for knowledge of what it was like to be a member of that group. There are also questions about the probability of acquiring sufficient factual knowledge in circumstances where an acquisition of knowledge by experience is impossible for an agent. Empathy might provide some additional evidence for the contention that the acquisition of the requisite information was not only possible but also not improbable. As I have argued throughout this chapter, empathy requires the imaginative adoption of the beliefs, attitudes, and desires of another, based on what it is that one believes about the other's particular experience. Empathetic emotion, when achieved, is a form of vicarious experiencing that may lead an individual to draw conclusions that might not otherwise have been drawn.

Consider the case of a couple, both philosophers. The husband ("H") believes that male professors are as well equipped to teach courses in feminist ethics as female professors. People of both sexes can understand socioeconomic oppression: it is a fundamental human experience. His wife ("W") is a bit less inclined to subscribe to this contention. W wonders whether men can fully comprehend the lot of women in the present culture and whether incomplete comprehension might not prove a liability in teaching a course based on the contemplation of that very lot. W and H travel to an APA meeting in a distant urban center. Immediately upon their arrival, they are accosted by large troglodytic strangers and narrowly escape being mugged. (They are, in fact, rescued by a heroic Jamaican cab driver, but that is another story.) Finally ensconced in their hotel room, they begin to discuss the attempted mugging. H is still very disturbed by it. In fact, he is horrified. What a loathsome city! W is considerably more sanguine. H inquires why W is not upset, why she is calmly leafing through

---

33. For instance, Donald W. Harward argues in this way in "Can I Know What It's Like to Be a . . . (e.g. Woman) and Not Be One?," *Journal of Value Inquiry* 14 (1980): 35–42.

the APA program and folding down page corners instead of resonating with retroactive distress. W tries to explain. She is used to it — not used to being mugged but used to exercising caution. She is physically small and female. She has been accosted in the street by strangers many times over the years. She is more inclined to wariness and distrust than is H. It is safer to be wary and distrustful. The attempted mugging was not as much of a shock to her as it was to H. H contemplates the idea of feeling as vulnerable as he did earlier that day (and still to some extent does) *most* of the time. He shudders. He begins to suspect that there is something to the claim that it is preferable to have women teach courses in feminist ethics.

The point of the above example is *not* that men should not teach feminist ethics, since I think H would probably do a great job. The point is that H's moment of empathy, stimulated by the analogous experience, brought home to him what theoretical discussion had not. Empathetic emotion simulates another's experience and may also provide a basis for further suppositions. The advantages in this context are twofold: first, the empathetic imagination provides the closest possible analogue to knowledge by acquaintance; second, it provides another source of hypotheses about experiences.

The fact that empathetic response is typical of the experience of fiction would therefore seem to suggest that fiction can aid in the development of capacities and habits of attention whose exercise is by no means confined to impractical flights of fancy and whose acquisition may legitimately be regarded as ethically important.

CONCLUSION

One interest that must be central for any philosopher wishing to establish a connection between ethics and literature lies in the similarities between empathetic response in nonfictional contexts and the construals we make when we respond empathetically to characters in fiction. Both involve imaginative extrapolation in an investigation of imaginary or hypothetical situations. According to Ronald de Sousa, "one component of the need for art is the desire to experience the emotions called forth by death, by sexual thrall, by revenge, or by painful or ridiculous alienation, by evoking the relevant paradigm scenarios [I would say, by making the relevant construals] without having to live through the actual events that are their natural causes."[34] This will figure in the next chapter's discussion of why it is we wish to undergo emotional experiences that could be regarded as harrowing in other contexts. For now, it is worth noting the relevance of this passage to an account of empathetic imagination, which allies our perspective with that of a character undergoing certain experiences. Empathetic engagement with fiction can be and often is ethically significant precisely because it allows us to explore experiences we have not had from perspectives that are not wholly our own but that we can make our own.

---

34. Ronald de Sousa, *The Rationality of Emotion* (Cambridge: MIT Press, 1990), 320–21.

7

The Satisfyingly Sad
and the Sadly Satisfying

"Tomorrow is another day." The last line of *Gone with the Wind* is met by a wail of anguish from my friend JoBeth. I later discovered that she had seen the film five times. She had read the book three times. Each of these episodes had been a six- or seven-handkerchief operation. On this occasion, JoBeth entered the theater armed with an entire box of Kleenex, most of which was used up during initial scenes in an orgy of anticipatory weeping. At fourteen (JoBeth was fifteen), I was painfully embarrassed. JoBeth was not a quiet crier. Her sobs, punctuated by loud, gurgling lamentations, attracted unwelcome attention. At last, I dragged her from the theater, hoping no one would recognize us. She mopped her swollen face with wads of wet Kleenex. "Wasn't it great?" she inquired damply. "Let's go back for the next show." I was dumbfounded. Why go through that again?

I should, in justice, have recollected my own inconsolable keening at the end of *Old Yeller*, a seven-handkerchief movie if ever there was one, and one that I had seen several times. That I did not understand JoBeth's reaction was probably due to the fact that I considered the dog a more worthy object of concern. Be that as it may, JoBeth and I had both, on separate occasions, undergone the experience of finding a fiction shatteringly sad. And we had both wanted to do it all over again. Why?

There are far more sophisticated versions of my question in both current and ancient philosophical literature. These are, nonetheless, centered on the same puzzle. Fictions can inspire in us emotions that are typically considered highly unpleasant: fear, sadness, pity, distress, revulsion, anger. It is strange enough that we voluntarily undergo such experiences, even pay money for the opportunity. It is stranger still that we appear to take pleasure or satisfaction in them, that we go in for repeat experiences and invite our friends to share them. This may have been part of what led philosophers like Kendall Walton to say that we do not feel genuine emotions when we respond to fictional states of affairs, led Colin Radford to call our emotional reactions to fictional events irrational, and led numerous other philosophers to employ terms like "art emotions," "fictional emotions," "imaginary emotions," and "aesthetic emotions" when describing emotional responses to fictional events—as if they were somehow fundamentally different in kind from emotional reactions to actual events.

I will focus on those accounts in which both the existence of our pleasure or satisfaction in a tragic or frightening fiction and the existence of our negative emotional responses to it are acknowledged. In the first three sections of this chapter, I will use different interpretations of Aristotelian catharsis as an organizing principle enabling me to group together theories and hypotheses that make related claims about the coincidence of pleasure and negative emotion in response to fiction. My intention is not to come to any definite conclusion about which interpretation is correct or preferable. The debate over how we are to understand the term *catharsis* as it is used in chapter 6 of Aristotle's *Poetics* has raged throughout this century and those before. I do not pretend to be privileged with some special insight that would allow its single-handed resolution. Neither do I intend to provide anything resembling a complete survey of the literature on Aristotelian catharsis, which is as vast as it is diverse.

I do wish, however, to reflect on variant interpretations of catharsis because many of them, whether true of the Aristotelian conception or not, convey important insights into our experience of a certain kind of fiction: the kind that gives rise to negative emotional reactions on the one hand and to some degree of pleasure or satisfaction on the other. All of the approaches that will be canvassed have one crucial feature in common: the object of the negative emotional response is said to be different from the object of the satisfaction or enjoyment. We do not entertain exactly the same thought with both distress and satisfaction. Hence, the dual reaction reflects no inconsistency.

ENJOYING EXCITEMENT AND EMOTIONAL RELEASE

In the *Poetics*, Aristotle speaks of tragedy's depiction of incidents "effecting through pity and fear [what we call] the *catharsis* of such emotions."[1] This is often linked to a passage in the *Politics*,[2] in which Aristotle describes persons who have fallen into a religious frenzy as a result of listening to sacred or mystic melodies and who are restored as though they had found healing and purgation. He continues by pointing out that "those who are influenced by pity or fear and every emotional nature must have a like experience . . . and all are in a manner purged and their souls lightened and delighted."[3] It has been suggested that the object of our satisfaction or delight would in this case be the relief or emotional release provided by the drama.

Alternative but not entirely unrelated accounts focus not on ridding ourselves of emotions like pity and fear but on *relishing* them. John Morreall makes the suggestion that our own negative emotions may be the objects of our satisfaction or pleasure, but his hypothesis is that they can play this role because we just, in certain controlled circumstances, *enjoy* negative emotions.[4] He uses mountain climbing and skydiving as examples of experiences that can involve both fear and pleasure. In an approach that is not dissimilar, Susan Feagin suggests that we like certain types of horror fiction because we "enjoy being grossed out." She indicates that certain aspects of our experience, "the adrenalin rush, the tingles, the queasiness," may come to be not only enjoyable but positively habit forming.[5] Marcia Eaton states that such accounts exemplify "the roller coaster theory" and acknowledges that in such cases the exhilaration one feels — or the pleasure — depends to some extent on the fear. There are simply times when we "like to feel our juices flowing."[6] Although I think

1. Aristotle, *Aristotle's Poetics*, Chapter 6, trans. James Hutton (New York: W.W. Norton, 1982), 60.

2. The connection with book 8 of the *Politics* is said to have been widely popularized by Bernays, for instance, by Stephen Halliwell, *Aristotle's Poetics* (Chapel Hill: University of North Carolina Press, 1986), 191, 353, and Leon Golden, "The Purgation Theory of *Catharsis*," *Journal of Aesthetics and Art Criticism* 31 (1973): 473–78.

3. Aristotle, *Aristotle's Politics* VIII, Chapter 7, trans. Benjamin Jowett (Oxford: Clarendon Press, 1920), 315.

4. John Morreall, "Enjoying Negative Emotions in Fictions," *Philosophy and Literature* 9 (1985): 95–103.

5. Susan Feagin, "Monsters, Disgust, and Fascination," *Philosophical Studies* 65 (1992): 82, 81.

6. Marcia Eaton, *Aesthetics and the Good Life* (New Jersey: Associated University Presses, 1989), 56–57.

that the satisfaction of the mountain climber or skydiver may sometimes be the kind of satisfaction one takes in one's own competence and in the ability to control one's own fear, there does seem to be truth in the contention that one would not find pleasure in such experiences were the element of fear to be entirely eliminated.

It is not clear to me, however, that fear itself can be characterized as the object of one's pleasure or satisfaction in such cases, or at any rate that it is specifically one's fear that is the object. What Morreall has to say about anger may shed some light on this. He indicates that we can take considerable pleasure in the arousal and excitement of getting angry and that, physiologically, this arousal is much like that associated with fear.[7] Perhaps what it is that we can enjoy outright is the component of excitement or physiological arousal in our fear or our anger, the physical sensation of having our adrenalin pumping, and so on. In that case, fear and anger are not precisely the objects of our satisfaction. What seems indisputable, however, is that the physiological component they have in common with excitement can be, under certain circumstances, a pleasant sensation. In that sense, of course, we can enjoy the experience of feeling our juices flow, and this could apply to our reactions to fictions as well as to real life situations, the parameters of which are controllable.

This caveat is made both by Eaton and by Morreall. The enjoyment of the negative emotion depends on control. The roller-coaster rider is in a controlled situation and he knows this. He does not believe that his car will fly from the rails. Likewise, neither the skydiver nor the mountain climber believes that she will plunge to her death. Otherwise, they would hardly take satisfaction in their experiences. They have control over the dangerous aspects of their respective situations that can be spelled out both in terms of their expertise and in terms of the reliability of their equipment. If their trust in their expertise or equipment proved misplaced, if the skydiver and mountain climber proved not to have the control over their situations they believed they had, any enjoyment they might have taken in either their emotional states or other features of their experience would be bound to dissipate very quickly indeed.

Similarly, any enjoyment we might get from some adrenalin-arousing response to a fictional event depends on our control of the situation. It seems that our experiences of fictions are by definition controllable: if

---

7. Morreall, "Enjoying Negative Emotions in Fictions," 85. This claim is not unrelated to some of those canvassed in Chapter 1. For instance, Schachter and Singer maintain that the same state of physiological arousal can be associated with any number of entirely distinct emotions (e.g., joy and fury) depending on the cognitions available to the subject.

they are fictions, we can always choose to withdraw our attention, leave the theater. Yet, just as we cannot enjoy a roller-coaster ride if we are attending to a suspicion that it has gone out of control or is likely to do so,[8] so we might not be able to feel any pleasure at all in our terror upon watching Hitchcock's *The Birds* if we have an irrational fear of birds, as Marcia Eaton has pointed out.[9] The fear of birds could simply get out of hand, despite the fact that we know we are dealing with a fiction.

I remember a scene from the film *Indiana Jones and the Temple of Doom* in which the heroine had to reach into a crevice teeming with hundreds of loathsome insects in order to pull a lever that would prevent her compatriots from being crushed. While the words "let them die" never passed my lips, I would not have been entirely unsympathetic had she done so. I suspect that my reaction was one of revulsion rather than fear. This is a revulsion the director, Steven Spielberg, undoubtedly intended his audience to feel, but not, I think, to the extent of having some of its members regard the heroine's possible desertion of her companions with equanimity. As in the case of Eaton's subject, my reaction to the scene was less than pleasant and almost involuntary. I have a deep and abiding dislike of anything with more than four legs. My response, moreover, was empathetic. The scene led me to imagine a tactile encounter with roachlike insects the size of Chihuahuas. For someone who suffered from a genuine phobia, entertaining these thoughts in imagination could lead to a reaction that was far more intense than mine.

Such fictions can tap into preexisting and very specific fears that are associated with previous experiences. Empathetic viewers might come perilously close to imagining their worst nightmares. Typically, phobic reactions are tied either to unjustified evaluative beliefs or to inconsistent imaginative construals. They are said to involve the inability to refrain from construing certain objects or events as dangerous or harmful, even in the face of strong counterevidence. William Lyons, for instance, states that an agoraphobe's fear "is based on an incontrovertible evaluation of open spaces as dangerous; he allows no evidence to count for or against his evaluative judgment."[10] A *New York Times* interview with Dr. Joseph

---

8. My friend Hanita Blair, a hater of roller coasters, assures me that this suspicion is a common one. Personally, I am very fond of roller coasters.

9. Marcia Eaton, *Aesthetics and the Good Life*, 60. Films could presumably also change our attitudes toward actual events. For instance, watching the Hitchcock film might produce a fear of birds in some subjects. However, the question under consideration is about what might cause a failure to control our imaginative engagement and absorption. It is Eaton's contention that a phobic reaction might sometimes have such results.

10. William Lyons, *Emotion* (Cambridge: Cambridge University Press, 1980), 72. Of

LeDoux, a professor of neurobiology at New York University, confirms this analysis: " 'You can tell the phobics all day long, "This will not hurt you," ' Dr. LeDoux said, 'but they don't believe it.' "[11] This suggests that a like construal could be almost involuntarily made in the course of empathetic engagement with fiction.

Similar reactions could occur when a painful or terrifying event of a kind previously experienced by a reader or viewer was described or depicted in the fiction. It has been suggested in earlier chapters that fictions can reactivate the emotions felt on account of past experiences and that there is a sense in which our emotional response involves the evaluation of an occurrent stimulus in terms of previous experiences. All this indicates the possibility that a particularly graphic and realistic rendering of an incident similar to one experienced by a subject can reactivate a previous emotion in a way that it is difficult for that person to control or prevent. Control, with fictions, seems to involve not a lack of imaginative absorption but an inability to curtail it.

David Novitz makes much the same point when he says that it is our "ability to move in and out of the imaginative mode which helps explain the pleasure we sometimes feel in being moved by a tragedy, or in being angered by the wickedness of the villain." But, while "a sophisticated and informed reader moves in and out of imaginative absorption with relative ease," this is not always the case. For instance, "a child finds this more difficult, becomes 'caught up in' the fiction."[12] Obviously, this need not be true only of children. A great many of us have dislikes or aversions, only some of which might be termed irrational, that can either prevent the possibility of imaginative absorption because of a refusal to focus attention or may provoke an excessive absorption from which it is difficult to extricate oneself.

This indicates that all responses of satisfaction to those of our encounters with fiction involving negative emotions (on account of our imaginative absorption) require of us a certain control over our own imaginative engagement. I am not claiming that imaginative distance is a requisite for the proper appreciation of a work, for this might imply that there is something inappropriate in our responses of pity or distress to fictional

---

course, the agoraphobe may also fear the possibility of experiencing a panic attack upon venturing out of doors. This is not the fear at issue in the present discussion, however.

11. Sandra Blakeslee, "Tracing the Brain's Pathways for Linking Emotion and Reason," *New York Times*, 6 December 1994, B11.

12. David Novitz, *Knowledge, Fiction and Imagination* (Philadelphia: Temple University Press, 1987), 85–86.

tragedy, and I do not believe there is. I do think, however, that one must have the capacity to distance oneself, to move out of imaginative absorption, if satisfaction or pleasure are to play any part in one's experience of a fictional tragedy or horror story.

In any case, provided one retains the capacity to regulate one's own imaginative engagement, it seems that talk of the pleasures of emotional release provides us with a different object of emotion than that which is the focus of our pity and fear. I may be both terrified and repelled while watching the film *Alien*. My fear and revulsion, however, take different objects than does my satisfaction. I fearfully entertain the thought of Ripley's peril. I entertain the thought of the alien's appearance with a kind of horrified revulsion. Yet these responses themselves may be instrumental to my feeling the pleasure of emotional release. My experience may somehow lead me to purge myself of negative emotions (e.g., as conveyed by the expression "blowing off steam") and this feeling of freedom may be pleasant. Alternatively, I may simply enjoy letting myself go. In other words, I get to yell and carry on and feel my adrenalin flow without paying the price of experiencing the context natural to an emotion like fear.

Of course, many philosophers have voiced serious objections to any view that allies catharsis with an (often pleasurable) emotional release. For instance, the clinical flavor that such an interpretation conveys concerning a work focused mainly on structural analysis has been found inappropriate, especially since it does not allow for the possibility of metaphorical usage.[13] Several commentators point out that the homeopathic approach to medical cures that the reading suggests is not one to which Aristotle can be held to have subscribed.[14] Numerous other objections to this reading have been voiced and equally numerous alternatives have been proposed. The purpose of this chapter, however, is to explore theories that account for the coincidence of pleasure with more negative emotion in reactions to the same work. I will therefore, with one further exception, focus on insights into the preceding puzzle that a survey of works related to Aristotelian catharsis may afford, rather than on claims about how the *Poetics* is to be interpreted.

The exception referred to above involves alternative readings of the

13. For instance, by Eva Schaper in *Prelude to Aesthetics* (London: Allen and Unwin, 1968), 107, and by Allen Paskow in "What Is Aesthetic Catharsis?," *Journal of Aesthetics and Art Criticism* 42 (1983): 60.

14. See, for instance, Jonathan Lear, "*Katharsis*," *Phronesis* 33 (1988): 301, and K. G. Srivastava, "A New Look at the '*Katharsis*' Clause of Aristotle's *Poetics*," *British Journal of Aesthetics* 12 (1972): 261.

catharsis passage that are important enough to note in passing, though they have no bearing on the present enterprise. These interpretations take the terms *pity* and *fear* or the term *catharsis* to characterize fictional events rather than spectator reactions. For instance, Charles Daniels and Sam Scully maintain that chapter 6 of the *Poetics* merely offers a characterization of the kinds of events appropriate for inclusion in tragedy, a classification of actions according to the typical but purely contingent reactions they may elicit.[15] Catharsis is simply the fitting or appropriate resolution to events that may be so classified. Gerald Else has put forward an interpretation of catharsis that, like the preceding, allies it with the dramatic structure of tragedy. Here, catharsis becomes a purification of the tragic act, a kind of exoneration of the tragic figure, whom we cannot pity or fear for until his lack of moral culpability is established.[16] The purification is an exoneration of the drama's protagonist; if the character were not so exonerated, we would not be able to pity him. The contention is that we can only regard the thought of the character's suffering pityingly when it is the thought of an *undeserved* suffering.

Catharsis thus has no immediate or obvious link with pleasure on this approach, that is, no link that would not require a separate explanation. Indeed, neither of these accounts suggests a conflict in the emotional reaction of the reader or viewer, for either the pity and fear, or their catharsis, or both, reside in the play and not in the subject. Else's approach does, however, ally pity with an indisputably normative evaluation of desert on the part of the subject; his approach also confirms some of the claims made in Chapter 4.

---

15. Charles B. Daniels and Sam Scully, "Pity, Fear and *Catharsis* in Aristotle's *Poetics*," *Nous* 26 (1992): 204–17. Daniels and Scully appear to make the move they do at least in part because of a view they ascribe to competing analyses. They maintain that some take the passage in the *Poetics* to convey the idea that the creation of emotion in the spectator (and its catharsis) is an essential characteristic of tragedy. However, the claim that catharsis is the telos of tragedy need not amount to the claim that nothing can count as a tragedy (or a good tragedy) unless it has aroused a catharsis of pity and fear. The purpose of a thing need not constitute an essential characteristic of that thing in quite so downright a way. Knives are for cutting, but there may be knives that have never cut. The point is, surely, that they have the potential to do so.

16. Gerald F. Else, *Aristotle's Poetics: The Argument* (Cambridge: Harvard University Press, 1967), 433–37.

ACHIEVING EQUILIBRIUM: REHEARSAL AND META-RESPONSE

There are alternative treatments linking catharsis to a type of moral or religious purification. Some of these do not take catharsis to involve the removal of an impurity but understand it as "a restoration of proper equilibrium,"[17] or a harmonizing of our emotions with our perceptions of and judgments about the world.[18] It is thought to involve a "process of psychological attunement or balance" that can shape our future capacities for response through habituation.[19] Humphry House and Stephen Halliwell both invoke Aristotelian concepts of moderation from the *Nicomachean Ethics* and remind us that, according to Aristotle, pity and fear are not in themselves undesirable but can be appropriate reactions to certain types of situations.[20] So a tragedy can be thought to rouse our emotions "by worthy and adequate stimuli; it controls them by directing them to the right objects in the right way; and exercises them, within the limits of the play, as the emotions of a good man would be exercised."[21] In light of the close association between emotion and normative judgment, especially since Aristotle himself sometimes allies emotion with evaluations or judgments, such a process might also be described as a rehearsal of our ethical evaluations. To the extent that catharsis, in this sense, can be considered pleasurable,[22] it would involve some satisfaction deriving from or felt on account of the achievement of a state of emotional equilibrium, a satisfaction in responding appropriately or having one's emotions appropriately exercised. Moreover, this kind of satisfaction might be linked to other accounts of our responses to tragedy.

It is clear that we can experience meta-responses, that is, responses to our own emotional responses. For instance, I remember a particular scene in David Lynch's series *Twin Peaks* in which a murder was performed in slow motion. My response to the scene was initially a response to the gorgeous quality of the light and the balletic, slow-motion choreography. It just *looked* beautiful, and I responded as if to a ballet or an expressionist painting. I was imaginatively absorbed in the fictional world to the extent that I was absorbed in how things looked in that world; I was not consid-

---

17. Humphry House, *Aristotle's Poetics: A Course of Eight Lectures* (London: Rupert Hart-Davis, 1961), 106.
18. Halliwell, *Aristotle's Poetics*, 201.
19. Ibid., 352.
20. For instance, in House, 108–10, and in Halliwell, 197.
21. House, *Aristotle's Poetics*, 109–10.
22. Halliwell, at least, ascribes our pleasure in the tragic to other sources (e.g., on 201).

ering how the effects were achieved. It was when I was admiring the vivid
red of a particular spray of blood against a gauzy white background that I
realized what I was doing and began to roundly curse David Lynch. I felt
guilty. I had entertained the thought of how things looked in the fictional
world without attending to thoughts of murder and assault. How could I
have done that?

Three separate facets of our emotional experience of fiction are illustrated by the above example. First, this example shows that we can have
responses to directors or directorial attitudes and manipulation, a phenomenon that will be discussed later in this chapter. Next, the example
illustrates how attention to some thoughts entertained in imagination can
either distract from attention to others or occur simultaneously with
attention that is otherwise directed. For instance, Alex Neill argues that we
can feel pleasure and pain concurrently and uses an example of a story
"about a man who confessed to feeling troubled by the fact that the most
beautiful sight he had ever seen was that of a Spitfire in flames . . .
against the backdrop of a night sky, and that he could have noticed and
been impressed by the beauty while he knew that he was witnessing the
violent death of a friend."[23]

The simultaneity of the aesthetic pleasure (tied in this case to a judgment
that something is beautiful) and the distress for the friend need not suggest
that the same thought was entertained with both distress and satisfaction
or that normative and aesthetic judgments were in outright conflict. The
thought of the appearance of the flames was entertained with aesthetic
pleasure.[24] The thought of the friend's death was regarded with distress.
Two aspects of the same situation were responded to in different ways at
the same time.

Finally, both of the preceding examples suggest that we can have a
response to our own emotional response. The individual whose situation
Neill describes entertained the thought of his own aesthetic delight with
some degree of distress, perhaps believing that no aspect of an incident
involving a death should give pleasure. The far less serious case of my
reaction to a fictional scene is not dissimilar. My own pleasure in the play of
color and light became the object of a kind of moral revulsion. In both
cases, reactions of aesthetic pleasure were themselves the objects of

---

23. Alex Neill, "On a Paradox of the Heart," *Philosophical Studies* 65 (1992): 58.

24. For the moment, such pleasure might be allied to the evaluation of a percept or
sequence thereof as having qualities associated with beauty, though I think a thorough
analysis must involve more than this. The subject will be briefly addressed in the last section
of this chapter.

negative emotion. The thoughts of our own reactions were entertained emotionally.

Susan Feagin suggests that our responses to fictional states of affairs as such (sadness about or pity for a character, for example) are not to be confused with meta-responses of the kind described in the preceding paragraphs.[25] The meta-responses Feagin brings to our attention can sometimes be emotional reactions of satisfaction directed toward our initial emotional responses to the imagined states of affairs. That is, we can take pleasure or satisfaction in our own sensitivity or moral responsiveness. Feagin has not claimed it is inevitably the case that those of us who feel both distress and a certain degree of satisfaction in the contemplation of a tragic fiction will feel that satisfaction for such a reason. Clearly, however, Feagin's account is often accurate. I remember how a college roommate of mine once bawled me out for failing to be saddened by *Love Story* (I had made the mistake of going to see it with my younger sister, who shared both my dislike of sentimentality and my fatal tendency to giggle at wildly inappropriate moments). Unlike herself, my roommate stated smugly, I was insensitive and unimaginative. Thick-skinned, that is what I was. Maybe morally underdeveloped. While the ensuing dispute did not involve thoughtful discourse, it does bear out Feagin's point.

Further, such reactions need not be smug (though I think they sometimes are). One may take one's negative emotional response of pity as a sign that one would be inclined to respond in a morally appropriate way to a given type of situation, and then find this assessment satisfying (just as I found my response to the scene in *Twin Peaks* rather horrifying). One may simply take one's emotional response as an indication of how vividly one is capable of imagining something, and find satisfaction in that. Again, we have candidates for the role of intentional object of our satisfaction in a tragic or frightening fiction: our own emotional responses of pity, distress, or fear. We can entertain the thought of our own responses emotionally. Alternatively, this kind of pleasure may sometimes be described as self-satisfaction.

Equally interesting is a possible link between an account of catharsis in terms of the development of appropriate moral dispositions and some of the ideas put forward by Ronald de Sousa. If art's raison d'être involves our desire to feel or undergo emotional responses to situations we have never experienced,[26] this could be in part explained by alluding to the desire to

---

25. Susan Feagin, "The Pleasures of Tragedy," *American Philosophical Quarterly* 20 (1983): 95–104.

26. Ronald de Sousa, *The Rationality of Emotion* (Cambridge: MIT Press, 1990), 320–21.

develop appropriate moral dispositions. De Sousa contends that literature educates us in how to picture and understand human situations, reinforces certain emotional dispositions, and enlarges our emotional repertoire.[27] This is not incompatible with some of the assumptions of House and Halliwell.

Jonathan Lear suggests that tragedy confronts us with possibilities for ourselves and our lives. Like de Sousa, he indicates that fiction permits us to imaginatively live life to the full without the risks attendant on actual experiencing. Here, fiction may enable spectators to apprehend more than they would through their ordinary experiences: a connectedness and unity of experience affirming hopes that the world is not wholly arbitrary and so is not devoid of meaning (given the Aristotelian requirement that events in the drama follow from one another of necessity).[28] Negative emotions would thus involve the contemplation of how one's own life might go and how one's own mistakes might affect the course of that life. More positive responses could be tied to an apprehension of the world's equilibrium, an apprehension of overall connectedness and order transcending the apparent chaos of the world of our experience.

In his discussion of the Aristotelian protagonist, Lear also suggests that tragedy may reinvest us with some conviction of control over the possibilities for our lives in that the tragic is not presented as being arbitrarily so. It thus may restore a sense of equilibrium insofar as it may give rise to an understanding of ourselves as genuine agents rather than objects at the mercy of forces beyond our control. In this case as well as those presented earlier, there is no single object to which we respond with seemingly incompatible emotions. Lear presents us with distinct reactions to distinct objects, thereby reinforcing the point that there need be no inconsistency in responding to the same work with both satisfaction and distress.

CLARIFICATION, COMPREHENSION, AND CONSTRUAL

The desire to experience emotions like pity and fear without experiencing their natural context, insofar as the former experiences are said to educate us in understanding human situations, may also be loosely associated with yet another treatment of Aristotelian catharsis, offered by Leon Golden. Golden describes catharsis as "a form of intellectual clarification in which

---

27. Ibid., 182–84.
28. Lear, "*Katharsis*," 325.

the concepts of pity and fear are clarified by the artistic representation of them." Catharsis is linked by Golden to the resolution of an inner demand for clarification of the human destiny.[29]

This is compatible with many of the claims I have made in preceding chapters. I have held that we can be moved by the perspectives on human life and human nature that a work affords in the course of responding emotionally to a fictional event we have imagined. Such perceptions and conceptions may sometimes be the objects of negative emotions, just as fictional events may. We may despair of human nature, fear the human capacity for cruelty, be angered or frustrated by the human potential for greed and self-interest. Our encounters with fictions can frequently involve responses to conceptions of life and experience inherent in a work, as well as responses to fictional entities and situations. When we consider such objects of emotion as these, it does not seem implausible to suggest that satisfaction can be associated with distressing, fearful, or sad insights—the satisfaction felt when something is finally clarified, understood, or elucidated. Indeed, Eva Schaper proposes that our enjoyment can be the pleasure of getting something clear, the pleasure of seeing things fall into place.[30] There can be satisfaction in the acquisition of understanding or the revelation of significance. One may also feel a certain satisfaction in having one's intuitions borne out or confirmed by the perspective on human experience associated with a given work.[31]

Other philosophers suggest that catharsis can effect a personal transformation. While some maintain that our emotions may be transformed or clarified by the experience,[32] others consider the possibility of a revelatory personal transformation effected by tragedy. That is, catharsis is allied not just with an outwardly focused revelation concerning humanity as a whole but with an inwardly focused exploration of one's own potentialities. When Stanley Cavell writes that a reader's (or spectator's) resistance to a work is like King Lear's failure to acknowledge genuine love, he may have in mind some impulse or inclination to avoid self-knowledge as well as a temptation to withdraw from the complexities of human interaction.[33] Alan Paskow suggests that identification or empathy with the protagonist may enable spectators to explore aspects of themselves they

---

29. Golden, "The Purgation Theory of *Catharsis*," 473, 478.
30. Schaper, *Prelude to Aesthetics*, 117.
31. The last suggestion comes from Lynne McFall.
32. For instance, E. P. Papanoutsos in "The Aristotelian *Katharsis*," *British Journal of Aesthetics* 17 (1977): 361–64.
33. Stanley Cavell, "The Avoidance of Love: A Reading of *King Lear*," in *Must We Mean What We Say? A Book of Essays* (New York: Charles Scribner's Sons, 1969), 267–353.

would normally repress or resist, that imaginative engagement with fiction may ultimately permit us to resolve moral or psychological conflicts within ourselves.[34] Again, the satisfaction may be found in the revelation, whereas more painful emotions are associated with the tragic route that must be imaginatively traversed before the revelation or realization is achieved.

On a slightly less serious note, but in keeping with our investigation of the satisfaction negative emotional responses to fiction can afford or accompany, the desire to have an experience involving negative emotions might also sometimes be explained as a desire to know what such experiences are like, because of an expectation of their eventually having to be undergone, or because of wishing to acquire knowledge of what actual people in certain circumstances can or do experience. The kind of satisfaction I have in mind is the satisfaction of curiosity. This can be linked to a clarification that is not precisely revelatory but that may in fact prove very satisfying.

Say, for instance, that I really want to know what it may have been like to live in medieval Europe. For this reason, I will eschew stories in the romantic tradition that are based largely on relatively inaccurate authorial imaginings. I might, however, thoroughly enjoy well-researched fictions that present us with what virtually amounts to the day-to-day life of a hypothetical person, with details about living conditions, medieval plumbing, and life expectancy thrown in. I have a friend whose academic specialty is medieval military history and who delights in the discovery of fictions dealing with the practical details of conducting a military campaign: how and where an encampment should be placed, which strategies should be employed given which terrain. She enjoys such fictions, she says, because they enable her to explore what it might have been like to have been in charge of such a campaign.

That is, even if fictional events evoke sadness or distress, there can be a good deal of pleasure in having aspects of one's curiosity satisfied by means of them. Indeed, a similar point has been made specifically in reference to horror stories. In his account of fictional horror, Noel Carroll indicates that our enjoyment of such works frequently involves curiosity and a desire for information. Monsters are cognitively intriguing, it is said. We want to figure them out and discover what it is that makes them tick.[35] Carroll maintains that "we accept the disturbing aspects of the genre in

---

34. Paskow, "What Is Aesthetic *Catharsis?*," 66–67.

35. Noel Carroll, *The Philosophy of Horror, or Paradoxes of the Heart* (New York: Routledge, Chapman and Hall, 1990), 181–85.

order to be fascinated by the genre's categorical anomalies," and these anomalies are just the ones manifested by fictional monsters.[36] Again, our satisfaction is that of interest or curiosity.

Such satisfaction is by no means restricted to the fictional. Chapter 2 gives several examples of the excitement and interest that actual disasters can arouse. This excitement and curiosity need not be perverse. My husband and I were teaching at the University of Central Oklahoma when the bombing of the federal building occurred. We felt the blast from a distance of twenty miles. Although we and our colleagues were horrified and distressed, nearly all of us were glued to our television sets for the next week (one local television station suspended all ordinary programming), eagerly awaiting the latest leads in the search for suspects. Many of us suspended our ordinary activities simply in order to follow the story. The very fact that we typically speak of the "satisfaction" of curiosity attests to what can be the only tolerable aspect of an otherwise terrible experience.

There can also be responses that are directed specifically toward what we take to be the attitudes of authors, directors, and even actors, attitudes expressed by the very mode of presentation in which they engage. That is, we can take a construal of the human condition or human nature associated with a given work to express the attitude of a particular person. Here again is a candidate object of emotion quite distinct from the purely fictional.

Such reactions need not be taken to occur only in cases involving fiction. When I was a teaching assistant, I was once required to assign a particular set of readings for one of my courses. Among these was an article that presented arguments against moral relativism featuring numerous examples of moral degeneracy and underdevelopment among the "cannibal savages in Africa." One of my students was black. He simply could not get past what he (not unjustifiably) considered the author's racism in order to appreciate the arguments that were being posed. He tried repeatedly, he told me, but every time he began to grasp the text, another cannibal savage from Africa would rise up to demonstrate a point, and he would founder in a morass of resentment. I have the same kind of response to films and television shows in which all the female characters apparently suffer from congenital brain defects. Instead of attending to the fictional events, I think about the attitude toward women that is conveyed by means of them, and so bid farewell to any possibility of imaginative absorption.

---

36. Carroll, "Disgust or Fascination: A Response to Susan Feagin," *Philosophical Studies* 65 (1992): 88.

Thus far, I have described negative emotional responses to authorial and directorial construals, responses that may on occasion mitigate our imaginative involvement. However, there can likewise be attitudes and construals we regard with pleasure or satisfaction, insofar as they bear out our own conceptions of the world or reveal to us a conception we believe to be accurate or true. Consider, for instance, that Margaret Atwood's feminist attitude, her pro-choice position, and her awareness of the liabilities of religious fundamentalism were at the core of many evaluations of *The Handmaid's Tale* (both the book and the film). That is, what many of Atwood's detractors and proponents responded to (with disapprobation or with satisfaction) were not the fictional events and not even the way they were depicted or described but rather what were taken to be Atwood's own political views. Both the novel and the film were treated as statements of certain political positions. By writing a story describing the eradication of civil liberties consequent upon a government takeover by the fundamentalist right, Atwood was taken to have expressed certain strong political convictions. It is my contention, therefore, that we can respond to such a conviction with pleasure when we respond to an otherwise distressing fiction. For instance, I responded with a certain satisfaction to Atwood's construals, though I feared for and pitied many of the characters in her novel.

Discussions of (and digressions on account of) Aristotelian catharsis alone have yielded several objects our satisfaction can take when we respond with pity and fear to a tragedy. We can enjoy the sensations and states of mind that come with emotional release or equilibrium. We can find satisfaction in having exercised our emotions appropriately, in having developed appropriate moral dispositions, or in having enlarged our emotional repertoires. We can find intellectual clarification, revelation, and insight satisfying. We can find authorial attitudes satisfying insofar as they corroborate or expand our own. We can certainly enjoy having our curiosity satisfied. All of these proposed objects of satisfaction confirm the claim that there is no inconsistency in the pleasure we take in sad or frightening fiction. There is no inconsistency in entertaining different thoughts in different ways.

FORM AND CONTENT

An investigation of the *Poetics* can suggest still further sources of satisfaction in tragedy, for we can also consider the pleasure Aristotle says we find in the excellence of imitations.[37] Marcia Eaton emphasizes Aristotle's contention that "human beings by nature delight in imitation. . . . [If an] object is cleverly imitated, they are pleased. Thus there can be pleasing pictures of unpleasant things, enjoyable dramatizations of unpleasing events. . . . People are sad about *what* is represented, but delighted by *how* it is represented."[38] Here, we have yet another object of satisfaction — another alternative to the imagined event that saddens us: the manner in which the fictional events are presented, where our response seems to be to authorial or artistic virtuosity on the one hand and to fictional events on the other.

Similarly, in "Of Tragedy," Hume allies our satisfaction or pleasure in tragedy with skillful depiction and eloquence. That is, our satisfaction in the tragic may sometimes be taken as a response to the author's, director's, or actor's ability rather than to the fictional states of affairs. Hume writes of what it is that raises pleasure from the bosom of uneasiness: "This extraordinary effect proceeds from the very eloquence with which the melancholy scene is represented. The genius required to paint objects in a lively manner, the art employed in collecting all the pathetic circumstances, the judgment displayed in disposing them; the exercise . . . of these noble talents, together with the force of expression and beauty of oratorial numbers, diffuse the highest satisfaction, and excite the most delightful movements."[39]

Although this may not be true of every case of our satisfaction in a fiction that also elicits responses of distress or pity from us, it seems to hold for a great many cases. Certainly it is possible to be moved to admiration or awe by the virtuosity with which a fictional state of affairs is presented, just as it is possible to be moved to contempt or irritation by incompetent writing or wooden acting. The latter, especially, seems frequently to prevent emotional response to fictional events on our part, probably because it focuses our attention on what is actually (rather than fictionally) the case.

However, the distinction between form, style, or mode of presentation and what is usually termed "content" is not always easy to determine. As I have already indicated in Chapter 5, the way in which a state of affairs is presented has a fundamental impact on what is presented, on what we imagine. Shakespeare's virtuosity with words is co-opted by his characters, just as an actor's appearance may be co-opted into the world of a

---

37. House, *Aristotle's Poetics*, 112.
38. Marcia Eaton, *Aesthetics and the Good Life*, 55–56.
39. David Hume, "Of Tragedy," in John W. Lenz, ed., *Of the Standard of Taste and Other Essays* (Indianapolis: Bobbs Merrill, 1965), 32.

performance. What *is* content? I have allied it with the states of affairs in a world's work and with what is true in that world. This comprises, after all, what a story is about, what it depicts and describes. Common ways of speaking suggest that two different performances of a single play are about the same thing, have the same content. They also suggest that two stories can be about the same thing.

Common ways of speaking are evidently more than a little deceptive. The states of affairs comprising the world of Shakespeare's *Henry V* (as text) are not the same as those comprising a play describing similar incidents in modern dialect, nor are the conceptions of life we can grasp by means of them. As Martha Nussbaum has indicated, conception and form are bound together. A paraphrase of a work "in a very different form and style will not, in general, express the same conception."[40] At the most basic level, the fictional world associated with a paraphrase of the original play would not contain the state of affairs of Henry having uttered a specific sequence of words (those Shakespeare wrote) when rousing his troops.

The worlds of the performances of Kenneth Branagh's *Henry V* and Laurence Olivier's *Henry V* differ in many respects: in how Henry acts, how he looks, in his beliefs about the nature of war. They also express very different conceptions of how life should be lived and of what war can mean for people. The world of the *Hamlet* performance starring Marianne Faithful as Ophelia differs considerably from that featuring Helena Bonham Carter in the same role. Inhabiting the first is a sultry and erotic Ophelia. Inhabiting the second is a shy and fragile woman liable to be shattered by the course of events. The distinctions between the world of *The Libation Bearers* of Aeschylus and the *Electra* of Euripides are more obvious: the characters say different things and behave in different ways. In the Euripidean world, Electra holds the sword with Orestes when Clytemnestra is killed. In *The Libation Bearers*, Electra is not even present at the death. The dramas make reference to the same state of affairs yet offer different conceptions of it.

However, distinctions based on mode of presentation go much further. Consider three descriptions of the same event, an auto accident:

1. There was a seven-car pileup on Route 27 at ten o'clock on Friday evening.

---

40. Martha Nussbaum, *Love's Knowledge: Essays on Philosophy and Literature* (New York: Oxford University Press, 1990), 5.

2. I couldn't see a thing in that rain. Then I turn the corner and there's this
   car smack in the middle of the road. Plowed right into it.

3. We are deranged, walking among the cops
   Who sweep glass and are large and composed.
   One is still making notes under the light.
   One with a bucket douches ponds of blood
   Into the street and gutter.
   One hangs lanterns on the wrecks that cling,
   Empty husks of locusts, to iron poles.[41]

The first description is a bald statement of fact. The second could be taken
as a personal narrative issued by one of the accident's victims. The third
description is an extract from Karl Shapiro's poem "Auto Wreck." If we
assumed that each description concerned the same event in the world, we
could accept the contention that each passage was about the same thing,
though each described it from a different point of view. Let us instead
assume that there has been no accident. Perhaps the three passages have
been fabricated on a whim. In any case, they are no longer anchored to the
actual world.

In the world of description 1, it is neither true nor false that people
involved in the accident had experiences such as those described in 2 and
3. It is neither true nor false in 1 that it was raining during the accident, that
the accident occurred near an intersection, that police personnel were
sweeping glass. In the worlds of the second and third descriptions, it is
neither true nor false that the accident occurred on Route 27 or that it
occurred on a Friday. In the worlds of 1 and 2, it is neither true nor false
that there was broken glass in the road.

The states of affairs projected by means of each description are radically
distinct and make entirely different things salient for the reader. The first
passage places the (imaginary) incident within a broader frame of geographic and temporal reference. The second gives a personal perspective
on the unavoidability of involvement. The third leads the reader to focus
on the (imagined) experience of the aftermath and evokes many
more associations than the other two. The point of commonality among
the worlds of these descriptions is the single state of affairs (among
many) of there having been (fictionally or imaginarily) an automobile

---

41. This is a stanza from Karl Shapiro's poem "Auto Wreck," included in his *Collected
Poems 1940-1978* (Random House, 1978).

accident. If the descriptions can be said to have the same content only insofar as they present the same states of affairs to the imagination, then the claim that they are about the same thing becomes debatable. Different descriptions would appear to yield different fictional worlds, though this is not to deny that such worlds can have states of affairs in common.

It was my contention in Chapter 5 that the use of metaphor, simile, symbolism, and other devices could significantly affect the states of affairs in a work's world, and I gave examples of how this might occur. At present, my intention is simply to stress that even the selection of turns of phrase, let alone the depiction of some features of a state of affairs as more salient than others, is crucial in determining the states of affairs that can be taken to comprise the world that a given subject imagines. John Gardner said it best when he pointed out that even individual words have associations,

> and groups of words form chains of association. To say the word *crate* to a native English speaker is to summon up an image of a crate and, with it, the natural background of that image, which is a different background from that summoned up by *casque* or *trunk* or *cube*. To say that a character is built like a crate is to suggest far more than just the character's shape: it is to hint at his personality, his station in life, even his behavior. . . . Thus the idea that the writer's only material is words is only true in a trivial sense. Words conjure emotionally charged images in the reader's mind.[42]

This is especially apposite when one considers Shapiro's comparison of wrecked cars with the husks of locusts. The associations that the metaphor brings to mind suggest a little of the complexity and depth that imaginative engagement can involve.

It is not just the writer's choice of words, of course, that is relevant here, for the writer's choices encompass the shape, the organization, the rhythms, the entire structure of a text, all of which can determine what is salient for a reader and express a unique authorial conception. An author's or director's organization and sequencing of fictional events can have an enormous impact on a subject's imaginative extrapolations and inferences. Presenting events in a certain sequence may even lead readers or spectators through a process in which they are forced to confront the inappropriateness of their own initial imaginative assumptions and expectations (as well as the beliefs on which these may be based).

---

42. John Gardner, *On Moral Fiction* (New York: Basic Books, 1977), 112.

As Louise Rosenblatt indicates, "content cannot be dissociated from the form in which it is embodied." She considers the effects that individual words can have, as does Gardner, but presents a more complex case that highlights something further about the manner in which a state of affairs can be presented. We are asked to consider two different versions of Keats's *Endymion*: one that begins "A thing of beauty is a constant joy," and another that begins "A thing of beauty is a joy forever."[43] While distinctions in the impact of the two versions may be in part attributable to variations in meaning and connotation between "constant" and "forever," these variations clearly cannot account for the whole of that difference.

Although this is not a book about poetry, it should be remembered that fictional states of affairs can be presented poetically. In describing the effects on the spectator of Shakespeare's poetic language, Stanley Cavell contends that attending to a line of poetry is like attending to a line of tonal music. This is not, he maintains, like the contemplation of prose, for the attitude demanded of the one who hears the poetry or music involves an experience of "continuous presentness." One's experience is said to have a quality of directedness other experiences lack.[44] I speculate that the rhythm and meter of poetry can, as with music, give rise to a different kind of expectancy than that involved in prose fiction, an expectancy that does not involve normative construals of fictional events but apprehensions of harmony, unity, symmetry, fittingness, or closure. These are clearly aesthetic responses, which comprise a topic I will briefly address in the last section of this chapter, though I do not pretend to do justice to either the complexity or the depth of the subject. It is important, however, to note that these apprehensions can be wedded to our awareness of a fictional state of affairs and can explain something about the nature and quality of our response that a simple awareness of what is fictionally the case may not.

We cannot regard "content" as something static and self-contained that can retain its identity across a variety of presentations and in a variety of forms. A manner of presentation informs what it is we take to have been presented. Style and form are not extraneous factors that can garnish the same content and dress it up in different ways. Content is not extractable from form of presentation, for there can be no content for us unless it *is* presented, any more than there can be a wholly contentless manner of presenting or a presenting of nothing. Form and content are not identical,

43. Louise M. Rosenblatt, *The Reader, the Text, the Poem: The Transactional Theory of the Literary Work* (Carbondale: Southern Illinois University Press, 1978), 35, 87.
44. Cavell, "The Avoidance of Love," 321–22.

but they are interdependent. With fiction, it is not a case of two different ways of presenting the same thing but a case of two different presentations or conceptions.

Naturally, this does not preclude the possibility of responding with pleasure or satisfaction to extrafictional objects while responding negatively to fictional ones. What is usually referred to as a response to style is often a response to authorial (or directorial or thespian) skill and virtuosity. None of these is encompassed in the world of the work, and there is clearly no difficulty or inconsistency in saying that we respond positively to authorial skill and negatively to fictional events. Yet there can be still other responses that can be held to constitute reactions to the form of a work and that are quite distinct from those described above.

APPRECIATING AESTHETICALLY

The emotional responses to fiction to which the bulk of this book has been devoted constitute only a portion of what may be termed an "aesthetic response," when that designation is taken to denote responses to works of art in general. In this chapter, I have begun to employ the term "aesthetic" differently, in order to distinguish the kind of response that could be allied with an apprehension of or judgment concerning beauty from emotional reactions to the fictional.[45] Immanuel Kant associates judgments of beauty with pleasure, and our pleasure in the tragic or the frightening is the topic presently under consideration. Further, Kant explicitly associates such judgments with form and composition. Thus, it seems that some investigation of Kant's contentions concerning these judgments can help to explain a kind of aesthetic satisfaction that has not as yet been explored and can provide us with some insight into what may be involved when one is said to respond to the form of a work.

Presumably, some type of aesthetic pleasure can be tied to the judgment that something is beautiful, just as anger can be tied to the judgment that something is unfair or unjust. However, in the case of an emotion like anger, I have claimed that one construes a certain action as possessing characteristics one believes sufficient for the classification or categorization of that action as unjust. Can we likewise maintain that one construes

---

45. Kant might maintain that the two were unrelated and probably incompatible, since the emotional reactions I have described do not appear to meet his criterion of disinterestedness.

a certain object as possessing properties—whatever it is decided that these may be—sufficient for the categorization of that object as beautiful?

Such a procedure seems questionable for several reasons. I do not think that many of us possess fully articulated or articulable beliefs about properties whose instantiation is sufficient for beauty. If we consider Kant's "purposiveness without purpose" as characteristic of the aesthetic response, the construals identified with such reactions could not involve beliefs about how items were to be classified or categorized and could not involve the subsumption of the content of our experience under concepts or categories. Perhaps the construal one would want to associate with an aesthetic judgment could be held to involve associations or habits or patterns of attention that operated at a prereflective level, as Cheshire Calhoun has proposed when considering different affective responses.[46]

But what is it that we can so construe? While Kant's discussion of judgments of beauty focuses most often on music and the visual arts, he does indicate that "it is what pleases by means of its form that is fundamental for taste," saying that it is possible to associate form with the play of sensations in time and offering composition as one of the proper objects of the pure judgment of taste.[47] He later maintains that form is the quality necessary for all the fine arts, no matter how media may be combined.[48] Judging a turn of phrase or a soliloquy beautiful, therefore, may involve a responsiveness to harmonies, rhythms, metrics, and tonal variations, as well as a responsiveness to the play of thoughts that can be taken to involve the apprehension of those aesthetic ideas the work expresses.

The former responsiveness calls Cavell's comparison of poetry and tonal music to mind once again, when we consider the "directedness" he says such experiences have and associate it with a Kantian purposiveness. The latter responsiveness involves a pattern of thinking—a synthesizing of concepts and apprehending of connections that expands and deepens what it is those thoughts embrace. Such syntheses may be involved in our responses to figurative language, for instance. A metaphor can enrich the *way* we think of something by giving rise to a multitude of images and associations or by enabling us to see it in a novel way—and can do so without rendering more determinate and categorizable what it is we think

46. Cheshire Calhoun, "Cognitive Emotions?," in Cheshire Calhoun and Robert C. Solomon, eds., *What Is an Emotion? Classic Readings in Philosophical Psychology* (New York: Oxford University Press, 1984), 327–42.

47. Immanuel Kant, *Critique of Judgment*, Sec. 14, trans. J. H. Bernard (New York: Hafner Press, 1951).

48. Ibid., Sec. 52.

about. I will speculate no further about a topic to which an enormous and impressive literature has already been devoted. Rather, I will pursue distinctions that may be drawn between such responses and those with which they can be conflated.

It is clear that an aesthetic pleasure of the kind described can be entirely distinct from responses to fictional events and entities as such. Consider once again the case of the soliloquy. To judge it beautiful and eloquent and to respond to it with aesthetic pleasure may be to respond to the rhythm and cadence of the very turns of phrase, or to attend to new conceptual syntheses that can enrich or can expand thoughts of what in other contexts might have seemed quite unremarkable. That is, we respond to the play and pattern of our sensations or our thoughts, a play the soliloquy can make possible in virtue of its form: its meter, its rhymes and rhythms, the metaphors and similes and symbols it employs. However, there are still other pleasures that can be associated with the beauty or the eloquence of the soliloquy that should not be confused with what has been termed aesthetic pleasure.

Eloquence can be regarded as evidence of a skill or talent in response to which our degree of satisfaction may vary, as opposed to something satisfying or pleasurable in itself. For instance, eloquence can be regarded as dangerous, as a skill liable to be put to inappropriate uses. When the title character of *Richard III* gloats "Was ever woman in such humor woo'd? Was ever woman in such humor won?"[49] he delights in an eloquence that has made possible the successful manipulation of another. Considering Richard's linguistic virtuosity dangerous may involve fear for those he manipulates or anger at the exercise of an unfair advantage. Considering such an ability a hallmark of talent and of ingenuity may involve admiration of the character's sheer Machiavellian finesse.

The first response is not to any linguistic object or exercise but to the thought of a misuse of talent and the consequences of that misuse for others. The second reaction is to the thought of someone's possession of an enviable and advantageous skill. In both cases, eloquence is regarded as an ability or talent of persons rather than a property ascribable to an utterance or a linguistic object. There is a difference between considering a sequence of words or turn of phrase beautifully eloquent and considering someone's facility with words, his very eloquence, either dangerously or laudably effective in the achievement of personal goals. There is a difference in what we attend to in the course of such responses and a difference

---

49. William Shakespeare, *Richard III* I.ii, in *The Riverside Shakespeare* (Boston: Houghton Mifflin, 1972), 717.

in how we attend to it, because there is a distinction between the appreciation of beauty and the appreciation of an excellent or successful exercise of skill.

Let us consider the second type of appreciation. The possession of linguistic facility, the possession of eloquence, is as readily ascribable to authors as it is to characters. Likewise, we can appreciate the grace of a character or of the actress who portrays her, and both of these responses seem distinct from that of taking a given movement or gesture as graceful or beautiful in itself. Perhaps responding to a character's utterance as eloquent or to a character's gesture as graceful can lead to a further response involving the judgment that linguistic facility or the capacity to orchestrate one's bodily motions in a certain way constitutes a trait or ability that has value both for its possessor and for others. Whatever the dependence of one response on the other may be, it remains the case that a focus of attention on the value of traits, skills, or abilities can sometimes lead us to focus not just on what we imagine but on those who make it possible for us to imagine what and as we do.

The preceding distinctions suggest that three varieties of satisfaction or delight in our experience of fiction have been identified. First, we can take aesthetic delight in the way something looks or sounds or is structured, in the pattern of relations it embodies or exemplifies, and in the pattern of experiencing and thinking to which it may give rise. This does not seem to depend in any exclusive way on what is fictionally the case. However, such a response can make it true that there is beauty, grace, or eloquence in the worlds that we imagine. It can also lead us to believe that existing things in the world are beautiful, that actors are graceful and authors eloquent.

Next, we may find satisfaction in imagining persons who possess certain skills or graces, and such satisfaction may involve admiration or may involve considering that certain properties or capacities are valuable ones to possess. Similarly, we can derive satisfaction from the contemplation of authorial, thespian, directorial, or cinematographic skill, and this satisfaction can be a pleasure we take in excellence, a pleasure in seeing things well done. The latter may, on some accounts, be considered an aesthetic pleasure as well, but it would be "aesthetic" in a different sense, for it involves the appreciation of an ability to create what is considered beautiful rather than the appreciation of beauty.

These three kinds of pleasure in or on account of a fictional work can obviously be interdependent, though it is not clear that they must inevitably coincide. One could presumably appreciate an author's eloquence and facility with words without regarding her characters as eloquent, if there can be eloquent descriptions of ineloquence or if eloquence is confined to omniscient narration. One can certainly appreciate and enjoy the eloquence of a character without sparing a single thought for the author, though the reader might in such a case be held to have some dispositional belief about the author's linguistic facility — a belief that is thought to be derivable from other reader beliefs about the sources of fictional descriptions.

Whether or not someone *could* enjoy and appreciate a character's or an author's possession of eloquence and fail to enjoy the eloquence of character utterances or authorial turns of phrase is another question. Presumably, one could believe that eloquence and linguistic facility were valuable skills and enjoy their exhibition by a favorite character or author (in the sense that the exhibition reflected positively on the favorites) without thereby enjoying the eloquence and beauty of the words themselves. It might be objected that, in responding in this way, someone could understand only the instrumental and not the aesthetic value of eloquence. It might even be held that such a person could not be aware that certain sequences of words *were* eloquent or beautiful. It may therefore be the case that any claims about the interdependence of such responses would have to rest on an individual's valuations of properties like eloquence or grace and, more important, on what it was that grounded such valuations.

Be that as it may, the kinds of satisfaction that have been identified can be associated with objects other than those to which there is a negative emotional response. Satisfaction in tragic or frightening fiction once again exhibits no inconsistency. Aesthetic appreciation in particular is of considerable significance, for Kant saw it as more than a pleasure. To respond aesthetically can be a way of extending or expanding one's cognitive powers and capacities.[50] Thus, to claim that we can take aesthetic satisfaction in a tragic work not only militates against contentions that our response to fiction signifies some flaw or incoherence in our thought but shows how contemplation of the fictional can be considered cognitively advantageous.

CONCLUSION

There are several explanations that might account for the satisfaction we take in fictions that arouse negative emotions. I am strongly inclined to

---

50. Mary A. McClosky so maintains in *Kant's Aesthetic* (New York: SUNY Press, 1987), 159.

concur with Marcia Eaton's conclusion that we do not have to assume that any single one of them must account for *all* cases in which being saddened by a fiction is somehow accompanied by satisfaction. Each of the candidates is applicable to some, but not all, situations.[51]

The explanations I have reviewed, all of which attempt to account for the presence both of satisfaction and negative emotion in some of our encounters with fictions, support the contention that the presence of both positive and negative emotions suggests no inconsistency, in view of the fact that each type of response has a very different type of object. Such divergent emotional responses can be associated with the entertainment of different thoughts. The negative emotional responses being considered at the moment — fear, pity, anger, sadness, distress — are often responses to what we have imagined. They are ways we entertain thoughts of fictional events and entities. We may also have negative emotional responses, as has been indicated elsewhere, to actual persons, possibilities, and conceptions of life, brought to mind by what it is that we imagine. The satisfaction or pleasure we can feel when contemplating fictions that give rise to fear or pity can likewise have several objects. We can take satisfaction in authorial or directorial skill, in beauty and eloquence, in what we take to be the attitudes of the author or director, in our own sensitivity, in "letting go," in the sensation of excitement or arousal, in the intellectual clarification and insight that even painful truths can afford, in having our curiosity satisfied, in the development of appropriate moral dispositions, and even in our own responses, provided that we retain the capacity to control the extent of our imaginative absorption.

---

51. Marcia Eaton, *Aesthetics and the Good Life*, 59.

Afterword

hat's Hecuba to the player, that
he should weep for her? Provided that Shakespeare's player is not merely
indulging in an excess of thespian histrionics, he may be moved by any of
several things. He may imagine Hecuba's plight, imagine her frustration
and despair, and entertain the thought of these compassionately. He may
be moved by the plights of actual persons whose experiences resemble
those of Hecuba, by the thought of the human capacity for cruelty, by the
real potential for tragic loss in every life, by some experience of his own
that resonates with that of Hecuba. Since he is an actor, perhaps he
imaginatively inhabits the worlds whose denizens he represents on stage.
It could be that he enters into Hecuba's perspective on the world, imagines her beliefs, desires, tensions, and impulses, shares her construal of her
situation, and shares the horror and despair with which she contemplates
her husband's death.

In this book, I have only suggested necessary conditions for an emotional response to fiction. To be distressed specifically by Hecuba's plight,
the player must imagine it and imagine her, must believe that to see a loved
one killed is a painful, indeed an intolerable, experience, and must construe Hecuba's situation as painful and intolerable. He must believe that a
situation of this kind could occur. If we were to consider conditions
sufficient for his being moved, further stipulations concerning the *way* the
player imagines Hecuba's plight would have to be made.

His attention would have to focus on those aspects of Hecuba's plight
that he himself believed were sufficient for assessing an experience as

intolerably painful. This focus of attention itself implies an absence of
distraction. A number of the player's beliefs would be rendered tacit, in
particular the belief that the events he contemplates are fictional. The
player would engage in a complex of mental activities, a pattern of extrapolation and association that expanded and deepened the states of
affairs in the story he contemplated (and told). He would make imaginative
inferences about Hecuba's state of mind, perhaps imagine experiencing
her horror and helplessness. He would desire vengeance and redress and
wish for Hecuba's relief. In short, the player would engage in a pattern of
thinking and imagining and attending that rendered *unavoidable* and
inevitable the focused, concerned, and serious construal of Hecuba's
situation as intolerable. To imagine Hecuba's plight in that way is to
imagine it with compassion and distress, focusing in particular on certain
aspects of it.

I believe that imaginative engagement characterized by the kind of
mental activity, involvement, and focus that I have described may, with the
other conditions specified, prove sufficient for an emotional response to
fiction. I am aware, of course, that difficulties inhere in any claim such as
this. How much mental activity is enough? What kinds of extrapolations
are requisite? Is it the quality or quantity of activity that counts, and how are
we to determine that? This is material for a second book at the very least,
and at present I will indulge in no speculations beyond those already
ventured, for these already indicate directions such investigations could
pursue. For the moment, I wish only to indicate that to weep for Hecuba is
not inevitably silly or trivial, inconsistent or phony, self-indulgent or inau-
thentic. It can, in fact, involve significant apprehensions of how life is or
ought to be. It can provide an alternate perspective, focus our attention in
a way that makes of what is fictional a lens by means of which we can
regard the world and our experience of that world. Thus, the pursuit of
ideas generated by his observation of an emotional response to fiction
leads Hamlet himself to assume that it is by means of fiction a conscience
can be caught.

Bibliography

Abbarno, John M. "Empathy as Objective Moral Value." In *Inquiries into Values.* Lewiston: Mellen Press, 161-71.

Allen, R. T. "The Reality of Responses to Fiction." *British Journal of Aesthetics* 26 (1986): 64-68.

Alston, William P. "Emotion." In *The Encyclopedia of Philosophy.* New York: Macmillan, 1967.

Aristotle. *Aristotle's Poetics.* Trans. James Hutton. New York: W.W. Norton, 1982.

———. *Aristotle's Politics.* Trans. Benjamin Jowett. Oxford: Clarendon Press, 1920.

———. *De Anima.* Trans. J. A. Smith. In *Aristotle: I* of *Great Books of the Western World*, vol. 8. Chicago: Encyclopedia Britannica, 1952.

———. *Nicomachean Ethics.* Trans. Terence Irwin. Indiana: Hackett, 1985.

———. *Poetics.* Trans. S. H. Butcher. New York: Hill and Wang, 1961.

———. *Rhetoric.* Trans. W. Rhys Roberts. In *Aristotle: II* of *Great Books of the Western World*, vol. 9. Chicago: Encyclopedia Britannica, 1952.

Armon-Jones, Claire. "Social Functions of the Emotions." In *The Social Construction of the Emotions.* Ed. Rom Harre. New York: Basil Blackwell, 1988, 57-82.

———. "The Thesis of Constructionism." In *The Social Construction of the Emotions.* Ed. Rom Harre. New York: Basil Blackwell, 1988, 32-56.

Aune, Bruce. *Knowledge, Mind, and Nature.* New York: Random House, 1967.

Battin, Margaret, John Fisher, Ronald Moore, and Anita Silvers. *Puzzles About Art: An Aesthetics Casebook.* New York: St. Martin's Press, 1989.

Bedford, Errol. "Emotions." In *What Is an Emotion? Classic Readings in Philosophical Psychology.* Ed. Cheshire Calhoun and Robert C. Solomon. New York: Oxford University Press, 1984, 264-78.

———. "Emotions and Statements About Them." In *The Social Construction of the Emotions.* Ed. Rom Harre. New York: Basil Blackwell, 1988, 15-31.

Bennett, Kenneth C. "The Purging of *Catharsis.*" *British Journal of Aesthetics* 21 (1981): 204-13.

Blakeslee, Sandra. "Tracing the Brain's Pathways for Linking Emotion and Reason." *New York Times*, 6 December 1994, B5, B11.

Boruah, Bijoy H. *Fiction and Emotion: A Study in Aesthetics and the Philosophy of Mind.* Oxford: Clarendon Press, 1988.

Bouwsma, O. K. *Philosophical Essays.* Lincoln: University of Nebraska Press, 1965.

Brentano, Franz. *On the Origin of Our Knowledge of Right and Wrong.* Excerpted in *What Is an Emotion? Classic Readings in Philosophical Psychology.* Ed.

Cheshire Calhoun and Robert C. Solomon. New York: Oxford University Press, 1984, 203-14.

Broad, C. D. "Emotion and Sentiment." In *Critical Essays on Moral Theory*. London: Allen and Unwin, 1971.

Calhoun, Cheshire. "Cognitive Emotions?" In *What Is an Emotion? Classic Readings in Philosophical Psychology*. Ed. Cheshire Calhoun and Robert C. Solomon. New York: Oxford University Press, 1984, 327-42.

Carroll, Noel. "Critical Study: *Mimesis as Make-Believe*." *Philosophical Quarterly* 45 (1995): 93-99.

———. "Disgust or Fascination: A Response to Susan Feagin." *Philosophical Studies* 65 (1992): 85-90.

———. "A Paradox of the Heart: A Response to Alex Neill." *Philosophical Studies* 65 (1992): 67-74.

———. *The Philosophy of Horror, or Paradoxes of the Heart*. New York: Routledge, Chapman and Hall, 1990.

Cavell, Stanley. "The Avoidance of Love: A Reading of *King Lear*." In *Must We Mean What We Say? A Book of Essays*. New York: Charles Scribner's Sons, 1969, 267-353.

Charlton, William. "Feeling for the Fictitious." *British Journal of Aesthetics* 24 (1984): 206-16.

———. "Radford and Allen on Being Moved by Fiction: A Rejoinder." *British Journal of Aesthetics* 26 (1986): 391-94.

Chisholm, Roderick M. *Perceiving: A Philosophical Study*. Ithaca: Cornell University Press, 1957.

Chismar, Douglas. "Empathy and Sympathy: The Important Difference." *Journal of Value Inquiry* 22 (1988): 257-66.

Coulter, J. "Affect and Social Context." In *The Social Construction of the Emotions*. Ed. Rom Harre. New York: Basil Blackwell, 1988, 120-34.

Currie, Gregory. *The Nature of Fiction*. Cambridge: Cambridge University Press, 1990.

Dadlez, Eva. "Fiction, Emotion, and Rationality." *British Journal of Aesthetics* 36 (1996):290-304.

Daniels, Charles B., and Sam Scully. "Pity, Fear, and *Catharsis* in Aristotle's *Poetics*." *Nous* 26 (1992): 204-17.

Deigh, John. "Empathy and Universalizability." *Ethics* 105 (1995): 743-63.

De Sousa, Ronald. *The Rationality of Emotion*. Cambridge: MIT Press, 1990.

Dewey, John. "The Theory of Emotion." 1894. Excerpted in *What Is an Emotion? Classic Readings in Philosophical Psychology*. Ed. Cheshire Calhoun and Robert C. Solomon. New York: Oxford University Press, 1984, 154-72.

Eaton, Marcia. *Aesthetics and the Good Life*. New Jersey: Associated University Presses, 1989.

———. "A Strange Kind of Sadness." *Journal of Aesthetics and Art Criticism* 41 (1982): 51-63.

Else, Gerald F. *Aristotle's Poetics: The Argument*. Cambridge: Harvard University Press, 1967.

Euripides. *The Medea*. Trans. Rex Warner. In *Euripides I* of *The Complete Greek*

Tragedies. Ed. David Grene and Richard Lattimore. Chicago: University of Chicago Press, 1972, 56-108.

Feagin, Susan L. "Imagining Emotions and Appreciating Fiction." *Canadian Journal of Philosophy* 18 (1988): 485-500.

———. "Monsters, Disgust, and Fascination." *Philosophical Studies* 65 (1992): 75-84.

———. "The Pleasures of Tragedy." *American Philosophical Quarterly* 20 (1983): 95-104.

Foot, Phillipa. *Virtues and Vices and Other Essays in Moral Philosophy.* Berkeley and Los Angeles: University of California Press, 1978.

Forabosco, Giovannantonio. "Cognitive Aspects of the Humor Process: The Concept of Incongruity." *Humor* 5 (1992): 45-68.

Gardner, John. *On Moral Fiction.* New York: Basic Books, 1977.

Golden, Leon. "The Purgation Theory of *Catharsis.*" *Journal of Aesthetics and Art Criticism* 31 (1973): 473-79.

Goldman, Alvin. "Empathy, Mind, and Morals." *Proceedings of the American Philosophical Association* 66, no. 3 (1992): 17-41.

Gordon, Robert M. *The Structure of Emotions.* Cambridge: Cambridge University Press, 1976.

Gribble, James. "The Reality of Fictional Emotions." *Journal of Aesthetic Education* 16 (1982): 53-58.

Hagberg, Garry. Review of *Fiction and Emotion,* by Bijoy H. Boruah. *Journal of Aesthetics and Art Criticism* 48 (1990): 246-48.

Halliwell, Stephen. *Aristotle's Poetics.* Chapel Hill: University of North Carolina Press, 1986.

Harre, Rom. "An Outline of the Social Constructionist Viewpoint." In *The Social Construction of the Emotions.* Ed. Rom Harre. New York: Basil Blackwell, 1988, 2-14.

Harward, Donald W. "Can I Know What It's Like to Be a . . . (e.g. Woman) and Not Be One?" *Journal of Value Inquiry* 14 (1980): 35-42.

Hickey, Leo. "The Particular and the General in Fiction." *Journal of Aesthetics and Art Criticism* 30 (1972): 327-31.

Hirst, R. J. *The Problems of Perception.* London: Allen and Unwin, 1966.

Hitchens, Christopher. "Stuck in Neutral: The Place of Feeling in Law and Politics." Review of Martha Nussbaum's *Poetic Justice* (Boston: Beacon, 1996). *Times Literary Supplement,* 15 March 1996, p. 9-10.

House, Humphry. *Aristotle's Poetics: A Course of Eight Lectures.* London: Rupert Hart-Davis, 1961.

Hume, David. *Essays: Moral, Political, and Literary.* Ed. Eugene F. Miller. Indianapolis: Liberty Classics, 1987.

———. *Of the Standard of Taste and Other Essays.* Ed. John W. Lenz. Indianapolis: Bobbs-Merrill, 1965.

———. *A Treatise of Human Nature.* Ed. L. A. Selby-Bigg. Oxford: Clarendon Press, 1967.

———. *A Treatise of Human Nature.* Prometheus Books: New York, 1992.

Iseminger, Gary. "How Strange a Sadness?" *Journal of Aesthetics and Art Criticism* 42 (1983): 81-82.

James, William. "What Is an Emotion?" *Mind* (1884).

Johnson, Mark. *Moral Imagination: Implications of Cognitive Science for Ethics.* Chicago: University of Chicago Press, 1993.

Kalin, Jesse. "Knowing Novels: Nussbaum on Fiction and Moral Theory." *Ethics* 103 (1992): 135-51.

Kant, Immanuel. *Critique of Judgment.* Trans., with an introduction, by J. H. Bernard. New York: Hafner Press, 1951.

Kenny, Anthony. *Action, Emotion, and Will.* Excerpted in *What Is an Emotion? Classic Readings in Philosophical Psychology.* Ed. Cheshire Calhoun and Robert C. Solomon. New York: Oxford University Press, 1984, 280-90.

Kupperman, Joel K. "Ethics for Extraterrestrials." *American Philosophical Quarterly* 28 (1991): 311-20.

Lamarque, Peter. "How Can We Fear and Pity Fictions?" *British Journal of Aesthetics* 21 (1981): 291-304.

———. Review of *Mimesis as Make-Believe*, by Kendall Walton. *Journal of Aesthetics and Art Criticism* 49 (1991): 161-66.

Lamarque, Peter, and Stein Haugom Olsen. *Truth, Fiction, and Literature: A Philosophical Perspective.* Oxford: Clarendon Press, 1994.

Lear, Jonathan. "*Katharsis.*" *Phronesis* 33 (1988): 297-326.

Leighton, Stephen R. "A New View of Emotion." *American Philosophical Quarterly* 22 (1985): 133-41.

Levinson, Jerrold. "The Place of Real Emotion in Response to Fiction." *Journal of Aesthetics and Art Criticism* 48 (1990): 79-80.

———. Review of *The Philosophy of Horror, or Paradoxes of the Heart*, by Noel Carroll. *Journal of Aesthetics and Art Criticism* 49 (1991): 253-58.

Lewis, David. *Counterfactuals.* Cambridge: Harvard University Press, 1973.

———. "Truth in Fiction." *American Philosophical Quarterly* 15 (1978): 37-46.

Liddell, Robert. *Robert Liddell on the Novel.* Chicago: University of Chicago Press, 1969.

Lord, Catherine. "A Representational Approach to Fearing Fictions." Paper presented at the annual meeting of the American Society for Aesthetics, Los Angeles, California, November 1984.

Lyons, William. *Emotion.* Cambridge: Cambridge University Press, 1980.

Mannision, Don. "On Being Moved by Fiction." *Philosophy* 60 (1985): 71-87.

McCloskey, Mary A. *Kant's Aesthetic.* New York: SUNY Press, 1987.

McCormick, Peter J. "Feelings and Fictions." *Journal of Aesthetics and Art Criticism* 43 (1985): 375-83.

———. *Fictions, Philosophies and the Problems of Poetics.* Ithaca: Cornell University Press, 1988.

———. "Moral Knowledge and Fiction." *Journal of Aesthetics and Art Criticism* 41 (1983): 399-410.

McGhee, P. E. *Humor: Its Origin and Development.* San Francisco: Freeman, 1979.

Moran, Richard. "The Expression of Feeling in Imagination." *Philosophical Review* 103 (1994): 75-106.

Morreall, John. "Enjoying Incongruity." *Humor* 2 (1989): 1-18.

———. "Enjoying Negative Emotions in Fictions." *Philosophy and Literature* 9 (1985): 95-103.

———. *The Philosophy of Laughter and Humor*. Albany: SUNY Press, 1987.

Morton, Adam. *Frames of Mind: Constraints on the Common-Sense Conception of the Mental*. Oxford: Clarendon Press, 1980.

Mounce, H. O. "Art and Real Life." *Philosophy* 55 (1980): 183-92.

Neill, Alex. "Fear, Fiction and Make-Believe." *Journal of Aesthetics and Art Criticism* 49 (1991): 47-56.

———. "Fiction and the Emotions." *American Philosophical Quarterly* 30 (1993): 1-13.

———. "On a Paradox of the Heart." *Philosophical Studies* 65 (1992): 53-65.

Novitz, David. "Fiction, Imagination and Emotion." *Journal of Aesthetics and Art Criticism* 38 (1980): 279-88.

———. *Knowledge, Fiction and Imagination*. Philadelphia: Temple University Press, 1987.

———. Review of *Fictions, Philosophies and the Problems of Poetics*, by Peter J. McCormick. *Journal of Aesthetics and Art Criticism* 47 (1989): 382-84.

Nussbaum, Martha C. *Love's Knowledge: Essays on Philosophy and Literature*. New York: Oxford University Press, 1990.

Papanoutsos, E. P. "The Aristotelian *Katharsis*." *British Journal of Aesthetics* 17 (1977): 361-64.

Paskins, Barrie. "On Being Moved by Anna Karenina and *Anna Karenina*." *Philosophy* 52 (1977): 344-47.

Paskow, Alan. "What Is Aesthetic *Catharsis?*" *Journal of Aesthetics and Art Criticism* 42 (1983): 59-68.

Pretorius, Elizabeth J. "Humor as Defeated Discourse Expectations: Conversational Exchange in a Monty Python Text." *Humor* 3 (1990): 259-76.

Quine, W. V. O. "Quantifiers and Propositional Attitudes." In *Reference and Modality*. Ed. Leonard Linsky. London: Oxford University Press, 1971, 101-11.

Radford, Colin. "Charlton's Feelings About the Fictitious: A Reply." *British Journal of Aesthetics* 25 (1985): 380-83.

———. "Emotions and Music: A Reply to the Cognitivists." *Journal of Aesthetics and Art Criticism* 47 (1989): 69-76.

———. "The Essential Anna." *Philosophy* 54 (1979): 390-94.

———. "How Can We Be Moved by the Fate of Anna Karenina? (I)." *Proceedings of the Aristotelian Society* 49, suppl. 6 (1975): 67-80.

———. "The Incoherence and Irrationality of Philosophers." *Philosophy* 65 (1990): 349-54.

———. "Philosophers and Their Monstrous Thoughts." *British Journal of Aesthetics* 22 (1982): 261-63.

———. "Replies to Three Critics." *Philosophy* 64 (1989): 93-97.

———. "Stuffed Tigers: A Reply to H. O. Mounce." *Philosophy* 57 (1982): 529-32.

———. "Tears and Fiction." *Philosophy* 52 (1977): 208-13.

Roberts, Robert C. "What an Emotion Is: A Sketch." *Philosophical Review* 97 (1988): 183-209.

Rosebury, B. J. "Fiction, Emotion and 'Belief': A Reply to Eva Schaper." *British Journal of Aesthetics* 19 (1979): 120-30.

Rosenblatt, Louise M. *The Reader, the Text, the Poem: The Transactional Theory of the Literary Work*. Carbondale: Southern Illinois University Press, 1978.

Roszak, Theodore. "When Movies Ruled Our Lives." *New York Times*, 30 June 1991, sec. 2, H18.

Ryan, Marie-Laure. "Fiction, Non-Factuals, and the Principle of Minimal Departure." *Poetics* 9 (1980): 403-22.

Ryle, Gilbert. *The Concept of Mind*. New York: Barnes and Noble, 1949. Excerpted in *What Is an Emotion? Classic Readings in Philosophical Psychology*. Ed. Cheshire Calhoun and Robert C. Solomon. New York: Oxford University Press, 1984, 252-63.

Sankowski, Edward. "Blame, Fictional Characters, and Morality." *Journal of Aesthetic Education* 22 (1988): 49-61.

Schachter, Stanley, and Jerome Singer. "Cognitive, Social, and Physiological Determinants of Emotional State." In *Readings for an Introduction to Psychology*. Ed. Richard A. King. New York: McGraw-Hill, 1966, 246-67. Also excerpted in *What Is an Emotion? Classic Readings in Philosophical Psychology*. Ed. Cheshire Calhoun and Robert C. Solomon. New York: Oxford University Press, 1984, 173-83.

Schaper, Eva. "Aristotle's *Catharsis* and Aesthetic Pleasure." *Philosophical Quarterly* 18 (1968): 131-43.

———. "Fiction and the Suspension of Disbelief." *British Journal of Aesthetics* 18 (1978): 31-44.

———. *Prelude to Aesthetics*. London: Allen and Unwin, 1968.

Scheler, Max. *Formalism in Ethics and Non-formal Ethics of Values*. Excerpted in *What Is an Emotion? Classic Readings in Philosophical Psychology*. Ed. Cheshire Calhoun and Robert C. Solomon. New York: Oxford University Press, 1984, 215-28.

Scruton, Roger. *Art and Imagination*. London: Methuen, 1974.

Shakespeare, William. *The Riverside Shakespeare*. Boston: Houghton Mifflin Company, 1974.

Sirridge, M. J. "Truth from Fiction?" *Philosophy and Phenomenological Research* 35 (1975): 453-71.

Skulsky, Harold. "On Being Moved by Fiction." *Journal of Aesthetics and Art Criticism* 39 (1980): 5-14.

Solomon, Robert C. "Emotions and Choice." In *What Is an Emotion? Classic Readings in Philosophical Psychology*. Ed. Cheshire Calhoun and Robert C. Solomon. New York: Oxford University Press, 1984, 305-26.

Sparshott, Francis. *The Theory of the Arts*. New Jersey: Princeton University Press, 1982.

Spiegel, P. Keith. "Early Conceptions of Humor: Varieties and Issues." In *The Psychology of Humor: Theoretical Perspectives and Empirical Issues*. Ed. J. H. Goldstein and P. E. McGhee. New York: Academic Press, 1972.

Srivastava, K. G. "A New Look at the '*Katharsis*' Clause of Aristotle's *Poetics*." *British Journal of Aesthetics* 12 (1972): 258-75.

Stein, Edith. *On the Problem of Empathy*. 3d rev. ed. Trans. Waltraut Stein. Washington, D.C.: ICS Publications, 1989.

Stocker, Michael. "Emotional Thoughts." *American Philosophical Quarterly* 24 (1987): 59–69.

Stout, G. F. *A Manual of Psychology*. London: University Tutorial Press, 1938.

Tanner, Michael. "Morals in Fiction and Fictional Morality (II)." *Proceedings of the Aristotelian Society*, suppl. 68 (1994): 51–66.

Thalberg, Irving. "Emotion and Thought." In *What Is an Emotion? Classic Readings in Philosophical Psychology*. Ed. Cheshire Calhoun and Robert C. Solomon. New York: Oxford University Press, 1984, 291–304.

Tong, Rosemarie. *Feminine and Feminist Ethics*. California: Wadsworth, 1993.

Van Inwagen, Peter. "Creatures of Fiction." *American Philosophical Quarterly* 14 (1977): 299–308.

Vetlesen, Arne Johan. *Perception, Empathy, and Judgment: An Inquiry into the Preconditions of Moral Performance*. University Park: Pennsylvania State University Press, 1994.

Walton, Kendall. "Fearing Fictions." *Journal of Philosophy* 75 (1978): 5–27.

———. *Mimesis as Make-Believe: On the Foundations of the Representational Arts*. Cambridge: Harvard University Press, 1990.

———. "Morals in Fiction and Fictional Morality (I)." *Proceedings of the Aristotelian Society*, suppl. 68 (1994), 27–50.

Warnock, Mary. *Imagination*. Berkeley and Los Angeles: University of California Press, 1976.

Weston, Michael. "How Can We Be Moved by the Fate of Anna Karenina? (II)." *Proceedings of the Aristotelian Society* 49, suppl. 6 (1975): 81–93.

Wilson, J. R. S. *Emotion and Object*. Cambridge: Cambridge University Press, 1972.

Wolterstorff, Nicholas. *Works and Worlds of Art*. Oxford: Clarendon Press, 1980.

Woolf, Virginia. *A Room of One's Own*. New York: Harcourt, Brace and World, 1929.

Yanal, Robert J. "The Paradox of Emotion and Fiction." *Pacific Philosophical Quarterly* 75 (1994): 54–75.

Index

Abbarno, John M., 192 n. 29
adverbial analysis
  of emotion, 4-5, 8, 84, 88, 92-103 passim, 138-39
  of sensing, 100-102, 100 n. 42, 101 n. 43
Aeschylus (*The Libation Bearers*), 214
aesthetic reading, 155
aesthetic response, 206, 217-23
Alien, 27-28, 31-32, 36-38, 63-64, 81-82, 100, 111-12, 138-39, 142-43, 145, 157-59, 180, 203
Allen, R. T., 48 n. 13
amusement. *See* humor
Angels in America, 77
Aristotle
  artistic virtuosity, 212-13
  catharsis, 198-212 passim
  De Anima, 17
  desire, 16
  emotion, 17
  imitation, 212-13
  Nicomachean Ethics, 17, 205
  Poetics, 114, 198-212 passim
  poetry and history, 112
  Politics, 199
  Rhetoric, 17
  spectacle, 114
  universals, 112
Armon-Jones, Claire, 18 nn. 26-27, 108 n. 2
artistic virtuosity
  authorial/directorial/thespian skill, 212-14, 218, 221-23
  prose style, 47, 143-44, 161, 213-18, 221
attention
  and distraction, 84, 141-42, 226
  and imagining, 92-103, 130, 141-42, 156, 190, 226
  and hostility, 98-99, 130
attitudes. *See also* emotion
  approval and disapproval, 6, 116-26 passim

authorial/directorial, 206, 211-12, 223
  influence of imagination on, 36, 177-78
attributes (properties)
  existential commitment to, 29
  ascription of, 29-38
Atwood, Margaret (*The Handmaid's Tale*), 90, 212
Austen, Jane (*Mansfield Park*), 119-21
authorial assumptions, 147-49
authorial/directorial attitudes, 206, 211-12, 223
authorial/directorial skills (as objects of emotion), 212-14, 218, 221-23

Beardsley, Monroe C., 147, 147 n. 11
Bedford, Errol, 13 n. 9, 14-16, 18 n. 27
behavior
  and analysis of desire, 61-64
  and behavioral dispositions, 14-16, 19, 61-63
  and conditions for emotion, 14-16, 19, 42, 47-48
  influence of imagination on, 32-33, 36, 177-78
belief
  about what is fictionally the case, 28 n. 50, 53-54, 173-74, 191
  alteration of, 6, 79, 96, 111, 115, 123-24
  conflict with emotion, 23-39 passim, 97-99. *See also* emotion, irrational
  dispositional, 113, 141-42
  evaluative. *See* belief, normative, universal
  existentially committed, 4, 9, 19, 22-39 passim, 42-44, 45-46, 48-49, 82, 84, 92, 111, 184-85
  false, 26, 28, 54, 76 n. 5, 87, 179 n. 17
  to imagine having, 7, 33-36, 58-60, 176-85, 188, 191, 225
  irrationality in, 21-22, 26, 28 n. 52, 109, 124, 166-67, 177-79 , 201-2

CPSIA information can be obtained
at www.ICGtesting.com
Printed in the USA
LVHW091033180121
676782LV00007B/49